# Becoming Jihadis

# CAUSES AND CONSEQUENCES OF TERRORISM SERIES

*Series Editors:*
Gary LaFree
Gary A. Ackerman
Anthony Lemieux

BOOKS IN THE SERIES:

**From Freedom Fighters to Jihadists: Human Resources of Non State Armed Groups**
Vera Mironova

**ISIS Propaganda: A Full-Spectrum Extremist Message**
Edited by Stephane J. Baele, Katharine A. Boyd, and Travis G. Coan

**Extremist Islam: Recognition and Response in Southeast Asia**
Kumar Ramakrishna

**Insurgent Terrorism: Intergroup Relationships and the Killing of Civilians**
Victor Asal, Brian J. Phillips, and R. Karl Rethemeyer

**Becoming Jihadis: Radicalization and Commitment in Southeast Asia**
Julie Chernov Hwang

**Proto-State Media Systems: The Digital Rise of Al-Qaeda and ISIS**
Carol Winkler and Kareen El Damanhoury

# Becoming Jihadis

*Radicalization and Commitment in Southeast Asia*

JULIE CHERNOV HWANG

# OXFORD
UNIVERSITY PRESS

Oxford University Press is a department of the University of Oxford. It furthers
the University's objective of excellence in research, scholarship, and education
by publishing worldwide. Oxford is a registered trade mark of Oxford University
Press in the UK and certain other countries.

Published in the United States of America by Oxford University Press
198 Madison Avenue, New York, NY 10016, United States of America.

© Oxford University Press 2023

All rights reserved. No part of this publication may be reproduced, stored in
a retrieval system, or transmitted, in any form or by any means, without the
prior permission in writing of Oxford University Press, or as expressly permitted
by law, by license, or under terms agreed with the appropriate reproduction
rights organization. Inquiries concerning reproduction outside the scope of the
above should be sent to the Rights Department, Oxford University Press, at the
address above.

You must not circulate this work in any other form
and you must impose this same condition on any acquirer.

Library of Congress Cataloging-in-Publication Data
Names: Chernov-Hwang, Julie, author.
Title: Becoming Jihadis : radicalization and commitment in Southeast Asia /
Julie Chernov Hwang, PhD.
Description: New York, NY : Oxford University Press, [2023] |
Series: Causes and consequences of terrorism |
Includes bibliographical references and index. |
Identifiers: LCCN 2022044683 (print) | LCCN 2022044684 (ebook) |
ISBN 9780197653005 (hardback) | ISBN 9780197653012 (paperback) |
ISBN 9780197653036 (epub) | ISBN 9780197653043 (online)
Subjects: LCSH: Religious militants—Southeast Asia. | Terrorism—Religious
aspects—Islam. | Terrorism—Southeast Asia. | Radicalism—Southeast Asia.
Classification: LCC HV6433.A785 C44 2023 (print) | LCC HV6433.A785
(ebook) | DDC 363.3250959—dc23/eng/20221115
LC record available at https://lccn.loc.gov/2022044683
LC ebook record available at https://lccn.loc.gov/2022044684

DOI: 10.1093/oso/9780197653005.001.0001

Paperback printed by Marquis, Canada
Hardback printed by Bridgeport National Bindery, Inc., United States of America

*For Sophia*
*I love you infinity*

# Contents

*Acknowledgments* ix
*Acronyms* xiii

Introduction 1

1. Motivations 33
2. Internal Pathways: Kinship and Schools 62
3. External Pathways: Study Sessions, Conflict, Prison, and Social Media 80
4. Commitment 111
5. Jihadi Activism 126

Conclusion 149

*Notes* 163
*Glossary* 191
*Index* 193

# Acknowledgments

I've been researching terrorist behavior, mostly in Indonesia, for the past 12 years. I have examined most every stage of the terrorist life cycle: why people join extremist groups; how they join; what actions they take to prove commitment; what roles they take on once they are members; how they are recruited into a terrorist operation; what motivates a person to move between terrorist groups; and how and why they choose to disengage from violence and reintegrate back into society. I've theorized on deradicalization based on the small handful of individuals I've met who I can say, with a reasonable degree of certainty, have deradicalized versus a larger portion who have revised previously held views on some issues but not others or who remain ideologically radical, although their behavior has changed.

Over the course of this research, I have been very fortunate. Members of Islamist extremist groups have agreed to meet with me, repeatedly, sometimes for coffee, conversation, and brief clarifications, and other times for interviews and follow-up interviews. To do this research, I worked with several guides—academics, founders and staff at terrorist rehabilitation nongovernmental organizations, and human rights activists—each of whom had developed trust relationships with a subset of members of Indonesian jihadist groups. Over time, the interviewees came to trust me. By conducting repeat interviews, I was able to meet someone shortly after release from prison and see them start a family, start a business, fail at a business, try something new, develop a post-group identity and post-group life, or lapse and return to prison. This kind of longitudinal analysis is quite rare in terrorism studies.

This book would not have been possible without the 97 Indonesians and 25 Filipinos who agreed to meet with me, answer my questions, and share their narratives and experiences with me between 2010 and 2019. To the *ikhwan* from Jemaah Islamiyah, Mujahidin KOMPAK, Ring Banten, Tanah Runtuh, Mujahidin Kayamanya, Jemaah Anshorut Tauhid, Jemaah Anshorut Syariah, Jemaah Ansharud Daulah, Mujahidin Indonesia Timor, and the Maute Group, thank you for trusting me with your journeys and perspectives so that I, in turn, could help others understand.

I feel deep and profound gratitude to my guides, Nasir, Taufik, Noor Huda, Adhy, Yusuf (may he rest in peace), Hakim (may he rest in peace), Badrus, Sherbien, and Nashiba. Thank you for opening up your networks of contacts, securing consent, accompanying me to meetings, and sharing your perspectives. Your friendship, advice, countenance, and support have been invaluable. Jha Nisa, thank you for translating for me in Marawi. Your indomitable spirit is an inspiration. I keep all of you in my heart. Thank you for being you.

This book was made possible by a generous grant from the Smith Richardson Foundation that funded four trips to Indonesia and two to the Philippines between 2017 and 2019. Allan Song, thank you for being a program officer extraordinaire, mentoring me in the art of grant writing, and for the flexibility you showed in letting me include the Philippines in the project after the fact. Thank you to the three anonymous reviewers who gave me superb advice on rounding out the grant. I also thank my colleagues on Goucher's Institutional Review Board, who have been working with me for a decade to ensure that I conduct my research ethically and consider all the angles and points of concern.

A special thanks to Anthony Lemieux, who approached me initially about submitting my book to Oxford University Press' (OUP) START series. Thank you to Tony, Laura, and Gary for welcoming me into the OUP START family. It's been a wonderful experience working with the START/OUP team. Nadina Persaud, you have been an extraordinary editor. Thank you for seamlessly shepparding the manuscript through the review process. Sarah Ebel and Kamala Palaniappan, thank you for your diligence, reliability, and follow through during the production process. A great many colleagues offered input at various junctures on research design and on chapters. Kirsten Schulze, thank you for reading the draft chapters and giving me not only a historian's perspective but also your careful, critical eye. I am deeply grateful not only for our working relationship but also for our friendship. You are a gem of a person and an extraordinary scholar. Sidney Jones, thank you for taking the time to do a thorough review of *the entire manuscript*. I greatly appreciated your excellent critical feedback and for always pushing me to be sharper and better. Joseph Liow, thank you for being a friend and colleague throughout this entire process, for giving me advice regarding research in Malaysia and the Philippines, and for reading the manuscript and suggesting big picture improvements. Anne Marie Baylouny and Victor Asal, you are two of my favorite people in our profession, and I am fortunate to count you both as friends; thank you for taking the time to offer detailed comments from a non-Southeast Asianist perspective. Dan Kim, thank you for responding to dozens of texts about proper military terminology and for your unstinting love, support, and encouragement. To the three OUP anonymous reviewers and to the START editorial board, thank you for your robust comments; you helped make this a better book, more grounded in the literature. Much gratitude to Navhat Nuraniyah, A'an Suryana, Solahudin, John Horgan, Bruce Hoffman, Colin Clarke, Jillian Schwedler, Bozena Welborne, Emy Matesan, Najib Azca, Michael Kenney, Chris Fair, Greg Fealy, Joseph Young, Ihsan Ali Fauzi, Khariroh Maknunah, Diah Kusumaningrum, and the late Rizal Panggabean.

To my parents, thank you for giving Sophia love and support while I was away on my fieldwork trips. I could not have done this work without you.

Sophia, you are the light of my life.

# Acronyms

| | |
|---|---|
| AKP | Ansharul Khilafa Philippines |
| AQMA | Al Qaeda in the Malay Archipelago |
| ASG | Abu Sayyaf Group |
| BIFF | Bangsamoro Islamic Freedom Fighters |
| DDII | Dewan Dakwah Islamiyah Indonesia |
| DI | Darul Islam |
| FPI | Islamic Defenders Front |
| HTI | Hizbut Tahrir Indonesia |
| ISIS | Islamic State of Iraq and Syria |
| JAD | Jemaah Ansharud Daulah |
| JAK | Jemaah Asharul Khilafa |
| JAS | Jemaah Ansharusy Syariah |
| JAT | Jemaah Anshorut Tauhid |
| JI | Jemaah Islamiyah |
| KOMPAK | Komite Aksi Penanggulangan Akibat Krisis |
| MILF | Moro Islamic Liberation Front |
| MIT | Mujahidin Indonesia Timor |
| MNLF | Moro National Liberation Front |
| NU | Nahdlatul Ulama |
| PKS | Partai Keadilan Sejahtera |

# Introduction

## Umar Patek

"Dulmatin was my neighbor," said Umar Patek.

> When we were children, he often asked me to play with him, even though he was four years older. I often called out his name from my house, "Joooo," because his [given] name was Joko, and he would come out of his house, and we would play together. Just like that.[1]

Patek attended Muhammadiyah[1] and al Irsyad[2] Islamic day schools through high school, and after graduation, he moved to the city of Yogyakarta to begin a computer certificate program. Around June 1991, while working on his computer courses, Dulmatin invited him to go to Malaysia to study Islam and to work. This appealed to Patek. They arrived in the Malaysian state of Johor and made their way to the town of Tiram. Within a few days, Patek was introduced to Ali Gufron, alias Mukhlas,[2] the director at the Luqmanul Hakim boarding school and a veteran of the Soviet–Afghan war. Mukhlas would go on to play a significant role in Jemaah Islamiyah (JI), both in the leadership, as head of Mantiqi 1, the division encompassing Malaysia and Singapore, and as a key plotter in the October 2002 Bali bombing. "I [began] attending his study sessions, where he shared stories about Islam and lectured on *tauhid* [the divine oneness of god], *iman* [faith], *aqidah* [belief]. At the time, I assumed he was just a regular *ustad*."[3]

---

[1] Muhammadiyah is a modernist Islamic mass organization in Indonesia withan estimated 30 million members. It is composed largely of urban, educated Muslims. They run schools and health clinics. Their members serve in every political party and in most Muslim social movements. Muhammadiyah members run the ideological gamut from progressive to radical. Together with the traditionalist Nahdlatul Ulama, with an estimated 50 million Muslims, these two organizations define the Indonesian Muslim mainstream.

[2] Al Irsyad is a conservative Islamic group, smaller than either Nadhlatul Ulama or Muhammadiyah. It also has schools in Indonesia.

After less than 2 months, Patek and Dulmatin were offered the opportunity to "study religion in Pakistan."[4] They accepted the offer. After they arrived in Peshawar, Pakistan, Patek learned that he would actually be studying military subjects at Harbiy Pohantun Mujahidin-e-Afghanistan Ittihad-e-Islami (also known the Mujahidin Military Academy or colloquially, As Saada, for its location in Saada, Pakistan), the training camp run by the Wahabi-sympathizing mujahidin commander, Abdul Rasul Sayyaf. "I then began participating in real *taklim* [study circles] where I learned about *fiqh*,[3] *jihad*, *tajwid*,[4] and other religious subjects "[5]

He was in the same batch as Sawad, Imam Samudra, and Ali Imron, men who would go on to play significant roles in the 2002 Bali bombing. Nasir Abas and Abu Tholut, who would go on to lead Mantiqi 3, the JI training region, were his instructors. Abu Tholut taught him how to assemble explosive devices.[6] Nasir Abas taught him to handle weapons, "from pistols to howitzers."[7] Patek explained, "He taught me about shooting and how to use a telescope to enhance accuracy."[8] Patek liked heavy weapons best.

He must have impressed his teachers because less than a month after he returned to Malaysia in 1995, he was tasked to work as an instructor in the Philippines, teaching demolitions, first at the Moro Islamic Liberation Front (MILF) Camp Abu Bakar and then at JI Camp Hudaibiyah within the Abu Bakar Camp on the island of Mindanao in the Philippines. He also worked in the weapons laboratory on the grounds of Camp Abu Bakar fabricating armaments for JI and the MILF, including RPG-2 rockets and bombs.[9] He was enamored by the experience of living in and fighting in jihad fronts. He liked meeting Muslim fighters from Afghanistan and the Philippines. He stayed in the Philippines until 2000, marrying a Filipino convert to Islam in 1998.

In 2000, soon after he and his wife returned to Indonesia, he reconnected with Dulmatin. To this point, Patek had studied at two infamous training camps in Pakistan and Afghanistan; he had trained men and fought in the jihad on Mindanao. However, his participation in acts of violence had been reserved exclusively for battlefields. With the re-entry of his childhood friend, Dulmatin, into his life, his pathway shifted from jihad experiences and training others for jihad to using his skills for terrorism.

---

[3] Fiqh is the term used to denote the operationalization of the broad principles and values of the sharia into distinct laws by Islamic jurists.

[4] Tajwid is the term used to refer to correct pronunciation of Quranic Arabic.

According to Patek, Dulmatin recruited him for two operations: the Christmas Eve bombing in 2000, where bombs exploded at 11 churches on Christmas Eve, and the 2002 Bali bombing. Patek claimed he initially protested when Dulmatin informed him they would make bombs for an operation attacking churches on Christmas Eve, taking issue with the target of the bombings (churches) and the timing (Christmas Eve). Destruction of houses of worship is prohibited in Islam.[10] However, Dulmatin persisted. "Just join with me."[11] Dulmatin asserted they already had permission. Patek relented. Dulmatin also brought him into the 2002 Bali bombing. He recalls, "after the bombing was [largely] planned, I was then asked to go to Bali. I went with Dulmatin to Bali."[12] At his trial in 2012, he admitted to mixing the chemicals and assembling the explosives used in the 2002 Bali bombing.[13]

Following the 2002 Bali bombing, he and Dulmatin fled to the Philippines, where Patek resumed his life as a trainer. Under the protection of a fellow Afghan veteran and friend, Mugasid Delna, a commander with the MILF, Patek and Dulmatin set up a training camp for Indonesians at Pawas on the island of Mindanao.[14] When the MILF asked them to leave in 2005, they joined Khadafi Janjalani's faction of the Abu Sayyaf Group (ASG).[15] When Dulmatin returned home in 2007, Patek joined yet another ASG faction before returning to Indonesia himself in 2009.

Patek's narrative of joining JI, participating in multiple jihad experiences, becoming a trainer, and taking part in two terrorist attacks centers on his relationships, most notably with his childhood friend and brother-in-law, Dulmatin. Dulmatin facilitated his entry into the Darul Islam circles that, in turn, enabled his travel to train at Saada and Torkham during the Soviet–Afghan war. Dulmatin vouched for him. Later, Dulmatin pulled him into the Christmas Eve bombings and the 2002 Bali bombings. Patek trusted Dulmatin implicitly, and that trust overrode his initial inclination to refuse to participate in terrorist attacks; he understood that the targets, timing, and locations of the attacks were improper. Why was Dulmatin allowed to bring Patek into the 2002 Bali bombing at such a late juncture? Many on the core attack team knew Patek intimately. Imam Samudra, who masterminded the attack, as well as Ali Imron and Sawad, two other members of the core team, had been in the same batch with Patek in Afghanistan. Thus, Imam Samudra, Ali Imron, and Sawad trusted Patek not only because of Dulmatin's word but also because they had trained with Patek. That shared, formative, and profound personal experience created thick social bonds.

The experience of Patek highlights the centrality of social ties in understanding how one joins an Islamist extremist group and how one comes to participate in jihad experiences, paramilitary training, and acts of terrorism. These bonds are thick because the people involved are either actual family or constructed kin tied together by shared experiences and a common purpose. Patek followed Dulmatin into an Islamist extremist group and into terrorism because he trusted him as a brother. Imam Samudra, Ali Imron, and Sawad agreed to bring Patek into their operation at the last minute to assist in bomb construction not only because they trusted his capacity to deliver but also because they trusted *him* due to their bond from Afghanistan. Commander Delna protected Patek due to that same shared bond of trust. These sticky social ties are at the roots of joining, commitment to, and participation in violent actions as part of an extremist group.

## The Book

Drawing on the experiences of 97 jihadists from Indonesia and 25 from the Philippines interviewed between 2010 and 2019, this book examines four interrelated questions about the process of joining an extremist group: Why does someone join an extremist group? What are the pathways via which individuals join such groups? How does one show commitment to an extremist group? Why does someone participate in acts of terrorism?

This book argues that joining an extremist group is joining a community of people who share beliefs, purpose, values, norms, goals, and, above all, a deep commitment to one another. These interpersonal relationships propel joining, perseverance through mundane tasks, and commitment. The loyalty inspired in these communities may be thick, positive affective bonds, based on love, trust, and affinity for one another, or thinner, exclusive, negative bonds, with an affinity based on rejection of outsiders and hatred of the other.[16] For members of Indonesian Salafi-Jihadi groups such as JI, their spinoffs, affiliates, and splinter factions, thick social bonds function as a deep, almost familial constructed kinship that can, in some circumstances, even displace family as those most dear. For members of takfiri groups such as Jemaah Ansharud Daulah (JAD), an umbrella for pro-ISIS groups, and its ideological predecessor, Tauhid wa'al Jihad, the social bonds are brittle and fragile, based on a rejection of all outsiders. In short, although individuals may be initially drawn to extremist groups by a variety of factors, what makes them stay, commit, and participate in licit, illicit, and even terrorist activities is ultimately social and emotional.

This social component holds true over five full pathways into extremist groups—kinship, schools, study circles, conflict, and prisons—as well as social media, which functions as a partial pathway. These pathways bring one into contact with activists from an extremist group or groups, where they gain exposure to the group's worldview and ideological positions and form bonds of friendship that transcend formal group activities. This, in turn, leads some potential members to adopt in-group ideological, behavioral, and social norms as they come to prioritize in-group friends and in-group activities over those with non-members. Their way of relating to women or outsiders more broadly may change. Their manner of dress may change. Their choice of music or whether they listen to music at all may change. In time—how much time varies across groups—individuals who show due commitment to the group are vetted and may be inducted as members.

It is important to note that some people gain exposure to and join an Islamist extremist group via a specific pathway, whereas in other cases, two pathways combine. Someone from a family affiliated with an Islamist extremist group may be sent to a particular boarding school to instill the right mindset, with the expectation that the young person will be inducted into the group following graduation. In conflict zones in Indonesia, one may attend study circles prior to the invitation to join a particular group.

Moreover, it is important to distinguish between internal pathways (kinship and schools) and external pathways (study circles, conflict, prisons, and social media). Someone who is a relative, especially a sibling or child, of an existing member may have an expedited pathway to entry into an extremist group because they will be trusted by virtue of familial ties.

External pathways are the means via which outsiders—those who did not attend a radical school affiliated with the movement or who do not have kinship ties to existing members of the movement—join. The most common external pathways in the sample are study circles and conflict zones. However, individuals may also join activities of certain groups in prison or via online study sessions. Individuals joining via external pathways choose to join and must show they are worthy of trust. The internality or externality of the pathways shapes the process of joining, the duration of that process, the steps involved, the role that social bonds play, the points at which they become salient and sticky, and how interpersonal trust is built.

## Understanding the Joining Process

Before exploring how someone joins and why someone joins an extremist group, it is important to first understand what it means to join a group or a movement. Joining is a gradual and incremental process of socialization into an exclusive alternative community. One may be born into the group, socialized into the group intentionally through attendance at specific affiliated schools, or one may choose to enter the group as an outsider. In the latter two cases, over a period of weeks, months, and, in some instances, years, one attends formal and informal meetings and in doing so gains exposure to the group and its members. One's personal and social activities may come to center around the group.[17] The group members come to trust them and vice versa. Friendships in the group come to be of greater importance than friendships outside the group, and eventually group members may come to supplant one's friends and even one's family of origin as their go-to, ride-or-die people. In time, one may also begin to filter information through the lens of the specific ideology of the group and adopt cultural, linguistic, and behavioral markers of the group.[18]

A person may join an extremist group for a variety of reasons, including knowing someone in the group, being part of an affiliated community, feeling a strong sense of altruism, or wanting to learn more about a specific religion or ideology.[19] In some cases, unresolved personal trauma interacting with a derailed search for identity, community, and purpose can make someone especially susceptible to recruitment into extremism.[20] In other cases, there is no such trauma. In Indonesia, in particular, one may sample a wide array of Islamist and Islamist extremist groups before settling on one specific group to join, or they may join a few groups conterminously.

Joining is also not a linear pathway that consistently ends with membership.[21] One can be active without being a formal member, and a formal member can go inactive or leave the group entirely.[22] Furthermore, members have differing levels of commitment. Some may be in the process of becoming committed members, others are already firmly committed, and still others may find their commitment to the group wavering or be in the process of leaving.[23] Some may never commit but may just exist on the margins of the group, interacting inconsistently with members via occasional attendance at mass prayers and study sessions. Others may migrate between groups in the network or may move in and out of the network itself as one's personal circumstances change.[24]

Once someone becomes a member, that person can play various roles in the group and engage to varying extents. For example, one can be a supporter and assist in small ways, such as attending religious events, providing transportation for specific leaders, clearing red tape to secure a building permit, or donating to the group. One can play a nonviolent role in the group but still one that requires a considerable commitment of time, energy, and resources—running a website or online chat, managing media, supporting and sustaining logistics, or teaching at an affiliated school. Through the anonymity of social media, women have taken a more active role running chats and doing fundraising. In the Philippines, women worked as recruiters for the Maute group.

One can also participate in short-term gray activities such as a paramilitary training and violent activities, including jihad experiences and terrorism. In this study, jihad experiences varied from a few weeks or months for participants in the communal conflict on the island of Ambon and in the district of Poso to 8 years for specific trainers and commanders in Afghanistan. For terrorist attack planning, there are also multiple roles, including masterminding the attack, identifying possible targets, surveillance, securing funds for the attack, procuring bomb-making materials, making the bombs, and setting the bombs.

Between terrorist attacks, one's role may vary. Someone who made a bomb for one attack may only be tasked with surveillance for another or be asked to rent the car. For example, "M.B.", a member of JI currently serving a life sentence for his role in multiple terrorist attacks in the early 2000s, was assigned to place a bomb in a church as part of the Christmas Eve bombing in 2000. However, for the Bali bombing in 2002, he was only asked to store some of the funds for it in his bank account.[25] Likewise, "Anas" built circuitry used in the bombs for the 2002 Bali bombing, whereas he was tasked to procure dynamite for the Australian embassy bombing.[26] Roles are typically not constant across attacks. Moreover, just because someone is brought into a terrorist attack does not mean that is their primary role within the group. Anas was part of the media wing. M.B. was a teacher. Both were, on occasion, brought into attacks. However, their daily roles in the network were quite different, ordinary, and possibly even mundane. Participation in terrorist attacks as well as jihad experiences, and paramilitary training constitute episodes in a person's time in an extremist group.[27]

It is important to stress that most members of extremist groups never participate in acts of terrorism. Those who do represent a tiny fraction of the overall group members and sympathizers.[28] In addition, even members who participate in terrorist attacks, as well as those who do not, may not be full-time members. They may have day jobs, be they affiliated with the network or even independent of it. In these latter cases, attack plotters groomed trusted family members (spouses, siblings, children, and nephews) to play roles in operations.[29]

## Islamic Terminology

Before proceeding further, it is necessary to unpack two terms that are used throughout this book: Salafi-Jihadi and takfiri. To do so, it is necessary to begin with defining Salafi. Salafi is derived from the Arabic word *salaf*, meaning "to go before," a reference to the first three generations of the Muslim community, whom Salafis view as the exemplars of proper Islamic behavior.[30] Today, the term Salafi is frequently used to refer to those Muslims who strictly adhere to the model of conduct set out by those early generations and who take the injunctions set out in the Quran and Hadith literally.[31] Wiktorowicz denotes three types of Salafis—purists, politicos, and jihadis—noting that most Salafis are purists, who focus on promoting the Salafi creed and eschew engagement in politics or jihad against the state, whereas politicos believe in accomplishing their goals through legislating.[32]

This book primarily centers on the third variant: Salafi-Jihadis. Although Salafi-Jihadis share the same creed as the purists and politicos, they differ insofar as they view violent jihad as the only way to achieve their goals.[33] Salafi-Jihadism rose to prominence during the Soviet–Afghan war, drawing on the ideas of Syed Qutb and Abdullah Azzam. Salafi-Jihadis differ significantly from Salafis concerning the conditions under which jihad is permissible, how that jihad may be conducted, what tactics are allowable, and the legitimacy of rebellion against a Muslim government.[34] In contrast to Salafis, who assert that jihad is permitted only with the authorization of the ruler, Salafi-Jihadis contend that because a Caliphate is the only legitimate form of government and no such Caliphate exists, Islamic groups can follow the direction of their commander or amir in deciding whether or not to wage jihad.[35] Abd al-Salam Faraj explained, "When jihad is an individual duty, there is no need to ask your parents to leave jihad. . . .It is thus similar to prayer and fasting."[36] Abdullah Azzam concurred, asserting that jihad in defense of Muslim lands was, in fact, an individual obligation incumbent on every able-bodied Muslim and that one may join jihad without consulting their parents, teachers, rulers, or creditors.[37]

Salafi-Jihadis also do not adhere to the ethics of war specified in the Quran and Hadith—to avoid targeting noncombatants, particularly women, children, and the elderly. They do not reject suicide bombing as a tactic. Instead, they contend that jihad may include terrorist attacks, civilians may be targeted, and suicide bombers are martyrs who will be assured admission into heaven. The late Mukhlas, one of the masterminds of the Bali bombing, was characteristic of this view. He argued,

> The pious were commanded by Almighty God to become *irhaabii* or terrorists, namely those who can make the enemies of Almighty God and their enemies, as well as enemies they are not aware of but whom Almighty god knows, tremble, be afraid, and be overwhelmed by fear.[38]

He further justified his actions for attacking civilians in the Bali bombing:

> In jihad jurisprudence, mujahidin are permitted to direct their weapons at their enemies, even if their enemies have women and innocent children with them and moreover have Muslim captives there, on the condition that the aim is to destroy the enemy and not to kill the Muslim captives, women and children.[39]

Takfiris are also examined in this book. The term takfiri is derived from the Arabic word for excommunication, *takfir*. The label "takfiri" is applied to individuals and groups which freely declare Muslims, Islamic and Islamist groups, and governments that do not conform to their specific expectations and rigid norms of behavior infidels in order to justify or legitimate violence against them. In Islamic dogma, *takfir* is a very serious accusation, for those who are excommunicated are considered apostates or infidels, and thus they can be killed.[40] Takfiris hold similar views to those of Salafi-Jihadis regarding the permissibility of suicide bombings and the slaughter of civilians. In Indonesia, pro-ISIS communities and networks would fall under this category, as would the Maute group in the Philippines. In Indonesia, JI and its affiliates and splinter factions would all fall under the category of Salafi-Jihadi.

## Joining and Radicalization in the Literature

Much of the literature on joining and radicalization falls into three areas of exploration: motivations, pathways or stages, and mechanisms. The first type of study explores why individuals join extremist groups. What are they seeking? The second type of research is frequently model-based, where scholars outline a series of stages via which individuals may either join extremist groups or adopt radical ideologies. Finally, the third analyzes causal mechanisms that undergird the process of joining. One point of relative consensus across these three types of research is that joining an extremist group is indeed a process.[41] Importantly, although scholars may reference "radical ideas,"[42] most would caution the importance of differentiating between radical ideas and violent actions.[43] One can commit acts of terrorism without radical beliefs and can hold extreme views without committing acts of terror.[44]

Research on causes of and motivations for radicalization has highlighted a wide variety of factors, many centering around relationships, emotions, identity, and purpose. These include the role of social exclusion,[45] a quest for self-esteem,[46] a search for adventure and a worthy cause,[47] personal identity crisis,[48] the salience of a collective social identity,[49] existential identity anxiety,[50] discrimination and marginalization,[51] and one's circle of friends.[52] Bloom identified social, emotional, and trauma-based reasons why women might participate in acts of terrorism, encapsulating the reasons in five R's—respect, redemption, revenge, rape, and relationships—highlighting social, emotional, and trauma factors.[53] Sulastri Osman, Mohammed Hafez, Julie Chernov Hwang, and Kirsten Schulze all emphasized the importance of kinship ties in joining violent extremist groups.[54] Ken Ballen took an emotional approach, illuminating different kinds of love—familial, romantic, and peer-to-peer—as a motivational force.[55]

Neil J. Kressel and Arie Kruglanski et al. take a psychological approach to understanding radicalization. Kressel sets four conditions that makes a person more susceptible to radicalization and extremism: (1) refusing to compromise with those who think differently, (2) taking up an ends justifying the means point of view, (3) feeling a deep willingness to assume the role of defending the honor of God, and (4) seeking to attain heavenly rewards.[56] Kruglanski et al explains the radicalization process as a quest for significance and a desire to matter.[57]

Other scholars emphasized an eclectic array of factors that do not align easily with any single category but instead reflect the complexity of joining and radicalization. Stern highlighted several motivations for participation in terrorism and violent extremism, notably a desire for adventure, friendship and peer pressure, humiliation, righting historical wrongs, alienation, and claims over territory.[58] William Rosenau and co-authors cited personal ties, being highly educated with a lack of job opportunities, a desire for a better life, and boredom as reasons why children and university-aged individuals joined the FARC.[59] Andrew Silke noted youthful disobedience, opportunity, a desire for vengeance, coercion, and, in some instances, status.[60] Guilian Deneoux and Lynn Carter identified historical narratives of victimization and existential threat; a shared vision of how society should be organized; culture-specific perceptions of what is fair and just; frustration, rage, fear, or anxiety at the injustices of the global system; and social isolation, exclusion, and marginalization.[61]

A second stream of the radicalization literature concerns the pathways via which one becomes radicalized. J. M. Berger highlights a series of "stages" through which individuals who are radicalized pass, including identification with the eligible in-group, negative views about the out-group, perception of crisis, curiosity about the extremist in–group, consideration of the extremist in-group, identification with the extremist in-group, self-critique, and escalation.[62] In this instance, these stages speak more to identification than activism. Highlighting the extremist group Al-Muhajiroun in the United Kingdom, Quintan Wiktorowicz proffered a linear four-stage process of radicalization: A personal crisis led to a "cognitive opening, which then sparked a desire to seek solace in religion. Through debate with Islamist extremists, one comes to share their worldview and finally becomes socialized into the group itself."[63] In contrast to Berger, Wiktorowicz highlights a process of becoming a member.

Moghaddam used the metaphor of a staircase to outline a set of steps via which, if an individual proceeds, will lead to joining an extremist group and committing acts of violence. According to Moghaddam, feelings of dissatisfaction, perceptions of a rigged system, and limited future prospects lead to displacement of aggression, which creates fertile soil for recruitment into a jihadi group.[64] As one travels up this "staircase" of terrorism, Moghaddam contends, individuals who succumb to that mental state would then adopt an us versus them mentality and seek affiliation, affinity, and friendship with like-minded individuals.[65] These affinity groups cut themselves off from the rest of society and adopt a moral code that legitimates terrorism, and subsequently, they join terrorist groups and come to have a role in those terrorist groups.[66] Hafez and Mullins employed the metaphor of a puzzle in which certain configurations of four factors—grievances, social networks, ideologies, and support structures—facilitate one's entry into terrorist groups.[67]

Marc Sageman characterized his stages as four prongs, avoiding the sequential determinism of a model. He contends that moral outrage at world events combined with specific cognitive frames such as "the West is at war with Islam" can lead someone to adopt a mindset conducive to radicalization, especially if these beliefs resonate with one's personal experiences of discrimination and repression.[68] John Horgan and Max Taylor eschew stipulating a specific path,[69] instead developing a model that highlights a series of factors that interact with one another to produce multiple "routes" into terrorism, rooted in one's political, economic, familial, and organizational context, on the one hand, and personal factors, including dissatisfaction with one's sense of self, on the other hand.[70]

Some of the most compelling work on radicalization and commitment has explored mechanisms of its perpetuation. McCauley and Moskalenko highlight a series of mechanisms that can facilitate radicalization, including grievances, love, slow movement toward greater illegality, a desire for risk and status, and the complementary phenomenon of "unfreezing" and "refreezing."[71] In the last, old attachments and commitments are lost or displaced due to trauma, death of close family, conflict, or war. This, in turn, leads to the development of new connections and exposures to new ideas and then a refreezing around a new social network that supports those ideas.[72] Similarly, Pete Simi and Robert Futrell address the mechanism of "Aryan free spaces," defining "free space" as a setting in which marginalized groups feel some measure of freedom in expressing identities and beliefs that run counter to the accepted mainstream.[73] They note these free spaces—these hidden social contexts, including homes, parties, online communities, private Aryan communities, and the White power music scene—enable the gathering together of Aryans to cultivate racial hate and, in doing so, enable the persistence and endurance of White racial nationalism in the United States.[74] They note, "Aryan free spaces offer members solidary, affection and support."[75]

Mary Beth Altier, Christian Thoroughgood, and John Horgan apply Rusbult's investment model, which highlights the mechanisms perpetuating commitment to terrorism.[76] The Rusbult model utilizes the following formula: Commitment = Satisfaction − Alternatives + Investments, where Satisfaction = Actual (Rewards − Costs) − Expected (Rewards − Costs).[77] According to Altier et al., terrorists who derive high rewards, in the form of achievement or social bonds, and low costs from their role in the group are likely to be highly satisfied with membership in the group and sustain commitment to the group.[78] The converse is also true. The lower one's satisfaction and the higher the perceived costs, the more dissatisfied one may feel, and should one have viable alternatives to participation, one may choose to disengage or leave the group entirely.[79]

One of the major points of relative consensus within the literature on joining and radicalization is that there is a social component to entry, involvement, commitment, and participation at various junctures, notably via kinship and constructed kinship ties.[80] This holds true not only for studies of terrorism but also for insurgencies, gangs, and cults.[81] Here, one does find resonance with Southeast Asia, particularly regarding the role of family, friends, and mentors.[82]

Sageman underscored the role of informal social networks, particularly friendship networks, in becoming a terrorist.[83] He highlighted how individuals who would go on to become members of Al Qaeda were friends, roommates, classmates, and family members with shared interests who were radicalized together.[84] These small and often tightly knit groups created echo chambers that reinforced radical beliefs and increased isolation, culminating in the group displacing one's prior social ties to family and friends.[85] What is notable, in this instance, is that it was not ideology that radicalized them but, rather, the patterns of friendship through extracurricular activities and study groups that propelled them to join.[86] This also at times extended to acts of terrorism. Four members of the cell that perpetuated the JW Marriott bombing in Jakarta in 2003 attended the same Islamic boarding school. More commonly, participants in acts of terrorism in Indonesia in the first two decades of the 21st century came from the same familial and friendship networks.[87]

In his later work, in 2017, Sageman unpacked the mechanism undergirding these social relationships, highlighting how coming to view oneself as a member of a social group transforms one's relationships with other members of that same group.[88] One is more likely to trust and respect fellow members of the group; develop feelings of belonging; and in so doing, coordinate collective action.[89]

The research on joining in Southeast Asia tends to echo the broader findings about the social and emotional components to the joining process.[90] Julie Chernov Hwang and Kirsten Schulze identified four pathways into Islamist extremist groups in Indonesia—kinship, schools, study sessions, and conflict—highlighting the role that social relationships play across the pathways.[91] Sulastri Osman and Sidney Jones also noted the role of kinship ties in joining in their respective articles.[92] Drawing on the model developed by Quintan Wiktorowicz, Nava Nuraniyah underscored the emotional component of joining in her research on why women joined ISIS, asserting that women were prompted by the interplay between personal crises and political grievances that, in turn, facilitated a process of religious seeking that led them to ISIS, where they found belonging and felt accepted.[93] Noor Huda Ismail also took an emotional approach, highlighting the role of militant masculinity in the process of becoming a member of an Indonesian extremist group.[94] Likewise, Kumar Ramakrishna explored how the phenomenon of "existential identity anxiety" can lead to radicalization, drawing on Indonesian cases.[95] Sidney Jones emphasized the social and organization dynamics that led 30–35 young men to join an ISIS cell in Cotabato on the island of Mindanao in the Philippines and bomb a market in the city of Davao.[96] Julie Chernov Hwang and Kiraloi Ingram both stressed the role of relatives in recruitment of young men and women into the Maute group.[97]

In addition to individual-level analysis on terrorist behavior as well as program evaluation, there is also extensive scholarship highlighting the history, decision-making, and strategies of specific extremist cells, organizations, or networks,[98] as well as country-specific studies analyzing trends in specific localities.[99] Taking a historical approach, Solahudin traced the rise of Darul Islam and the splintering off of JI.[100] Emy Matesan analyzed tactical change within both Darul Islam and JI.[101] Julie Chernov Hwang explored JI's decision to prioritize *dakwah* (Islamic propagation) before jihad, focusing on three critical junctures in the network's development: the realization of the costs of the 2002 Bali bombing, the splintering off of the pro-bombing wing, and the series of arrests that followed the Densus raids on the JI home base at Tanah Runtuh in 2007.[102] More than a decade earlier, Ken Ward also examined this same shift within JI from violence to *dakwah*.[103]

Kirsten Schulze focused on local jihads in Ambon and Poso, asking what national-level jihadi groups "learned" in the Ambon jihad that they then transferred to the Poso jihad.[104] Quinton Temby highlighted the terrorist threat in Indonesia in the aftermath of ISIS[105] as well as the threat of the Maute group in the Philippines in the aftermath of the Marawi siege.[106]

Finally, some studies took a global perspective that emphasized, and at times overemphasized, the role of groups such as ISIS and Al Qaeda in mapping the landscape of jihadi groups in Southeast Asia.[107] The strongest of these, drawing on original fieldwork and rich with primary source knowledge, was "Jihadists Assemble: The Rise of Militant Islamism in Southeast Asia," by Quinton Temby, which contended that a regional jihadist assemblage of overlapping networks and groups created opportunities that made the region particularly attractive to global jihadists.[108] His dissertation most accurately established the extent of relationships between specific members of JI and Al Qaeda, their duration, and the results of those ties.

## Why Joining in Southeast Asia?

Although the policy community may have awoken to terrorism in Southeast Asia in the aftermath of the September 11, 2001, attacks (9/11), when a flurry of scholarship questioned whether Indonesia specifically and Southeast Asia more broadly was Al Qaeda's "second front" in the War on Terror,[109] Islamist extremism in Southeast Asia dates back prior to the Soviet–Afghan war. In the Philippines, Bangsamoro militant nationalism can be traced back to the 1968 Jabidah massacre, in which between 10 and 68 Moro Muslims were executed by the Marcos regime.[110] In Indonesia, there has been a violent Islamist extremist fringe dating back to the post-independence period, when the Darul Islam rebellions in the provinces of West Java, Aceh, South Kalimantan, and South Sulawesi attempted to actualize an Islamic state.

The Soviet–Afghan war marked an opportunity for Indonesian, Malaysian, and Filipino Islamist extremists in Southeast Asia to forge critical cross-national ties, as they trained together in the same training camp, Harbiy Pohantun Mujahidin-e-Afghanistan Ittihad-e-Islami, which was run by Abdul Rasul Sayyaf.[111] The Indonesian government contends that 350 Indonesians were sent to train in Pakistan and Afghanistan.[112] Some 200 of them came from Darul Islam.[113] Two Darul Islam members who would go on to found JI, Abdullah Sungkar and Abu Bakar Ba'asyir, became the conduit for Darul Islam—Indonesian and Malaysian—members who wanted to obtain paramilitary training in order to fight the Suharto dictatorship. Between 1985 and 1994, Darul Islam sent approximately 12 batches of recruits, with between 10 and 59 persons per batch.[114] By comparison, only approximately 13 Moros trained in Afghanistan.

The purpose of Darul Islam sending its members to Afghanistan was not to join the Afghan mujahidin in their fight but, instead, to gain valuable training experience, which they could bring home to the fight against the repressive New Order regime. However, Darul Islam members developed close ties to other groups in both Southeast Asia and the Middle East. Indonesians, Malaysians, and Filipinos trained together. They also developed relationships with Islamist extremist groups from the Middle East, cooperating with fighters from Egypt's al Gamaah al Islamiyah and participating in a training at one of al Gamaah's camps in Afghanistan's Khost Province.[115]

The relationships built during this period laid the foundations to enable JI to establish its own training camp inside the MILF's Camp Abu Bakar in 1994, a year after it broke away from Darul Islam. Moreover, it also fostered friendships between specific JI members and other individuals who went on to play a significant role in Al Qaeda, including Hambali, the leader of JI's fundraising division, Mantiqi 1, which was based in Malaysia, and Khaled Sheikh Mohammed, the mastermind of the 9/11 attacks. Through Hambali, members of the Malaysia-based Mantiqi 1 fundraising wing were to go for training at Al Qaeda Camp al Faruq between 1999 and 2001.

This, in itself, would make Southeast Asia a salient region to study, albeit not an exceptional one. What makes Southeast Asia particularly worthy of examination, however, is the sheer number of Islamist extremist groups that coexist with Islamist groups and Islamic organizations. There is a wealth of choices, particularly in Indonesia and the Philippines, if one wishes to join an Islamist extremist group, and many of these groups exist either semi-clandestinely or openly, which enables researchers to study why, indeed, one would join a particular Islamist extremist or Islamist group. However, to date, only a few models for understanding joining have considered Southeast Asian cases, and those are primarily authored by Southeast Asians or scholars who specifically focus on Southeast Asia.[116] However, Southeast Asia is where one finds the most open civil societies in the Muslim world and the most political liberal regimes. Thus, it is important to utilize Southeast Asian cases in understanding how and why one joins Islamist extremist groups, rather than beginning with the more authoritarian Middle Eastern societies.

## Why Indonesia?

With a population of 255 million people, 87 percent of which are Muslim, Indonesia is the largest Muslim nation in the world and the world's only Muslim democracy. Its total Muslim population exceeds that of Pakistan (181 million), Afghanistan (32.6 million), and Saudi Arabia (27.7 million) combined. Indonesia is a democracy, albeit a flawed one, with a multiparty system, free and fair elections, some respect for civil liberties, and tolerance for those who advocate for the implementation of Islamic law. However, it is also home to high levels of corruption and an oligarchic and personalistic party system.

## Terrorist Attacks

Indonesia has struggled with terrorism far more than its Southeast Asian counterparts. During the New Order era, from 1967 to 1998, terrorists attacks were largely carried out by Darul Islam members. Although Darul Islam went quiet following the arrest and execution of its leader, Sekarmadji Maridjan Kartosuwirjo, in 1962, it continued to exist as a community bound by common experiences, marriages, friendships, and familial ties.[117] In the 1970s, it re-emerged as an underground Islamic extremist network, launching a recruitment drive, employing the *usroh* (cell) method pioneered by the Muslim Brotherhood to organize clandestinely, and becoming a space in which those who opposed the New Order dictatorship's crackdown on political expressions of Islam found voice. Some members of Darul Islam launched terrorist attacks during the New Order period. Most notable were a series of bombings by a shadowy faction of Darul Islam known as Kommando Jihad in 1976 and the bombing of Borobodur temple in 1985.[118] JI, which splintered off from Darul Islam, would not begin to mount terrorist attacks until 1999.

During the initial decade following Indonesia's transition to democracy, Indonesia suffered iterated terrorist attacks largely targeting symbols of Western influence: hotels, bars, and churches. Initially, the masterminds of these attacks were part of a Malaysia-based pro-bombing faction within JI. This faction sought to incite civil war between Christians and Muslims and carry out Osama Bin Laden's 1998 *fatwa* calling for attacks against Westerners. The "pro-bombing wing" mounted a series of terrorist attacks, including the 2000 Christmas Eve bombing, the 2001 Atrium Mall Bombing, the 2002 Bali bombing, and the 2003 JW Marriot bombing. After JI distanced itself from this pro-bombing wing in 2004, the bombers, led by Malaysians Noordin M. Top and Dr. Azhari Husin, split off to form Al Qaeda in the Malay Archipelago (AQMA), a title pointing to admiration for Al Qaeda rather than any overt linkage. JI, in turn, eschewed terror attacks, outside of legitimate zones of conflict, favoring a strategy of *dakwah* and capacity building before jihad. AQMA would carry out the 2004 Australian embassy bombing, the 2005 Bali bombing, and the 2009 Marriot and Ritz Carlton bombing. After Noordin Top, the founder of AQMA, was killed in a shootout with police in 2009, AQMA was no longer operational. In the 5 years that followed, terrorist attacks were carried out by a host of smaller and often ad hoc cells.

Since 2014, terrorist attacks have been carried out not by JI affiliates and splinters but by pro-ISIS groups, most notably the umbrella JAD and tiny Poso-based Mujahidin Indonesia Timor (MIT). JAD attacks included the bombing of the Starbucks on Jalan Thamrin in 2016; the failed attack on the presidential palace, also in 2016; the police station attack in Solo in 2017; the attack on the Kampung Melayu bus terminal in 2017; the 2018 Surabaya church bombings; and the 2021 bombing of the Sacred Heart of Jesus Cathedral in Makassar. MIT attacks have been smaller in scope but are notable for their brutality, terrorizing local villagers into providing them with assistance. Recent attacks included the throat slitting of a father and son in Tanto village in 2019, the beheading of three farmers in September 2019, and the kidnapping and beheading of a cacao farmer in 2020.[119]

## The Fragmented Indonesian Islamist Extremist Ecosystem

The landscape of Indonesian Islamist extremism is highly fragmented. Although JI has been the best-known Southeast Asian terrorist group, other groups have formed and a few even went inactive or merged, most of which were splinters of preexisting groups. These included Mujahidin KOMPAK, a militant offshoot of the humanitarian aid organization, KOMPAK; Ring Banten, a violent splinter faction of Darul Islam; the aforementioned AQMA; Tanah Runtuh, JI's affiliate in the district of Poso; Mujahidin Kayamanya, Mujahidin KOMPAK's affiliate in the district of Poso; and many smaller groups. A detailed discussion of recruitment into Tanah Runtuh and

Mujahidin Kayamanya and the role of JI and KOMPAK in the Poso district can be found in Chapter 3.

Jemaah Islamiyah was and remains the most influential clandestine Salafi-Jihadi network operating in Indonesia. Its membership and its relevance have ebbed and flowed as it shed its pro-bombing wing, reacted strategically to state crackdowns, and took the necessary steps to avoid being arrested into insignificance. Although it initially struggled with a membership divided between a minority who sought to carry out terrorist attacks and a larger segment who advocated a strategy of *dakwah*, capacity building, education, and paramilitary training prior to launching violent actions, currently the network appears unified behind the latter position. However, with so many trained cadres having returned from Syria, whether that remains true in the future is uncertain.

Two other notable groups in the Indonesian Salafi-Jihadi ecosystem are Jemaah Ansharut Tauhid (JAT) and Jemaah Ansharusy Syariah (JAS). In 2008, JI co-founder Abu Bakar Ba'asyir established JAT, which would go on to supplant JI as the most active militant group of the period. It was easier to become a member of JAT because, unlike JI, it accepted newly released prisoners, and it was aboveground, not clandestine. Thus, JAT was a viable alternative that came with a bona fide JI founder at its head. When Ba'asyir swore loyalty to ISIS in 2014 and required his followers do likewise, however, most of the JAT leadership refused. An estimated 90 percent of JAT members, including Ba'asyir's own sons, broke off from JAT and formed JAS, taking rejection of al Baghdadi's Islamic State as a central principle.[120] JAS committed itself to socializing Islamic law and the concept of an Islamic state via *dakwah*, eschewing terrorism. The relationships among JI and its affiliates are shown in Figure I.1.

In contrast to JI, its splinters, and its affiliates, there were other groups that embraced takfiri ideology, often radicalized by the teachings of one man: Aman Abdurrahman. Although he had never fought in a jihad, Abdurrahman was respected for his prolific translations of jihadi texts from Arabic into Bahasa Indonesia.[121] He advocated some of the most extreme positions regarding the conduct of jihad.[122] Various groups and branches of groups fell under his influence, including Tim Hisbah, a local anti-vice militia based in a particularly crime-ridden neighborhood in the city of Solo.

The fragmented Indonesian extremist ecosystem would cleave sharply in 2014 as groups sorted themselves into pro- and anti-ISIS. Pro-ISIS groups swore loyalty to Abu Bakar al Baghdadi and had contacts among Indonesians

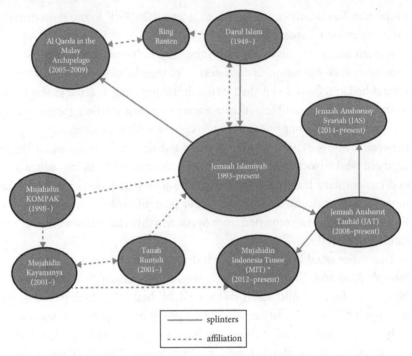

**Figure I.1** Jemaah Islamiyah and its affiliates. Dotted lines denote affiliation. Solid lines denote splinters. *MIT broke away from the JAT branch in Poso. It recruited heavily from former members of Mujahidin Kayamanya.

fighting with ISIS in Syria. The largest groups, JI and JAS, opposed ISIS. JI rejected Baghdadi's caliphate, preferring to send members for 3–6 months of training with Jabhat al Nusra and Ahrar al-Shams. Aman Abdurrahman was among the first senior Indonesian jihadists to swear loyalty to ISIS in November 2013; he quickly became the center of Indonesia's pro-ISIS community.[123] Two key figures who would travel to Syria, join ISIS, and set up a special division for Malaysian and Indonesian fighters, Katibah Nusantara—Bahrum Syah and Salim Mubarok alias Abu Jandal—were students of Aman Abdurrahman.

The most significant pro-ISIS group was the umbrella organization, JAD, which was first conceptualized in late 2014 by Aman Abdurrahman and a group of his followers visiting him at the Kembang Kuning prison where Aman was serving a sentence for his role in a cross-organizational jihadi training camp in the province of Aceh in 2010.[124] The network was formally established in November 2015 with Aman Abdurrahman at the head. Initially, one goal of JAD was to send its members to Syria; Aman Abdurrahman believed that because the Caliphate had been established, making *hijrah* (migration) to Syria was an obligation incumbent on supporters of ISIS.

However, Aman Abdurrahman's perspective changed in mid-2016 following an instruction from then ISIS spokesman, Abu Muhammad al Adnani, who contended that because it had become difficult for ISIS supporters to get to Syria, they should carry out *amaliyat* (lit. actions) in their home countries.[125] Adnani asserted, "If the tyrants have shut the door to *hijrah* in your faces, open the door of jihad in theirs."[126] JAD members turned their attention to launching terrorist attacks at home, although many still continued to try to make their way to Syria.

At the outset, JAD had an extensive regional structure in eight provinces: East Java, Central Java, West Java, Greater Jakarta, Lampung, Kalimantan, Sulawesi, and Maluku.[127] JAD excelled in poaching, preferring to recruit individuals from other Salafi-Jihadi and takfiri groups who did not need to be wholly indoctrinated. Multiple small groups, most of which had preexisting ties to Aman Abdurrahman, joined the fold. In addition, branches of long-established groups switched affiliation. For example, the Lamongan branch of the Islamic Defenders Front and parts of the Bandung branch of Darul Islam migrated to JAD.[128] Their greatest coup was gaining the support of Abu Bakar Ba'asyir, the head of JAT, who swore loyalty to ISIS in 2014, following a persuasion campaign by Aman Abdurrahman and his supporters. With him came members of JAT who remained loyal to him and, importantly, the JAT structure. With the entry of JAT into the JAD network, in large parts of West and East Java, the JAD structure was built atop of what was once JAT.[129] Between 2016 and 2019, JAD members were responsible for some of the most egregious terrorist attacks in Indonesia. However, JAD did not have the staying power of a JAS or a JI. By 2021, the network had been decimated by arrests and was woefully short on funds. Entire branches went inactive.

A handful of other small groups supported ISIS but eschewed membership in JAD. These included MIT, Ring Banten, Jemaah Ansharul Khilafa (JAK), Firqoh Abu Hamzah, and Tim Hisbah. Tim Hisbah was an anti-vice militia with ties to Syria via Bahrun Naim, an ISIS recruiter who came from their neighborhood. Ring Banten was actually divided; some members flirted with ISIS after one of their leaders, Iwan Dharmawan, shared a cell with Aman Abdurrahman in prison. However, the group was not united in its support of ISIS. MIT grew out of JAT-Poso in 2012. MIT, with between 30 and 50 members at its height, was best known for operating training camps in the mountains around Poso. It drew upon long-standing relationships within the Tanah Runtuh and Kayamanya communities and a desire for revenge against police for excesses. It was the first Indonesian jihadi group to swear loyalty to ISIS, likely in an effort to garner support and attention.

Jemaah Ansharul Khilafa was established in 2014 by Abu Husna, who was actually a founding member of JI. Subject to the same campaign of persuasion by Aman Abdurrahman and his supporters as Abu Bakar Ba'asyir at Pasir Putih prison because he was very close to Ba'asyir, he became an ISIS supporter.[130] However, Abu Husna did not join JAD. Instead, he created JAK, which initially he called Katibul Imam. JAK is the "mostly non-violent face of ISIS", conducting fundraising, undertaking humanitarian efforts, providing food and medical services to the poor, and running mosque study sessions, schools for Quran memorization, and educational programs.[131] In contrast to violent pro-ISIS groups—JAD, Tim Hisbah, and MIT—nonviolent JAK has largely been left alone by authorities.

Finally, there were also self-affiliated pro-ISIS cells, varying from less than a dozen to several hundred members.[132] They were typically constructed around social ties: family members, friends, neighbors, university classmates, or fellow participants in a religious study session.[133] Few lasted very long.[134] The relationship among pro-ISIS groups is specified in Figure I.2.

JAD, JAK, Tim Hisbah, and MIT had separate connections to specific Indonesian "link men" already in Syria. These included Bahrumsyah, the commander of the Indonesian-Malay unit, Katibah Nusantara; Salim Mubarok, alias Abu Jandal, former leader of the breakaway unit, Katibah Masyaariq, until his death in Syria in November 2016; Abu Walid, who was believed to be close to ISIS central leadership; Bagus Maskuron, a small-time jihadi who served time for participation in a bank robbery and migrated to Syria; and Bahrun Naim, who, until his death in 2017, functioned as a recruiter and funder for terrorist attacks in Indonesia.[135]

The rich fragmented landscape of Indonesian Islamist extremism makes it an ideal case for studying how and why individuals join Islamist extremist groups because with such a variety of groups comes a diverse set of pathways and motivations for joining. In certain groups, such as Darul Islam, JI, and JAT, internal pathways like kinship and schools were key. Individuals followed parents, siblings, teachers, and peers into the network. Mujahidin KOMPAK, by contrast, had no schools and was not operational long enough for kinship ties to play a role in joining. However, communal conflict on the

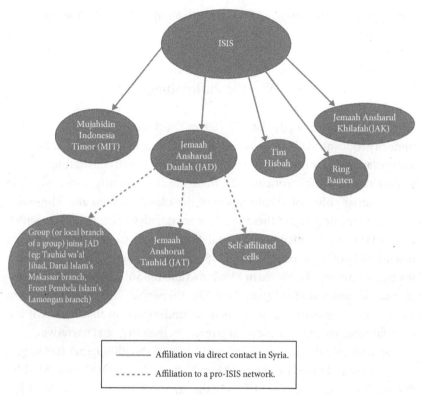

**Figure I.2** ISIS in Indonesia.

island of Ambon and in the district of Poso between 1999 and 2002 inspired many to join KOMPAK as a way to fight in a jihad to protect Muslims from attacks by Christians.

In Indonesia, individuals may move from one group to another. Thus, it is possible to meet someone who started out in JI, migrated to the AQMA splinter due to ideological affinity with the latter, shifted to JAT after prison, and then migrated again to JAS after Ba'asyir declared loyalty to ISIS. Thus, they can speak comparatively not only about motives for joining but also about the specific differences in recruitment and activities. Among pro-ISIS groups, people often joined via either social media or study circles. Many were poached from other organizations. However, prison was also a venue for recruitment. In short, Indonesia presents an empirical richness in the sheer array of groups that is absent in the Philippines and also in the broader Muslim world. This offers scholars the opportunity to explore a wider array of pathways to entry and motivations for joining than they otherwise could.

## Why the Philippines?

The Philippines is majority Catholic (80.6%), with a small 5.6 percent Muslim minority concentrated on the islands of Mindanao, Palawan, and in the Sulu archipelago. This immediately sets joining Islamist extremist groups in the Philippines in a different category than Muslim majority Indonesia. The post-colonial policy of Filipinization of the islands of Sulu and Mindanao resulted in the flooding of these Muslims areas with Christian settlers, which reduced the indigenous Muslim population from 70-80 percent at its height to a minority of 30 percent.[136] The 1968 Jabidah massacre ignited a separatist insurgency among the Moros in Mindanao and the Sulu archipelago that displaced millions and killed more than 120,000 people.[137] Islamist extremism in Muslim Mindanao and Sulu has to be understood in that regard. It has been far more rooted in these local grievances than in global narratives.

The academic discussion of militant Islam in the Philippines has largely revolved around three groups: the Moro National Liberation Front (MNLF), the MILF, and the ASG. The MILF and the ASG both broke from the MNLF—the MILF in 1977 and the ASG in the early 2000s. The MILF and MNLF both behave far more like insurgent groups in that they seek to capture and retain territory. The ASG is loosely organized, more as a confederation of armed bands with deep roots in their local communities on Basilan and Sulu than the quasi-military structured MILF and MNLF.[138] These groups cleave largely along clan lines, with the MNLF and ASG being largely Tausug and the MILF Maguindanao and, to a lesser extent, Maranao.

The landscape of Moro Islamist extremism continued to fragment throughout the first decade of the 21st century, most notably when the Bangasamoro Islamic Freedom Fighters (BIFF) splintered from the MILF in 2010 after the MILF decided to return to peace talks with the government.[139] After the death of its leader, Ameril Umbra Kato, it too splintered into three factions. There were also smaller groups that emerged, such as Ansar al Khilafah Philippines (AKP), Ghuraba, and, eventually, the Maute group (Figure I.3).

With the emergence of ISIS, there was a cleavage similar to that which occurred among Indonesian groups, with specific factions and smaller

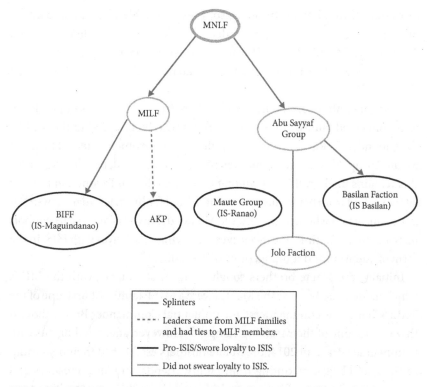

**Figure I.3** Islamist extremist groups in the Philippines. Solid lines denote splinters. Dotted lines indicate that leaders came from MILF families and had ties to MILF members. BOLD: pro-ISIS/swore loyalty to ISIS; FADE: did not swear loyalty to ISIS.

groups supporting ISIS while the larger ones rejected it. In the latter category, the MILF, the MNLF, and some factions of the ASG opposed ISIS. In the former category, the Basilan faction of the ASG led by the late Isnilon Hapilon swore loyalty to ISIS in July 2014, with pledges from one faction of BIFF, Ansar al Khilafah Philippines, and Ghuraba the following month.[140] In 2015, these groups made a video of themselves uniting and declaring Isnilon Hapilon as their Amir.[141] In 2016, the Maute group emerged from Ghuraba, began referring to themselves as IS Ranao, and swore allegiance to Abu Bakar Al Baghdadi.[142] I conducted interviews for this book with members of the Maute group, many of whom came from MILF families.

Although the Maute group may have been small, they are notable for what they accomplished in a short period: the 5-month takeover of parts of Marawi City in 2017. In doing so, they were able to build a coalition of pro-ISIS groups that transcended clan, bringing together Maranao, Tausug, and Maguindanao. This included Isnilon Hapilon's faction of the ASG, an ISIS cell from the town of Cotabato, and AKP based in Sultan Kudarat.[143]

Omar and Abdullah Maute, two brothers from a wealthy and politically well-connected family in the town of Butig who had studied in the Middle East, founded IS Ranao, which the Philippine government referred to as the Maute group.[144] At some point, they became radicalized, but the trigger for this remains unclear. It is known that Omar married an Indonesian but was later expelled from her family's boarding school for his strict Salafi views.[145] It is also uncertain whether initially, the Mautes deployed Islamic state symbols instrumentally. In time, the incentives for allying themselves with ISIS, in the form of attention and funding, proved irresistible.[146]

Initially, the Maute brothers sought to form an alliance with the MILF, which made sense because the Mautes were a MILF family. At first, one of the MILF's "renegade commanders," the influential Commander Bravo, allowed them to use one of their training camps.[147] However, after a falling out with Commander Bravo in 2014, the Maute brothers established their own camp in Butig and began recruiting from family, friends, and local mosques and communities in Butig, Piagapo, and Marawi.[148] In 2017, the coalition took over Marawi.

According to Quinton Temby, the goal of the Marawi takeover appeared to be carving out territory in an attempt to gain official recognition as part of the Caliphate, as the East Asia Province.[149] The government launched a massive counterattack, deploying 22 battalions drawn from its army, air force, and navy and shelling large portions of the city. In the end, the Mautes lost control of the city center and approximately 360,000 persons were displaced.[150]

It is important to examine the Maute group because it provides important counterpoints to groups based in Indonesia. The joining process has similarities, insofar as kinship plays a significant role in many narratives, but also critical differences. First, the Bangsamoro grievance narrative drove participation in a manner that differed even from those Indonesians living in conflict zones. Bangsamoro were raised with the grievance narrative about the historical injustices against their people. Second, several of those interviewed were from MILF families. Their fathers and uncles had participated in the jihad against the government. They grew up going to MILF camps for periods of weeks, months, or even living at the camps. Thus, jihad and paramilitary training were part of their lives in a way that they simply were not for the Indonesians.

Third, clan ties play a significant role in the Philippines, whereas they are absent in Indonesia. Fourth, the time horizons for joining were far shorter in the Philippines, with some recruited for specific battles. For these young men, participation was short term and situational. Fifth, financial incentives featured prominently for the majority of those interviewed. Finally, although the leaders of the Maute group were highly educated, those interviewed were, overall, poorer and less educated than their counterparts in Indonesia. Thus, inclusion of the Maute group introduces important variation.

## Methodology

This book is based on original fieldwork conducted between 2010 and 2019 in Indonesia and the Philippines. Over 12 trips to Indonesia during those years, I conducted more than 150 interviews with 97 jihadists from 14 Islamist extremist groups in Indonesia, including Darul Islam, Jemaah Islamiyah, Mujahidin KOMPAK, Ring Banten, Tim Hisbah, Tanah Runtuh, Mujahidin Indonesia Timor, Mujahidin Kayamanya, Al Qaeda in the Malay Archipelago, Jemaah Ashorut Tauhid, Jemaah Anshorusy Syariah, Jemaah Anshorut Daulah, and other pro-ISIS factions. These interviews took place in 11 cities: Pekanbaru, Bogor, Jakarta, Yogyakarta, Solo, Semarang, Kudus, Surabaya, Poso, Palu, and Ampana. As often as possible, I endeavored to meet with the same individuals on multiple occasions over the 9 years in order to build rapport and establish trust, which, in turn, increased the reliability of the information garnered. I also compiled 11 additional profiles of Indonesian Islamist extremists from primary source and open source documents, including autobiographies of specific militants, jihadi writings, official documents, sermons, publications, and websites; court documents and other government materials; as well as reports from international organizations, newspaper articles, and think tank reports. Most of these were individuals from the pro-ISIS community.

I utilized two sampling methods to identify respondents: identifying current and former members by working through guides (purposive sampling) and asking interviewees to identify other potential respondents (snowball sampling). As a complement, in February and July 2019, I interviewed 25 jihadists from three Islamist extremist groups in the Philippines (Maute group, ASG, and MILF) in three cities (Manila, Marawi, and Butig). The decision to add in the Philippines in 2019 means that the sample is bifurcated, but I contend it adds value by bringing in variation on ideology (more pro-ISIS individuals), education, gender, the role of study sessions, and the role of conflict.

As a rule, I conducted interviews in locations where the respondent felt most comfortable. In Indonesia, this included a restaurant during off hours, coffee shops, outdoor areas during prison visiting hours, and homes. In the Philippines, I interviewed in our translator's home or shop; in the homes of the interviewees; in a room on the grounds of a government complex; on the grounds of the former Darul Iman training camp in Butig; and, on several occasions, in the middle of fields a few hundred yards away from homes.

At the start of the interview, I shared who I was, the nature and goals of the project, and the ethics and obligations for the researcher. I explained that I had the duty to protect their identity to the best of my ability, that they were under no obligation to answer a question that made them uncomfortable, and that we could end the interview at any time. I sought permission to use an audio recording device, to quote them, and I asked them to select an alias or a general title via which I would refer to them in the book. When interviews were conducted in prisons, which occurred in Indonesia but not the Philippines, my guides first sought permission from the jihadi himself, and upon obtaining that permission, they then sought permission from the relevant authorities in the Department of Corrections. Closer to the date, interviews were reconfirmed with the jihadi. I received permission from the Goucher College Institutional Review Board (IRB) to conduct these interviews, including the informed consent language, which we agreed would be delivered orally. In prison, interviews were conducted in public areas such as a garden, an outdoor visiting room, a conference room, and, on one occasion, the cell.

In Indonesia and the Philippines, it was critically important to me to respect interviewee privacy and protect their rights. I worked in conjunction with the IRB at Goucher College to develop protocol that I carried through both *Why Terrorists Quit* and *Becoming Jihadis*. I also worked with many of the same guides in Indonesia, who had received MAs or PhDs in Australia and the United Kingdom and were familiar with ethics protocols. In cases in which I worked with new guides, we discussed IRB protocols, notably the importance of informed consent, voluntary participation, and protection of identities. Individuals approached for interviews had multiple opportunities for refusal: when initially contacted by the guide, when we sought confirmation closer to the date, and by going quiet at the interview. However, in most instances in Indonesia, those contacted accepted the interview. In the Philippines, because of the way interviews were procured, the power to refuse was entirely in the hands of the interviewee.

I made an effort to interview people who were at all stages of joining. This included individuals who had joined, become members, and left the group; joined, become members, and gone inactive; flirted with joining but never completed the process; joined multiple groups at once; joined, left, and joined other groups; and never actually joined anything but were pulled into a battle or an action by a relative or by material need. I do not doubt that many of those I interviewed obfuscated. When I interviewed a person the first time, they tended to be more cautious in what they chose to share compared to when we met a second or third time. These conversations are not easy ones. This highlights why conducting repeat interviews is so important. It enables clarification and trust building so that over time, one can obtain a fuller picture of why and how someone joined an extremist group. Every time I met with a person again, I learned new details about his or her life. We would delve into detail on new subject matter or dig deeper to unpack old questions. Slow research—in these instances, rapport building and trust building—is necessary for truly learning someone's narrative. People are like onions.

Finally, over the course of the research, I did my best to vary the sample. It is important to admit that the 25 Filipinos and 97 Indonesians were certainly a self-selecting group. In doing interviews with individuals who are inactive or former members of clandestine movements, it is impossible to be completely scientific in selection. However, I maximized variation in the sample by conducting interviews with members of 14 groups in Indonesia and three in the Philippines in 11 cities in Indonesia scattered across three islands and three cities and towns in the Philippines scattered across two islands.

Within and between the Indonesia and Philippines samples, however, there was considerable variation on multiple measures, including gender, education levels and types, roles in extremist groups, causes of radicalization, whether they participated in a jihad, motivations for joining extremist groups, duration of time in extremist groups, and the extent to which they have disengaged from violence and/or left the group.

A supra majority of those interviewed were men, across both samples. In the Philippines, four out of 25 were women, and in Indonesia, four out of 97 were women. Among the Indonesian male portion of the sample, 18 were or had been leaders in either JI, Mujahidin KOMPAK, JAT, JAS, or a pro-ISIS group; and 41 were operatives, meaning they participated directly in a terrorist attack, by making bombs, setting bombs, surveillance, gathering bomb-making materials, or planning aspects of the attack. Forty-one were rank-and-file members who played supportive roles.[151]

Among the Philippines sample, 22 participated in battles in Piagapo, Butig, or the Marawi siege. Among women, in the Philippines two out of the four were recruited for battles. However, in Indonesia, women's roles were confined to attending study circles and working at or attending specific Islamic boarding schools. It is important to note that this is specific to the particular sample. Increasingly, women have played roles in jihadi networks via social media—fundraising, recruiting, and managing chat rooms—and, in more recent years, in terrorist attacks themselves, notably the failed attack on the Presidential Palace in 2016 and the May 13–14, 2018, church bombings in Surabaya. Although some of these cases are highlighted in the book, the information is gleaned from primary source documents.

There was also considerable variation in education in terms of both level and duration of Islamic education. Among the Indonesians, 45 attended Islamic schooling, and of those, 16 attended Islamic boarding schools that were explicitly affiliated with JI or JAT for some portion of their education. The remaining 44 attended secular schools.[152] The majority were high school graduates. However, 16 attended university, whereas five stopped their schooling at middle school and one did not complete elementary school. There was also variation in the Philippines sample. Three had attended college; six had attended some high school but did not finish; the remaining 16 either attended elementary school before dropping out or never went to school at all.

Viewed from this perspective, the sample is quite diverse. One may ask why the interviews did not include individuals who were former members of other extremist groups—Christian extremists or former members of communist groups. Here, it is a matter of access. My guides simply do not have connections to these groups. Yet, it should also be acknowledged that the literature on why individuals join extremist groups lacks an understanding of the process in Southeast Asia. The existing literature is replete with cases drawn from the Red Brigades, the IRA, far right ultranationalists, and skinhead gangs as well as Al Qaeda, ISIS, and other groups based in the Middle East. Southeast Asia lags behind.

## Glancing Ahead

Chapter 1 explores the theme of motivations: why one joins Islamist extremist groups. Drawing on original fieldwork, it highlights specific push and pull factors that facilitated initial entry and forays into militant groups. It underscores the important pull of having family or friends already in the group. It then unpacks the roles played by various forms of seeking: redemption, revenge, the desire to effect change for Muslims, additional income, and knowledge about Islam and jihad.

Chapter 2 is the first of two chapters highlighting the processes and pathways via which individuals join extremist groups. It explores internal pathways to entry into jihadi groups. This chapter centers mostly on the experience of members of Jemaah Islamiyah and its affiliates in Indonesia, although it also draws on members of the Maute group in the Philippines. It underscores the role of kinship ties, on the one hand, in expediting the pathway to entry into militant groups, and radical educational institutions, on the other hand.

Chapter 3 explores three external pathways facilitating entry into militant groups and one partial pathway. In this instance, individuals were not born into the networks. They did not go to school at a radical *madrasa* (Islamic day school) or *pesantren* (Islamic boarding school). Instead, they encountered Islamist extremist groups in prison, living in a conflict zone, attending study circles, or in online chats. This chapter draws on examples from Indonesia and the Philippines, paying particular attention to the processes and pathways via which individuals join pro-ISIS groups.

Chapter 4 unpacks the various ways that commitment is expressed when one joins an extremist group. This includes changes in dress, where one chooses to live, and social norms to which one adheres. It also delves further into how brotherhood is felt at the commitment stage and how it comes to be expressed.

Chapter 5 explores the activities one engages in once they are a member of an extremist group. It highlights how most roles are quite mundane: *dakwah* (Islamic propagation), teaching, studying, and attending religious functions. It underscores how, often, those invited to participate in paramilitary training or terrorist attacks have a relationship with those facilitating entry into these activities and that participants in terrorist attacks often know each other. They may be relatives, friends, or even from the same nuclear family. This chapter draws primarily on Indonesian cases.

The Conclusion highlights the major trends that have emerged from the preceding chapters and discusses the implications of those trends for the broader study of joining, radicalization, and terrorism in both the Muslim world and the West. Where pertinent, it highlights parallels and similarities between joining an Islamist extremist group in Southeast Asia, and joining ISIS.

# 1
# Motivations

Considerable research has been conducted at the individual level exploring motivations for joining and committing to extremist or insurgent groups.[1] Scholars acknowledge a diverse array of factors that motivate or create the conditions for someone to join a terrorist group. These include grievances,[2] familial and peer social networks,[3] social identification with group goals,[4] vengeance,[5] conscription,[6] and opportunity and a desire for status or adventure.[7]

This chapter unpacks the push and pull factors[8] that motivated individuals in Indonesia and the Philippines to join Islamist extremist groups. Some of these echo the points from the broader literature, and others, far less so. The most notable pull factors center on actual and constructed kinship ties, those familial and peer networks mentioned above. In short, if one's family members, friends, or teachers are already in the group, one is more likely to join that particular group. In addition to relational pull factors, various push factors can motivate a person to join a particular group. In this research, the most common push factors were seeking ideological affinity or practical knowledge about jihad, personal redemption, and revenge in Indonesia; seeking jihad and financial compensation in the Philippines; and the ability to improve Muslim lives by redressing injustice and improving circumstances in both countries.

Through an examination of individual narratives and broad patterns data, this chapter explores *why* individuals join Islamist extremist groups. It highlights how one's motivations for joining are often a result of the interaction between who one knows (i.e., relational pull factors) and what one seeks (i.e., purpose-driven push factors). The chapter shows how, in most instances, individuals were initially attracted to a particular group by a combination of factors, with one reinforcing another. An individual may be very interested in learning more about jihad, for example, and may be sampling different study circles in order to do so. Then, a trusted friend invites them to join a particular study group. Here, friendship and a desire to learn about jihad reinforce each other.

This chapter stresses how, in Indonesia and the Philippines, relational factors are typically paramount. It is rare that someone found their way to extremist groups by themselves, without any aid from family members, friends and acquaintances, or mentors. This chapter stresses how and why those factors are particularly salient.

## Who You Know: Family, Friends, and Mentors

### Rashid

"Rashid" came to Malaysia from Indonesia in 1977 as an illegal migrant when he was 2 years old with his mother and father.[9] His parents were members of the Darul Islam movement. They sent him to state primary school, but starting in middle school between 1988 and 1990,[10] they sent him to Mahad Ittiba' As Sunnah in the town of Kuala Pilah in Malaysia's Negeri Sembilan state. This particular Islamic school was friendly to the men who would go on to found Jemaah Islamiyah, Abu Bakar Ba'asyir, and Abdullah Sungkar. Sungkar and Ba'asyir would sometimes visit his school. He remained at the school for the first through third years of middle school.[11]

Although his parents were ordinary rank-and-file members in Darul Islam, his father still intended to socialize him into the Darul Islam worldview. He contends his father taught him about Islam and jihad from a young age, but it "was not focused."[12] When he was 15 years old and in his third year of junior high school, his parents decided it was time to intensify his Islamic education. They asked him to attend sermons alongside his father led by Abu Bakar Ba'asyir and Abdullah Sungkar. Rashid noted, "I preferred Abdullah Sungkar as he had a soft voice, made jokes, and was interesting. Abu Bakar Ba'asyir was too serious. I would fall asleep."[13] That year, in 1990, he also met Mukhlas, then newly returned from Afghanistan, where he trained on the Afghanistan–Pakistan border. Mukhlas took him under his wing and began to teach him about Islam and to guide him in basic paramilitary training—physical fitness.

> He delivered sermons about *i'dad* (preparations for jihad) and about how to defend Islam. He once asked me to jog with him in the morning. He said,

"We need to jog so our body is strong and healthy . . . to defend Islam, we have to be strong and healthy. If conflict breaks out, we are already ready."[14]

Gradually, through the sermons and through Mukhlas, Rashid was becoming socialized into the worldview and mindset of a Salafi-Jihadi.

That year, three notable things happened. First, Rashid swore *bai'at* (loyalty oath) to Sungkar, affirming that he would defend Islam and follow sharia, obeying the leader unless the leader's order ran counter to sharia.[15] Second, he began attending small home-based Darul Islam religious study groups. Third, once it was determined he was ready, he was sent to the boarding school founded by Sungkar and Ba'asyir: Ngruki. Mukhlas had a plan for him. He would study at Ngruki and become a teacher in his own right. Then, Rashid would return to Malaysia to teach at Luqmanul Hakim, the boarding school Mukhlas was founding that would teach Salafi-Jihadi ideology along the lines envisioned and preached by Sungkar, Ba'asyir, and Mukhlas.

Rashid's progress to this point was entirely a result of who his parents were. He had started attending sermons at the request of his parents. He was accepted because they were members. He came to know Sungkar and Ba'asyir through his parents. Mukhlas took him under his wing, not only because he saw something in him but also because he knew he could trust him as the son of members in good standing. Due to his familial ties to the group, he was given the oath at 15 years of age and sent to Ngruki, the radical Islamic boarding school founded by Sungkar and Ba'asyir for further Islamic education and indoctrination. None of these opportunities would have been present for him had his parents been ordinary Indonesian migrant workers and not Darul Islam members.

The most important motivation for joining an Islamist extremist group is knowing someone already in the group (Figure 1.1). In 97 interviews with Indonesian Islamist extremists and another 11 profiles constructed from a combination of primary source and open source documents, having a family member, teacher, or friend in the group was a key pull factor in 49 instances. Likewise, in 19 out of 25 interviews with former members of the Maute group, having immediate or extended family, friends, or imams propelled them to join. This held constant across gender, with 6 out of 8 women across Indonesia and the Philippines citing following family or being invited by friends.

Having family members already in the group was most important, with 23 individuals citing it. This was typically a parent, sibling, or uncle. Being

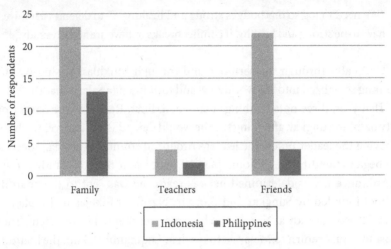

**Figure 1.1** Pull factors: Family, teachers, and friends.

born into Darul Islam and Jemaah Islamiyah families meant that youth were socialized from a very early age into the network's worldview, often sent to schools affiliated with the network to ensure that they would, at the very least, grow up to be sympathizers, if not members in good standing. Moreover, the bonds of kinship are not only social but also emotional. One loves, trusts, and respects one's parents. Thus, if one's parents belong to the community, it is very difficult to choose another path. There may be more flexibility with siblings and uncles. However, if one has a deep emotional bond with or admiration for a particular sibling or uncle, it may motivate them similarly to that of a parent.

The late "Sam," a member of Ring Banten, a violent offshoot of Darul Islam, explained that he joined Ring Banten "because my family was there. It was a family matter. There were also soft pressures. 'You went to Ngruki, right?' You understand."[16] In short, it was expected. His uncle was the head of Ring Banten. Sam was sent to the Ngruki *pesantren* (Islamic boarding school).[17] Darul Islam was where he belonged.

The salience of kinship is not simply a Jemaah Islamiyah and Darul Islam phenomenon, however. Dita Oepriarto, the mastermind of the May 13 and 14, 2018, church bombings in Surabaya, Indonesia, led a cell of the pro-ISIS umbrella, Jemaah Asharud Daulah, composed of three families: his immediate family, including his wife, teenage sons, and two young daughters; a family of six, including a husband, wife, and three children; and another family of five.[18] The parents were inspired by jihadi eschatology.[19] They believed the end-times were coming, and the only way to ensure they and their children would all end up in heaven was to martyr themselves together.[20] The children were not in a position to refuse their parents. They loved their parents, respected them, and trusted them implicitly. They would not defy them.

Twenty-two individuals shared that friends initially approached them. In these instances, it is important to note that friends rarely inducted someone into a group. Far more typical, friends would invite someone to participate in a study circle or a mass prayer that was a vetting mechanism to begin the pathway to possible recruitment into an Islamist extremist group. Thus, friendship served as a gateway for individuals seeking to learn more about Islam and jihad, opportunities to improve the well-being of Muslims, redemption, or revenge. For example, Mujahidin Indonesia Timor (MIT), a tiny Poso-based group that was the first in Indonesia to swear loyalty to ISIS, relied heavily on pre-existing friendship ties and the sense of camaraderie they inspired. In interviews, three members of MIT shared that their prior relationship with Santoso, the founder of MIT, and their affinity for him were the key factor in their joining and swearing the oath of loyalty.[21] Second to that was a desire for revenge against the police counterterrorism team (Densus 88) for excesses, including the January 22, 2007, shootout at their base in the neighborhood of Tanah Runtuh that resulted in the deaths of 14 of their friends.[22] Likewise, several members of Jemaah Islamiyah, who joined via study circles, explained that they were invited by friends to attend study sessions.

In four instances, a teacher or mentor invited someone to join an Islamist extremist group. This occurred in two ways. A teacher or mentor could encourage someone who had no prior affiliations with Islamist extremist groups to join such a group. Alternatively, if a teacher or mentor left a particular Islamist extremist group to found another, existing members who were loyal to that particular teacher or mentor could follow. Here, too, emotions underpin motivation. One agrees to join or follows a particular mentor out of trust and deep and abiding respect.

Teachers and mentors often offered an expedited pathway to entry. Whereas someone recruited by a friend or acquaintance might have to go through months or even years of study circles, a teacher or mentor who was a high-ranking or venerated figure in the group could enable someone to enter into the extremist network via his recommendation alone. In doing so, the mentor plays an outsized role in the motivation. As with kinship, a person may join a group or migrate between groups based on pressure or persuasion from the mentor, with little else reinforcing it.

For example, Ahmed Junaidi, who would travel to Syria to join ISIS, was invited to become a member of Jemaah Anshorut Tauhid (JAT), a breakaway faction of Jemaah Islamiyah, by Salim Mubarok alias Abu Jandal.[23] Mubarok was a religious teacher who lived in Junaidi's neighborhood and recruited for ISIS.[24] According to two members of the JAT leadership at that time, someone who wanted to join JAT had to go through 6 months to 1 year of study circles before being vetted to join the group.[25] However, Mubarok's recommendation gave Junaidi a shortcut to entry. Rather than attend 6 months of study sessions, he simply went to Ustad Achwan, who was at the time heading up JAT in the town of Malang, and told him, "I have instructions from Abu Jandal to join JAT."[26] After praying, they went back to Ustad Achwan's house and he administered the *bai'at* (loyalty oath). Ustad Achwan trusted Abu Jandal's recommendation. Although Junaidi professed that he thought about joining JAT for upwards of a week before going to Ustad Achwan, he gave no reason why.[27] He had grown up and been active in the Islamic mass organization, Muhammadiyah; he was not seeking knowledge about Islam. He did not claim he was seeking revenge or redemption, and he expressed no altruistic motive. Instead, he emphasized the role played by his relationship with Salim Mubarok. In fact, he washed out of JAT-Malang after 7 months and joined study sessions again only when Salim Mubarok was leading them.[28] When he went to Syria to join ISIS, it was with the encouragement of Salim Mubarok.

Likewise, several former members of JI reported that they migrated to JAT after JI co-founder Abu Bakar Ba'asyir founded it. They left JI either because Ba'asyir specifically asked them or because they felt loyalty to Ba'asyir and wanted to be part of the group he led, irrespective of whether or not they were invited. For example, 3 former members of JAT reported that they joined JAT because Ba'asyir requested their help to build either the central network or a specific branch of that network. One explained, "Ustad Abu [Bakar Ba'asyir] left JI and then established a [new] organization. Because I have a *bai'at* bond with Ustad Abu, I will follow him wherever he goes. This is a consequence of having sworn *bai'at*."[29]

Although kinship ties are no less important among recruits to the Maute group in the Philippines, there are important familial differences in terms of *who* pulls someone into an extremist group. Whereas in Indonesia, family typically refers to parents, uncles, or siblings, in the case of the Maute group, family can be siblings and uncles, on the one hand, or "relatives," on the other hand. *Relatives* is a loose term referring to extended family. This could be second, third or fourth cousins or in-laws. Sometimes, one's teacher, imam, or best friend is also a relative. These are further reinforced by clan ties. The division between friend and teacher, on the one hand, and family, on the other hand, tends to be less explicit in the Philippines compared to Indonesia. That fusion of family with best friend or teacher or imam made it difficult to refuse the call to join the Maute group, especially in cases in which the person recruiting was a Maute leader. It also makes friendship function similarly to kinship because so often there is kinship in friendship and it generates the same emotional bonds: love, affinity, trust, and respect.

Fourteen former Maute members cited being invited or encouraged by relatives in the Maute group, particularly uncles, cousins, or in-laws, as a primary motivator for them joining. Five of them were related to the imam of the Tambo mosque in the municipality of Piagapo, who was an avid recruiter for the Maute group in that area. Imam Abilino Dimakaling held study circles and preached about jihad and Islamic rights in the years leading up to the Marawi siege. "Jamal" explained,

> [Imam] was my uncle. My mother's brother. I attended daily prayers at his mosque starting at age 12. He recruited many of the youth in Piagapo. He taught me that if we did jihad and we died, we'd go to heaven and get the virgin angels.[30]

In cases in which relatives were the same age, sometimes the peer pressure was quite intense. "Ryan" shared that he left his six children and his wife to join the Maute group 10 days into the Marawi siege after 17 of his friends and relatives showed up at his house and told him it was time to participate in *jihad qital* (battle) by joining the battle in the Marantao municipality.[31] Four others followed same-aged friends, who were not relatives, into the Maute group. In each of these instances in which an individual followed their friends or same-aged relatives, the relationship itself was not sufficient. The individual was susceptible to recruitment by a friend because they needed extra income, wanted to participate in a jihad, or sought a channel for personal redemption. For example, Ryan's cousins not only used peer pressure by showing up en masse to entice him to join the fight but also promised him

50,000 pesos ($1,012) and a job.[32] When asked if he would have joined the battle had only one relative come to his home instead of 17, he said he would have because the prospect of 50,000 pesos and a job was too good to pass up.[33] Thus, the financial reward may have outweighed the personal connection in this instance.

The salience of kinship ties and constructed kinship ties in Indonesia and the Philippines is not surprising. That pre-existing familial and friendship ties facilitate recruitment is among the most robust findings from research on social movement activism, gang and cult membership, terrorism, and religious extremism.[34] Why do family, friends, and mentors have such an outsized impact on whether one joins Islamist extremist groups? Kinship, constructed kinship, and friendship can intensify bonds of love, trust, and loyalty.[35] From the perspective of someone already in the group, who better to target for membership than one's own blood, one's favorite students, or one's closest friends? From the outside, who better to trust than one's own siblings or parents? There are also emotional bonds underpinning kinship and constructed kinship affinity and affection among friends, esteem and veneration for mentors, and love and respect for parents. Trust for all of them. What is compelling is that this finding holds true across groups, whether one is a member of a pro-ISIS group or a member of a group that is anti-ISIS, and whether one is male or female. The motivation to join an Islamist extremist group is shaped, at least in part, simply by the company one keeps.

## What You Seek

Joining an extremist group is influenced not only by whom you know but also by what you seek (Figure 1.2). Although having friends or family in the movement is likely a necessary condition for joining, it is seldom sufficient on its own. For a person to join an extremist group, they need to gain some form of emotional, psychological, or material satisfaction from doing so. In short, it must fulfill a need.

Such needs may include a desire to learn more about Islam, jihad, or the search for ideological affinity; opportunities for altruism and a greater sense of purpose through improving the lives of Muslims; redemption; revenge; and financial or material rewards. Ideological affinity, altruism, and redemption were factors present in both Indonesia and the Philippines. Revenge was prevalent among respondents in Indonesia, whereas financial rewards

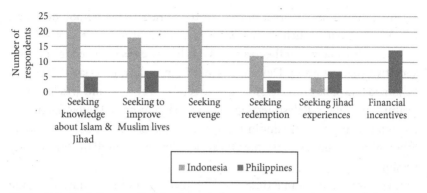

**Figure 1.2** Push factors: Seeking knowledge, experience, purpose and altruism, financial benefits, or emotional vindication.

were a key factor among respondents in the Philippines. Far less frequent, one woman in the Philippines cited coercion as key to her involvement in the Maute group. Of the five who sought to join the Caliphate, in each case, this was not the start of their entry into extremism but, rather, a waystation along the way. For example, two were dealing with multidimensional personal crises; leaving for Syria provided an escape and a solution. For people who migrate between groups, they may have different motivations undergirding each switch. What they seek may vary depending on time, place, circumstance, and desire.

Many who seek ideological affinity or opportunities for altruism or even redemption may do so through mainstream Islamic or Islamist groups. That is why the interaction effect between knowing someone in the group and what one is seeking is important. Without the connection and community, one may never have found their way into the extremist group. However, without the desire, one may never have been tempted in the first place.

## Seeking Knowledge and Ideology Affinity

### Abu Ayyas

"Abu Ayyas" was born in the Kelapa Dua neighborhood in the city of Depok at the dormitory for the Police Mobile Brigade. He came from a police family. His father and older brother were police officers. They were not a religious family. He attended Technical Vocational School Budi Utomo, a school infamous for street brawls. In the library at the school, he found Islamist magazines such as *Sabili, Intilaq,* and *Al-Islam*.[36] It was 1992 or 1993, and Bosnia was in the headlines. He had friends involved in the conservative Islamist group Dewan Dakwah Islamiyah Indonesia (DDII), and he joined one of its protests. He began to read more books and articles about Islamic struggle in Palestine, Algeria, Burma, Southern Thailand, and the Philippines and the mujahidin groups in Afghanistan. He began to study religion, collect books, learn the Quran, and involve himself in Quran study sessions.

It was around this same time that he joined the Tarbiyah movement, the precursor to what became the Prosperous Justice Party, and soon became enamored with the concept of *ghazwul fikri* (war of thought):

> This was a turning point for me; I became a more radical person. When I learned about *ghazwul fikri,* I hated Western civilization and the global injustice that claimed Muslims as victims. I blamed the United States. These disappointments turned me into a more radical person.[37]

After graduating from technical school in 1996, he attended Islamic boarding school to study Arabic and learn the Quran. In 1997, he joined the police force at the urging of his mother, who insisted he follow his father's example.[38] He continued to study with Tarbiyah.

Beginning in late 2001, Abu Ayyas started to become interested in JI. He read books published by key JI figures and followed the Ambon conflict closely. After the October 2002 Bali bombing, he became more overtly sympathetic to JI. A friend on the police force gave Abu Ayyas a phone number of a jihadi notable at Cipinang prison; he did not specify whom, and they began corresponding via text message.[39] He began visiting JI members at Cipinang prison, including Urwah and Ubeid, both members of Noordin M. Top's splinter network, which he called Al Qaeda in the Malay Archipelago; Abdullah Sunata, a former senior leader in Mujahidin KOMPAK; and eventually takfiri ideologue, Aman Abdurrahman.[40] The knowledge he sought interacted with whom he came to know. He came to see himself as Urwah's student,[41] although, by 2006, he had also become a sympathizer of Aman Abdurrahman.

> I was astonished by Aman Abdurrahman's thought, and it interested me. I thought that it was a new *manhaj,* a new ideology. I had never been

exposed to a religious understanding quite so brave in branding certain persons as infidels. Since I was a police officer, my friends who were members of Aman Abdurrahman's group, viewed me cynically. They said I was un-Islamic, because I was a serving police officer. I was not comfortable with this group. But the ideology stayed with me.[42]

As he moved deeper in jihadi circles, he used his connections in the police force to open a recreational shooting company while still an active duty police officer.[43] In 2008, he resigned from the police force.[44]

By 2009, he shifted from simply adopting their mental frames of reference and worldview to taking action. He began holding paramilitary training for members of jihadist groups together with a paratrooper from the Police Mobile Brigade force, who was also a student of Aman Abdurrahman.[45] Moreover, he took up the cause of jihadis restarting paramilitary training camps, taking a key role in establishing a training camp for members of different extremist groups in the province of Aceh in 2010.

In short, Abu Ayyas found his way into the jihadi community by a desire to learn more about Islam and jihad. Initially, he was drawn to the worldwide mujahidin struggle, but this, on its face, would not be enough to pull someone into an extremist group. Many Muslim youth are enamored with the stories of the mujahidin struggle much as young American children may be enthralled by the military. Abu Ayyas initially sought to satisfy his curiosity by joining conservative Islamist groups such as Tarbiyah, reading Islamic magazines and books, and attending Islamic boarding school for a year. After the 2000 Christmas Eve bombing and after the terrorist attacks of September 11, 2001 (9/11), however, he began to be intrigued by JI and books authored by JI leaders and significant figures. Due to his contacts as a member of the police force, he connected with JI, KOMPAK, and the Al Qaeda in the Malay Archipelago members in prison and, in time, Aman Abdurrahman. At this point, as he was exposed to the debates within the Salafi-Jihadi and takfiri communities, his thinking became radicalized. At every juncture in his decade-long journey, Abu Ayyas sought to learn more about Islam and jihad, but he was attracted to militant interpretations, not mainstream ones. As he became exposed to Salafi-Jihadi and takfiri interpretations, he found ideological affinity and he shifted from simply holding radical views to holding paramilitary trainings.

Of those interviewed in Indonesia, 24 cited a desire to learn about jihad in a practical way or to find ideological affinity as an important motivating force for why they joined a specific Islamist extremist group. Its important to stress that the majority of Muslims who seek knowledge about jihad do so via mainstream Islamic and Islamist groups. However, some seek practical paramilitary knowledge about performing jihad. For example, "Hajir" was "searching for the meaning of jihad."[46] He attended many study sessions and read many books on the subject, but all the answers he found were unsatisfactory. They were banal. Then, his friend brought him to a study session run by the late Subur Sugiarto in Semarang, an affiliate of the late Noordin M. Top, mastermind of the 2005 Bali bombing and the 2009 Marriott and Ritz Carlton bombings.[47] His friend claimed it would satisfy his curiosity about jihad

> in a practical way. Like how to use a weapon. How to shoot well. How to survive in the jungle and on the battlefield. My idea of jihad had been troops facing each other. Kill or be killed. I was interested in "Pak Subur" because I could know more about how to practice jihad.[48]

"Anas" echoed these sentiments when he explained why he joined JI study groups, although he did not realize it was JI at the time: "I joined because I wanted to learn more about jihad. I was like a small boy seeing something new. [I liked these study circles] because the study of jihad in them and subsequently in the Madrasa Diniyah [after-school Quran study run by the same people] was more robust."[49]

Others were not seeking knowledge about jihad per se but about Islam more broadly, and they were attracted to expressions of Islam that were more Salafi. Thus, they were seeking a specific ideological affinity—finding a certain type of Islam that satisfied them. One former member of Aman Abdurrahman's community, Tauhid wa'al Jihad, shared that he had been looking for Salafi *pengajian* (study sessions) after returning to his home province; he had attended Salafi study groups in college. He stumbled into a Salafi-Jihadi study circle, however. He explains, "Their views influenced me strongly because all of it was new. I had no filter. All their views penetrated."[50] He would travel from Salafi-Jihadi circles to takfiri circles propelled by what he called a "thirst for knowledge."[51]

In the Philippines, the five individuals who stated they joined the Maute group to learn more about Islam and jihad were speaking about Islam on a more basic level. "Nabi," "Omar," and "Naga," for example, all joined the Maute group because they wanted to learn to read the Quran.[52] Since they were either part of the Maute family or a relative of Imam Abilino Dimakaling, that desire was channeled through Maute or Maute-sympathetic figures, whereas otherwise they might have sought to attend an Arabic language school.

The search for knowledge about Islam, jihad, and ideological affinity is typically innocuous. Most who engage in this search, especially in Indonesia with its surfeit of Islamic movements and organizations, will find a mainstream Islamic or Islamist group that satisfies their curiosity. They will find community and connection in those groups. However, some who engage in that search will not be satisfied with the answers they receive in the mainstream and Islamist groups. They will seek that practical knowledge and experience of jihad and find fulfillment, answers, and community in Salafi-Jihadi groups. Perhaps they will value the absolute certainty that comes with being a member of a takfiri group. Alternatively, they may seek the ideological affinity that comes from being part of an exclusive community bound by the same worldview seeking revolutionary change. These ideological factors served as primary motivations, as in the case of Hajir, who searched for practical knowledge about jihad and Abu Ayyas, whose captivation with the mujahidin struggle led him first to Islamist groups and then to Salafi-Jihadi and takfiri groups, until he finally took it upon himself to become a paramilitary trainer for those groups.

However, neither Hajir nor Abu Ayyas would have found their way into Salafi-Jihadi/takfiri circles without connections from friends who vouched for them. Thus, the connection between what one seeks and whom one knows becomes apparent. Without a desire to learn more about the practicalities of jihad, neither man would have associated with the extremists. However, without friends who made those introductions, it is unlikely they would have had the opportunity to gain entry into those communities.

## Seeking to Improve the Lives of Muslims: Altruism and Purpose

### Amar

"Amar" was a student at Muhammadiyah University–Surakarta in Central Java studying electrical engineering when the September 11, 2001, terrorist attacks occurred in the United States. Up to that point, his life had been that of a mainstream Indonesian Muslim. His family had been members of Muhammadiyah, Indonesia's second largest Indonesian Islamic mass organization, which has an urban educated membership and a more Middle Eastern orientation. He had attended Muhammadiyah schools and public schools in his hometown of Solo.

The 9/11 attacks sparked his interest, and he began to follow online media. He paid particular attention to news about different Islamist movements. One group caught his eye: The Islamic Defenders Front (FPI). It seemed like the perfect balance for him. FPI was a paramilitary organization, but it was licit. It was a militant group, but it was not Salafi-Jihadi. It conducted anti-vice "sweeping" operations, breaking up and destroying bars and clubs, and it attacked groups it deemed to be religiously, socially, or sexually deviant.[53] However, it did not mount terrorist attacks. FPI aimed to make Indonesia more sharia compliant but was not revolutionary. Amar stated,

> I saw that FPI is a legal organization. It supported Islamic struggle.... Therefore, I was interested in that organization.... I joined FPI initially because I wanted to fight to change the community from one that is far from Islamic values to a [true] Islamic community. I wanted to contribute to that fight.[54]

The altruism inherent in his statement is clear. He and his younger brother, who shared his vision and view of Islam, joined together. He goes on to explain,

> I saw the wrongdoing and vice that was rampant across Indonesia. Police were not able to work well. I wanted to change this. I believed that FPI was one of the vehicles I could use [to help tackle these wrongdoings]. Before we can attain the level of jihad, we have to perform *amar ma'aruf nahi mungkar* (enjoining the good and forbidding the bad) first.[55]

At some point, likely between 2006 and 2009 (Amar did not specify the year), while he was still active in FPI, he also began joining in sweeping activities with another related area group, Tim Hisbah. He did not see this as a migration between groups. He asserted "at times, FPI members joined Tim Hisbah in performing anti-vice activities."[56] He saw his activities in Hisbah as a continuation of those in FPI. However, Hisbah was a fundamentally different organization.

In 2008 or 2009, Tim Hisbah's leaders became enamored with Aman Abdurrahman's teachings. Sigit Qardhowi, then the head of Tim Hisbah, set up monthly *pengajian* (study sessions) via phone for Aman and its members. Aman's takfiri arguments caused a shift in the focus of Tim Hisbah from anti-vice to anti-government.[57] This had an impact on Amar. He explained that as an FPI member, "my mindset was to perform *amar ma'aruf nahi mungkar*."[58] He was critical of the government, viewing it as hopelessly corrupt, but he did not reject it outright. He asserts that Aman Abdurrahman's ideas changed his mindset: "I became closed. I saw Indonesia as an area at war and I had to perform *amaliyah* [lit. actions]."[59]

Around 2012, having moved to Jakarta, his brother, Arif, became active in pro-ISIS circles and began attending activities at the Al Fatah Mosque in the neighborhood of Menteng.[60] He also reconnected with a former classmate, Bahrun Naim, a man who would become renowned as a recruiter and terrorist facilitator for ISIS.[61] Still in Solo, Amar also became attracted to ISIS, not surprising because Aman Abdurrahman was a key ISIS booster. Amar says he was particularly impressed with ISIS' successes in Syria and its boldness in standing up to Bashar al-Assad. Even as he became more active in ISIS activities in Solo, he continued to participate in FPI and socialize with fellow FPI members. In his own words, "I was FPI with ISIS flavor. I left FPI little by little."[62]

He asserts his activities in pro-ISIS circles came through his brother, Arif, who was his connection to Bahrun Naim's group.[63] He participated in the group's Telegram chats. He watched the videos Naim sent from Syria. However, he contends there was a limit to his involvement. He recruited people for the group at the behest of his brother. He hid a member of the cell fleeing from the authorities. However, he stayed away from terrorist attacks. "There was a chat to assemble bombs, but I did not join it. That would have been very risky. For security reasons, I didn't want to join activities that were risky."[64]

In short, Amar stayed in FPI for 11 years, was active in their *dakwah*, joined in their fights at least two or three times per week, and rose to the position of treasurer for his branch. As FPI was a licit aboveground organization, he did not need to know someone to gain entry, although he and his brother joined together. What he sought carried more weight. He was motivated by a desire to make society less vice-prone and more Islamic. He liked that, at the time, FPI was a recognized legal entity.[65] Thus, he was cracking down on vice and getting into fights, but he was doing so within the bounds of the law. Driven by the same motivation, he also joined in activities of Tim Hisbah. Exposure to the ideas of Aman Abdurrahman while part of Hisbah primed him to be open to ISIS ideology. His final shift from Tim Hisbah to ISIS and Bahrum Naim's group is a product of a different interplay of factors. Here, there is no emphasis on altruism and purpose. Instead, his motivations were tied to his brother, who had a previous relationship with Bahrun Naim, and ideological affinity with the group's members. This indicates that as an individual migrates among groups, it is likely they will have differing motivations undergirding differing shifts. However, a primary motivation for Amar, at least until he fell under the sway of Aman Abdurrahman's takfiri ideology, was indeed altruism and purpose. He wanted to clean up his neighborhood.

Of the 97 Indonesians interviewed for this book, 18 expressed altruistic motivations. They wanted to improve the lives of Muslims. Some sought to combat criminality, gangs, and vice in their neighborhoods. Others were motivated by a desire to come to the aid of oppressed Muslims. These endeavors gave them a sense of purpose and direction.

For example, five of those interviewed reported that after communal violence erupted on the island of Ambon and in the district of Poso in 1999, they wanted to help protect Muslims from attacks by Christian paramilitaries. One former member of Mujahidin KOMPAK explained he joined the group because "I heard what had gone on in Ambon and I wanted to lend a hand."[66] Another, who lived in a KOMPAK dormitory in the town of Solo when fighting escalated between Muslims and Christians in Ambon, noted that because "there was no resolute action from the state and Muslims were being slaughtered, I concluded it was my duty to help them to the extent I was capable."[67] That he was living in a KOMPAK dormitory at the time created another element of peer pressure because all of those around him were joining as well. Thus, all of the youth living in the dormitory could reinforce each other's conviction. "Agus" had attended study sessions at a mosque near his house where the organization Dewan Dakwah Islamiyah Indonesia (DDII) disseminated information about the violence in Ambon. One day, in June 1999, a sign-up sheet was circulated after prayers for those who would be interested in going to fight.[68] He and his friend, Abdullah Sunata, signed up.[69] He explained,

> When the conflict broke out in Ambon, I wanted to travel there to help because [I had learned that] Muslims were being evicted from their homes and slaughtered at prayer. I was sympathetic to the people in Ambon. I pitied my [Muslim] brothers and sisters.[70]

For another five young men who lived in a particularly crime- and gang-ridden neighborhood in the city of Solo, the desire to "clean up the neighborhood" led them to join a local anti-vice militia, Tim Hisbah.[71] According to "Khoirul," a former member of Tim Hisbah, "I just wanted to dignify Islam and die a martyr. I didn't have the patience for joining JI. The process was too lengthy. This was local."[72]

The majority of people looking to improve Muslim lives do so through mainstream Islamic and Islamist groups. With FPI, Amar chose a group that skirted the boundaries of militant Islamism and violent extremism. Others joined Salafi-Jihadi extremist groups. The difference between those who exercise their altruism via mainstream Muslim organizations and those who do so via extremist groups in these instances lies in "location," where they live and with whom they interact. Had the young man who lived in the KOMPAK dormitory lived in a dormitory run by a mainstream Islamic mass organization such as Muhammadiyah, his desire to help the Ambonese might have manifested in a different way. Perhaps he would have simply collected supplies for humanitarian relief, and that would have been the sum total of his involvement. However, because he was living in the KOMPAK dormitory, he went through KOMPAK, and this provided an entry into the Mujahidin KOMPAK paramilitary once he was on the ground in Ambon.

In Marawi, on the island of Mindanao in the Philippines, the opportunity to better the lives of Muslims manifested slightly differently than in Indonesia insofar as it centered on the opportunity to seek redress of long-held grievances. Seven out of the 25 interviewed cited the opportunity to rectify injustices against the Maranao community as a secondary motivator. These could be personal experiences of marginalization, or they could be echoing the rhetoric that they had heard in study sessions at the mosque or from Moro Islamic Liberation Front (MILF)-affiliated family members. Personal injustices included abuse and bullying by teachers or police and *rido* (feuds) with family members over land. At the mosque, "Faisal" found discussions about "military injustices" particularly persuasive.[73] "Abu Islam" said that Maute commander, Abu Dar, would speak to the need for the Maranao Muslims to have power. "If we could have power, we could fix everything."[74] Other themes included "do jihad and go to heaven" and the need to "raise Marawi" and "fight for Islamic rights."[75] The desire to remedy injustice often went hand in hand with the desire to participate in a jihad and go to heaven. These youth had been raised with the stories of the MILF and Moro National

Liberation Front members who had fought in jihads before them. There was glory in fighting in a jihad for Islamic rights for the Maranao people, to clean up the city from crime and drugs, and to secure power. The MILF was now in peace talks with the government; they were no longer fighting. This jihad would be their generation's opportunity.

In short, those who joined Islamist groups due to altruistic motivations sought to either improve the lives of Muslims or redress historical grievances and rectify injustices. In instances in which individuals joined Islamist extremist groups in order to improve Muslim lives, there is an interaction effect at work between relationships and location, on the one hand, and altruism, on the other hand. Faisal and Abu Islam in Marawi are indicative of that. Most Muslims, however, who seek to redress injustice or seek to improve the lives of Muslims do so via mainstream Islamic or Islamist groups or work through groups that skirt the boundaries of Islamist and extremist. Individuals who join Islamist groups and licit anti-vice militias may not require a friend to vouch for them in order to gain entry. However, for Salafi-Jihadi and takfiri groups, who one knows still intersects with what one seeks.

## Revenge

### Fauzan

"Fauzan" was in college at the Malang Institute of Technology in the province of East Java when the Poso conflict broke out. He had grown up in Poso and gone to primary and secondary school there. By his own account, he was neither a particularly good kid nor a bad kid. "I was not brutal. I was naughty like ordinary young kids,"[76] he explained. At the beginning of 2000, he decided to take a break from university to return to Poso. When the Walisongo massacre took place in May of that year, he decided he would never go back; the massacre ignited a desire for revenge in him.

He explains that most of his relatives lived in the area around Walisongo, also known as "Kampung Kilometer 9": "Some 80% of my relatives lived in Kampung Kilometer 9. 43 in all were slain. My grandfather, my uncle, my cousins."[77] He alleges that he tried to get to Kampung Kilometer 9, but he was stopped by soldiers and the Sector Police Chief for Kampung Kilometer 9 who told him, "It's ok. Go back. Everything is fine."[78] The next day, he heard that everyone was dead. Then, he saw the bodies in the river:

Bodies floating . . . headless, limbs missing. It was so sadistic. I'm just human, and those are my relatives. Of course, I wanted to avenge. I wanted revenge against the perpetrators. In Poso, everyone knows everybody else. We knew who they were.[79]

Fauzan then talked about what came next:

I joined Tanah Runtuh. Almost all the young people in Poso did. We were just preparing. Just about everyone was called upon to join. We were trained to assemble homemade weapons. Everyone made preparations in [the neighborhood of] Gebang Rejo and elsewhere. Everyone. We wanted revenge.[80]

Just as the Walisongo massacre was both a personal trauma for Fauzan and a collective trauma for Muslims in Poso, the desire for revenge was both personal and collective as well. According to Fauzan, he and his friends started going to the Baitul Makmur mosque for Quran reading. His teachers were JI "*ustads*" from Java; he asserts that at the time, he did not know they were affiliated with JI:

I used to be ignorant and knew it was time to stop all this nonsense. My relatives had been massacred. I couldn't go on like this. I started with an intention. I wanted to change. I joined Quran reading groups and started going to the mosque. This was sometime in 2002 or 2003.[81]

He was not alone in going to the mosque. This was a collective experience among many of his friends. "All the young people just came. We were all told to come to join the Quran reading at the mosque. We could learn praying. Everything else. It was cool."[82] After a certain point, he also attended paramilitary training. He became part of the hit squad that launched attacks against Christian targets between 2003 and 2007 in the name of revenge.

For 26 individuals based in the district of Poso in the province of Central Sulawesi, revenge was their primary motivation, following the escalation of communal conflict between Muslims and Christians in their district. Although the causes of the outbreak of violence in Poso were not religious, the fighting took on a religious hue because mosques and churches were common targets.[83] The galvanizing event was the May 2000 massacre of between 100 and 300 men and women at a mosque and Islamic boarding school at Walisongo.[84] Some of those interviewed lost upwards of a dozen family members at Walisongo. They channeled grief into anger and a deeply personal desire to avenge the dead. Others were inspired by a sense of vengeful solidarity and partook in the collective trauma at what they witnessed in the days that followed.

In the weeks following Walisongo, trainers and preachers from Mujahidin KOMPAK and JI began arriving in Poso. Mujahidin KOMPAK set up its base in the neighborhood of Kayamanya, while JI made inroads into the neighborhoods of Gebang Rejo and Tanah Runtuh. Mujahidin KOMPAK offered a quick 3-week course of paramilitary training, whereas JI required individuals to commit to a month of religious indoctrination before some were selected for paramilitary training.[85] The indoctrination and training provided by JI and Mujahidin KOMPAK members legitimated that desire for revenge that was already present and gave it a specific Islamic lens that validated it, making it not only desirable but also an actual obligation.[86]

This desire for revenge would continue to be a motivator for some, long after the Poso conflict had ended. On January 22, 2007, a team from Densus 88, the police counterterrorism unit, raided the compound at Tanah Runtuh, resulting the deaths of 14 militants and more than a dozen arrests.[87] Five years later, when remnants of Tanah Runtuh and Mujahidin Kayamanya formed MIT, the first Indonesian extremist group to swear loyalty to ISIS, many were still driven by revenge, but this was revenge against the police for the 2007 raid on Tanah Runtuh as opposed to revenge on Christians. One early member explained, "I joined to seek revenge against Densus for arresting and killing my friends in 2007."[88] Another concurred, noting,

> After the events on January 22, 2007, Jemaah Islamiyah had no activities; there was no military training. JI focused only on *dakwah*, and I was not interested in doing *dakwah* at that time. Densus killed my teacher and many of my friends on January 22, 2007. I wanted to take revenge.[89]

He counted MIT founder, Santoso, as a friend. Therefore, when Santoso started MIT, this was a natural affinity and meeting of minds.

In summary, personal and, especially, collective experiences of trauma can motivate a desire for revenge that can, in turn, motivate individuals to form or join extremist groups. In Poso, the Walisongo massacre on May 29, 2000, and, to a lesser extent, the Densus 88 raids on the Tanah Runtuh compound in January 2007 motivated youth in Poso who either lost relatives or bore witness to the carnage that followed to seek to avenge the dead. When JI and Mujahidin KOMPAK arrived in 2000, they offered these youth fulfillment of that purpose: the opportunity to exact revenge more deliberately and systematically than before, the weapons and training to carry it out, and a religious lens to legitimate it. The establishment of MIT in 2012 continued that theme.

## Redemption

Abu Usama

"I grew up as a kid in a very open community," "Abu Usama" began. "I was not a practicing Muslim. I did not pray. I had my vices. I drank. I smoked. These were normal teenage things. I was very ignorant of my own religion."[90] His parents had been religious people, so his self-professed teenage "rebellion" caused tensions, but he also attributed this to normal teenage behavior. Abu Usama was a black belt in karate. He loved hiking and mixed martial arts, and he had a wide array of friends, some of whom he drank alcohol with and others with whom he practiced karate.[91]

It was during college around 2013 that something shifted in him, and he wanted to know more about Islam.[92] At that time, there were many mass religious gatherings. Abu Usama learned more about the fighting in Syria and Palestine. He began watching international news and browsing the internet, particularly regarding the fighting in Syria. His fluency in English made this easy. Around the time his curiosity was peaking, a friend of his invited him to an Islamic seminar in Butig, a small town in the mountains of Lanao Del Sur, a 3-hour drive from Marawi on the island of Mindanao in the Philippines.[93] Having never been to Butig, he thought the trip would serve two functions: He could learn more about Islam and also hike in the mountains because Butig was lush and beautiful.

What followed was a 4-day seminar. On the first day, he met Omar and Abdullah Maute, two brothers from a very influential family in Butig, who formed the Maute Group. He felt wowed by them because they had finished their education abroad. Abdullah Maute impressed him. "The guy was a preacher. At the same time, he was a fighter. And he was doing indoctrination."[94] Abu Usama contends that whereas other seminar attendees were farmers, he was different—one of only three college-educated participants—so it was difficult for them to convince him. However, in the end, Omar and

Abdullah succeeded because he was ignorant about Islam and because of his vices.[95]

Abu Usama said, "Initially, Abdullah spoke about Islam—what is the meaning of Islam. Islam as a way of life. Submission to God. However, after that, they moved onto a topic that touched him: sin and the corresponding punishments."[96] What had begun as a desire to learn more about Islam and events in the Muslim world outside of the Philippines suddenly became personal. He learned that should one commit adultery, the only way he or she could be forgiven by Allah would be to submit to death by stoning. Moreover, Allah would not receive the prayers of someone who consumed alcohol for 40 days. Abu Usama felt overwhelmed by guilt. He thought about his vices. He began to consider what would happen to him should he suddenly die. "After that," he shared, "they had my emotions."[97] Whereas he had attended the seminar originally in pursuit of knowledge, now he sought redemption. One motive reinforced the other.

It was at this point at his most vulnerable and with his emotions raw that Omar Maute introduced the group to jihad: what it was, why it mattered, and why it was an individual obligation:

> After teaching about the importance of jihad, it came to me that jihad was important. They started to bring Iraq and Syria into the conversation. Then, little by little, they introduced *daulah Islamiyah* [the Islamic state]....Then, they asked, "Are you willing to be part of the Islamic community?" Since it was the height of my emotions, I felt like I wanted to be a part of this Islamic community and defend Islam. They asked—"Are you willing to fight for the Islamic community because if you are willing to fight, we will train you." And we all said yes.[98]

Training began immediately thereafter.

Abu Usama was invited by a friend to join the seminar. He was not married. He had no children. However, biographical availability and friendship did not propel him to attend or to stay at the seminar the full 4 days. The key factor for Abu Usama was that he felt ashamed by his sinful behavior, and Omar and Abdullah gave him a road map for how to redeem himself. That is what motivated him to agree to training and to join the Maute group. They gave him a purpose, a path to his own rehabilitation. Initially, after the seminars and two trainings, with the words and experiences fresh in his mind, he felt committed. He began castigating relatives for behavior he deemed *haram* (forbidden according to Islam). However, as time went on, with no regular activities to reinforce connection, community, and commitment to the group, he returned to alcoholism. He rejoined only after the battles in Butig in late 2016 and early 2017 commenced. Abu Dar, a Maute commander, contacted him, extolling him to come to Butig to fight.[99] He confessed that he had gone back to drinking in the interim, and Abu Dar responded that Allah was forgiving.[100] With that, he joined the jihad, again seeking redemption for his sins.

In Indonesia, for eight of those interviewed, redemption was a powerful motivator, sometimes functioning in tandem with revenge as a secondary factor and, at other times functioning secondarily to having a friend in the group or independently. Redemption has a religious component in this research. In short, it is the idea of turning away from mistakes one made in their life, most notably those aspects that would be unacceptable in Islam—alcoholism, drug dealing and drug abuse, murder for hire, promiscuity, and sex out of wedlock—and seeking to live a purer and more Islamic life going forward. Among those interviewed in this research, the most common reasons male interviewees sought redemption were alcoholism, drug abuse, drug dealing, bankruptcy, killing someone whether by accident or on purpose, and divorce. This was true in both Indonesia and the Philippines. Among Indonesian women, about whom data were gathered from primary and secondary sources, the most common redemptive reasons were dysfunctional family dynamics and divorce.[101]

Redemption also served as a secondary motivator, often alongside having a family member or friend already in the group in the Philippines. Redemption was salient for five individuals either who had a history of alcoholism, drug abuse, or criminality or who had gone through a traumatic event such as a serious illness or divorce. Calls to "make your life worth living" and "do jihad and go to heaven" resonated especially with this subgroup.[102]

Interestingly, three of those who cited redemption also went through multidimensional personal crises. "Ivan" was dealing with the realization he had been adopted, a divorce, alcoholism, and sepsis when a childhood friend suggested that "if you wanted to go to heaven, you should join [the Maute] jihad. No one can help you now, but we can make your life worth living. Do jihad and go to heaven."[103] This appealed to him. He believed he was dying, and this was an opportunity to seek forgiveness for his sins before Allah. Similarly, "Abu Hamdan" had been a hitman for a drug gang, a drug dealer, a gun runner, a thief, and a carjacker in Manila. After going through a divorce, he returned home to the town of Butig with only one of his five children to take stock. He was a member of the Maute family; Omar and Abdullah Maute were his first cousins. The Maute brothers wanted him to join their group given his extensive experience with guns and killing. He, however, joined them for redemptive reasons:

> There came a time that I felt horrible for all my horrible mistakes and choices in my life and I wanted to quit drugs and quit being gun for hire. I wanted to cleanse my heart, and Omar [Maute] would help me to cleanse my heart. He would teach me Islam, so I would know how to live as a Muslim. I told my mother, "I want to cleanse everything. Veer away from drugs. From vices. I feel sorry for all the horrible things I have done in the past. I want to join Omar because maybe he can help me." Immediately, my mother grabbed her car, and we went to Omar.[104]

Among Indonesian women, "potholes"[105]—episodes that cause one's life to veer off course—such as divorce or having a baby out of wedlock caused several women to turn to religion in an attempt to live a less sinful life or open up a new chapter in their life, shedding past trauma.[106] For example, in 2011, "Icha" decided to make such a shift after suffering through her own multidimensional personal crisis. After suffering through an abusive marriage, divorce, and then loss of custody of her children, her parents rejected her when she asked them for help.[107] She learned to live independently, starting a small snack-selling business and reading Islamic books in her spare time.[108] In 2014, her business partner introduced her to ISIS and suggested they move to Syria to live in the Caliphate together. She noted,

> After the divorce, I thought my life was over. I wanted to move far away and start a new life somewhere. Then a few years ago ISIS was booming, all the media talked about it. I was curious. I read more about it.... But to me, the main thing is that I wanted to open a new chapter in my life ... and what better place to do that than *Sham* (Syria)?[109]

In short, redemption was another key factor that motivated individuals to join an Islamist extremist group. It typically functioned in tandem with knowing someone in the group, either a relative or a friend. In these instances, one could be experiencing a multidimensional crisis, both personal and financial; a familial crisis caused by the death or deterioration of a core family member; or a personal crisis—addiction, divorce, loss of custody of children, estrangement from parents. Any of these could leave someone in a vulnerable state that a family or friend in an Islamist extremist group could exploit.

## Financial and Material Assistance

### Aisha

"Aisha" was the second of seven brothers and sisters. At age 10 years, her parents sent her to an all-girls boarding school that taught Arabic. Of all of her siblings, she was the only one sent to Arabic school. When she was 15 or 16 years old, a friend of hers at the school started approaching her to join the Maute group as a recruiter. This friend chatted her up. They talked about their lives, about social status. Aisha opened up about her family and the fact her father was a *tuk tuk* (a motorized rickshaw) driver. Knowing Aisha was poorer than many of her classmates and that this was a source of insecurity for her, the friend promised her money if she joined. Initially, Aisha disregarded her friend's invitation. She did not want to join. However, something happened that changed her mind:

> My father's *tuk tuk* burned up. [It was an accident.] A piece of cloth from a skirt was caught in it. That was our only livelihood. When the tricycle was burned, they could only gather vegetables from the river and because we were a big family, it was not enough. [When my friend approached me again], she emphasized I would be compensated.[110]

It is fair to say that Aisha was primed to accept the ideology of the Maute group and the idea of *daulah Islamiyah* (Islamic state) from her school:

> We were taught about jihad and that jihad was *fisabililah*. It was religious war in the way of Allah. We were taught that no innocent people should be involved; there should be no collateral damage. Also, when you die, you go to heaven.[111]

However, she did not agree to become a recruiter because of ideological affinity. She repeatedly refused, even though she personally wanted money to buy better clothes and a phone so she could be like the other girls at the school. She was not seeking personal redemption from sin or revenge.

Aisha only consented to recruit for the Maute group once her family's financial circumstances became dire. Initially, they paid her between 4,000 and 5,000 pesos per month, but when the siege neared, they paid her 8,000 pesos per month. Now, her family could buy rice and other foodstuffs. They did not have to resort to gathering riverweed to survive. She stressed she was unaware that the Maute group was going to occupy Marawi. She knew the group would fight in a jihad, but she contends she was not informed of the plan to take over the city:

> When the city was destroyed, I felt sorry because I realized I was a part of it. I played a part in the devastation of my city. When we were in the evacuation camp, we were sleeping on the floor. It was so cold. I felt this was my greatest mistake. I cannot sleep. I just cry. I cannot eat. . . . When I saw the devastation on the news, I was living in a camp and I thought, "What have I done?"[112]

Her parents were furious. Her father asked her, "Why did you do this?" She answered, "I did it for you."[113]

Financial and material incentives can also motivate a person to join an extremist group, especially if the group is offering payment for participation, employment, protection, or other goods and services. In some instances, people joined motivated, in part, by a need for resources. In these instances, one's motivation is not altruistic, emotional, or ideological. They may or may not feel ideological affinity at the start; that may come later. However, they are joining because the group is fulfilling a direct material need.

Fourteen individuals cited financial or material assistance as a primary or secondary motivator for joining the Maute group. Recruits were typically promised between 10,000 and 50,000 pesos ($200–$1,000) for joining, although Aisha reports being paid far less for recruiting.[114] For individuals from large families of 7–10 children, who might, at times, be existing on rice, salt, and river vegetables, the prospect of such a windfall for joining a jihad seemed too good to pass up. It would ensure they could provide for the family basic needs. To be clear, the leaders of the Maute group and core commanders were highly educated. However, among those interviewed, 16 had either never gone to school or terminated their education in elementary school.[115] For example, Abu Dar, one of the Maute commanders, promised Abu Islam that he would give him money. Abu Islam stated, "This was the most important thing. We only really ate when we went to see our relatives. With [that] money, we could get rice. We could get fish. Abu Dar promised me everything we needed, so I joined."[116]

All four women interviewed cited financial incentives as key to their decision-making calculus, and all came from families in dire financial straits. Parents died. A father abandoned the family. A home was burned. A mother became mentally ill. As daughters took on responsibility for the family in lieu of their parents, it made them vulnerable and more susceptible to recruitment in order to provide for the basic needs for themselves and their siblings. They joined, propelled by feelings of obligation and love for their families and financial desperation. This degree of dire financial circumstances was far less prevalent among those interviewed in Indonesia.

In Indonesia, material assistance shaped motivations in one key arena: prisons. One reason why people gravitated toward Islamist extremist groups, be it JI or ISIS, was a desire for access to better food, supplies, and money. By joining with the extremists, a person could get access to such resources, even a cell phone.[117] Outside of prison, however, financial incentives seldom[118] shaped the decision to join. This was likely due to higher levels of education and standards of living of respondents in Indonesia vis-à-vis in the Philippines. The Filipinos interviewed, particularly those living in the district of Piagapo, were simply in a far more desperate financial strait, living on rice and salt and river vegetables, often with larger families of six to eight children. Thus, the Maute group could prey upon that absolute poverty through its offers of financial incentives in a way that Indonesian recruiters for ISIS and JI simply did not.

## Conclusion

This chapter identified several key motivations for joining. In short, joining is largely a result of the interaction between whom one knows and what one seeks. This holds true among respondents from Indonesia and the Philippines, from pro-ISIS and anti-ISIS groups, and irrespective of gender. Kinship and constructed kinship ties via immediate and extended family, friends, and teachers/mentors are key. Parents, uncles, and older siblings socialize a person into the movement's worldview and expedite pathways to entry. Teachers and mentors function in the same manner. Friends and same-aged relatives open doors to study circles and to jihad experiences. The decision and desire to follow a family member into the group may happen via socialization and familial expectations as well as via the emotional bonds of love, respect, affinity, and trust. Friends, extended relatives, and mentors typically open doors to a new community by tapping into unmet desires and aspirations. These include seeking opportunities for altruism and purpose, revenge, redemption, financial or material assistance, or ideological affinity/ seeking practical knowledge about jihad. Without relationships, there is no way into a Salafi-Jihadi or takfiri movement. Without an emotional or psychological need, there is no reason.

Some of these motivations—notably the desire for ideological affinity and seeking to better the lives of Muslims—can manifest as easily in systemic Islamic and Islamist movements as they can in anti-system Islamist extremist groups. What makes a difference between pursuing licit or illicit avenues in seeking opportunities for altruism is interaction with specific persons or locations affiliated with the extremist group. Seeking ideological affinity and knowledge of jihad can be and is typically accomplished through mainstream Islamist and Islamic groups. However, when one seeks practical knowledge about performance of jihad or becomes enamored with Salafi-Jihadi and takfiri interpretations of Islam, this can motivate one to join and participate in extremist groups.

Collective and personal experiences of trauma as well as multidimensional personal crises motivated individuals to join Islamist extremist groups seeking either redemption or revenge. Multidimensional crises and personal trauma can prompt a search for redemption. Collective experiences of trauma can motivate persons to seek revenge, such as in the case of the 2000 Walisongo massacre in Poso. In this kind of situation, who one knew prior to entry was less important. The collective experience of trauma and the desire for revenge played a more significant role. The contacts were out there, in the local mosques, waiting for the youth to attend.

Finally, as individuals migrate among groups, as is common, particularly in Indonesia, their motivations may change. There can be variation on the basis of whom one knows or what one seeks. Perhaps one is born into a Salafi-Jihadi group, but at a particular juncture, they migrate following friends, mentors, or former *pesantren* classmates into either a different Salafi-Jihadi group or a pro-ISIS group. Alternatively, one may be attracted to a particular group seeking opportunities for altruism and a sense of purpose. However, they may shift to a different extremist group on the basis of ideological affinity. Of course, some individuals also may migrate among extremist groups, motivated by a common search—for revenge, redemption, knowledge, or opportunities for altruism. Others, however, will have divergent motivations, depending on timing, opportunity, need, and relationship.

# 2

# Internal Pathways

## Kinship and Schools

### Abu Muslim

"Abu Muslim" came from a Jemaah Islamiyah (JI) family, the oldest of 10 children. His parents were JI members in good standing. His father, a veteran of the Ambon conflict, had taught him about the spirit of jihad from a young age. "He taught me general lessons. This is *fard ayn* [an individual obligation] and this is *fard kifayah* [a collective obligation]. This one is a friend. This one is the enemy."[1] JI members, particularly those from the pro-bombing faction, frequented his house, including bombing masterminds Noordin M. Top, Saifuddin Zuhri, and Top's facilitator, Urwah.

When he turned 12, the age for middle school in Indonesia, in 2000, his parents sent him to Pesantren al-Muttaqin in Jepara, Central Java, in order to socialize him into the JI worldview. He took classes on Islamic jurisprudence, Arabic, English, Bahasa Indonesia, *tauhid* (the divine oneness of god), and martial arts. He cites the sense of brotherhood as particularly important to him at that time. "In Al-Muttaqin, we lived together, ate, slept, and studied together. Islamic boarding school was like that. We were together all day every day."[2] His friends became a surrogate family.

In 2003, his father decided to send him to Poso to study at the Al-Amanah boarding school in the hope he would have the opportunity to participate in paramilitary training, which Al-Muttaqin did not offer to middle schoolers. He spent his high school years at Al-Amanah. Haji Adnan Arsal, the founder of Al Amanah and head of the Tanah Runtuh community, was his teacher. JI members from Java cycled in and out. He noted that "Al Amanah was a place [where JI] nurtured its cadres."[3] Even more than at al-Muttaqin, he felt the strong pull of brotherhood and belonging. "Poso was a conflict area. We felt that we were part of the same destiny. Whether we lived or died, we would fight together."[4] He finished high school at Al Amanah, and Ustad Adnan Arsal administered the *bai'at* (oath).

Abu Muslim's pathway into JI and, subsequently, Tanah Runtuh was a product of two types of thick social bonds: kinship and schools. His father socialized him into JI, exposing him to Salafi-Jihadi ideas about jihad, introducing him to key figures in the JI pro-bombing wing from a young age, and sending him to al-Muttaqin to further his education and gain greater exposure to the JI worldview. However, when al-Muttaqin was not militant enough, his father sent him to a conflict zone, Poso, to study at Al-Amanah. Over time, Poso became his home. Al Amanah and the members of Tanah Runtuh became his family. Constructed kinship ties, born from the experience in JI/Tanah Runtuh schools, supplanted blood kinship ties. However, both were critical to him joining Islamist extremist groups. The longer he stayed in Poso, the more constructed kinship ties outweighed familial ties. He would eventually leave JI and Tanah Runtuh and join Mujahidin Indonesia Timor (MIT) in 2013 due to his close relationship with MIT founder, Santoso.

This chapter is the first of two chapters that explore how individuals join the activities of Islamist extremist groups and, in many cases, become members. Much of the literature on joining lays out either a single pathway[5] or proposes a collection of mechanisms that may or may not interact with one another.[6] Both this and the next chapter show there are multiple paths to becoming a committed member. This chapter unpacks the role of two internal pathways: kinship and schools. Kinship, in this instance, highlights familial ties: parents, siblings, uncles, and extended family or "relatives." Schools refer to specific radical boarding schools run by or affiliated with the extremist groups. This chapter affords special attention to the JI-Jemaah Anshorut Tauhid-Jemaah Ansharusy Syariah schools network in Indonesia because schools have played a greater role in JI and its splinter factions than they have in groups outside it in Indonesia and in the Maute group in the Philippines.

It is important to note that the pathways to joining the Maute group in the Philippines via kinship ties varied depending on whether one joined the Maute group early in its formation due to being a member of the Maute family or whether someone was recruited for a specific battle. In the former, the pathway was often longer in duration because certain relatives were cultivated as assets or groomed from childhood. In the latter, the pathway was expedited because fighters were needed for battles. The Maute group did not have schools, but two women reported being recruited at schools, in one instance from a fellow student who was recruiting at the school and in another instance from outsiders who came into the school to preach and recruit.[7]

## Kinship Pathway

The literature on terrorism notes that kinship is an important mechanism for recruitment.[8] This is especially true for jihadi groups in Indonesia and the Philippines. Kinship provides unmatched loyalty and unconditional support because it is not only the ties of in-group solidarity that bind but also the actual familial ties that ensure commitment. Love for a parent, sibling, or uncle can lead an individual to take on added risk out of love, trust, loyalty, and affinity.[9] Social ties are already thick. They already feel connected to the community. Moreover, knowing that one's relationship to a group stretches back to grandfathers may cause someone to believe that this is their inevitable path.

Kinship ties may also create more flexible pathways to entry. In some instances, they expedite the route into the group. In conducting illicit activities, familial ties reduce the likelihood of infiltration.[10] Kinship also makes disengagement far more difficult because one risks severing ties with parents, children, spouses, and siblings should one depart the group.

Kinship can function in one of four ways: intentional socialization, expectations, pressure, and admiration. In the first instance, one's parents are part of the group and they bring one up in the group. Members of the group are coming in and out of your house from the time you are small. Your father brings you to study sessions. He constructs your connection to the community. If you come from a JI family, when you are old enough, you are sent to the right schools to be socialized into the group's mindset. Related to this are expectations. One may join not with active intent but as a passive choice. You were part of this family so, of course, you joined because that is what you do. In addition, a relative may cajole you into joining or you may feel peer pressure to join. Finally, you may follow a sibling or a relative into the group because you idolize that person and want to be just like them.

Due to the long-standing history of Indonesian extremist groups, there are multigenerational jihadi families, in which the parents were members of Darul Islam (DI), who subsequently joined JI following the split in 1993. Some sent their children to JI schools. When they married and had children themselves, they followed the same path. The multigenerational jihadi tradition and its intersection with a radical Islamic education in a handful of boarding schools is possibly unique to Indonesia.[11] It has also been largely unique to JI, its affiliates, and its splinter factions. JI is the only Salafi-Jihadi community in Indonesia that has an extensive school network, although other groups, such as Jemaah Anshorut Tauhid and Jemaah Ansharud Daulah, have schools of their own.

Of those interviewed in Indonesia, 25 out of 97 joined via kinship. In the Philippines, of those interviewed, 19 out of 25 who joined the Maute group were invited either by uncles or by extended family. There are four main routes.[12] The most common is through parents, where one is born into jihad, socialized by parents into the jihadi worldview, and sent to the right schools to be groomed to become a member of a Salafi-Jihadi organization. The Salafi-Jihadi community is at the core of one's social network from childhood. The second route is through siblings. Here, the pattern is that older siblings often recruited younger siblings, although they do not necessarily persuade their older siblings to follow them. The third is through extended family members, typically uncles who grooms a specific nephew to follow them from a young age. The fourth is through marriage, which serves to consolidate in-group social ties and commitment to the organization.

One example of being born into a jihadi family is JI spiritual leader, Abu Rusydan, son of DI leader Haji Muhammad Faleh.[13] Due to his family ties, Abu Rusydan's pathway into DI and subsequently JI was expedited. He explained, "My circumstance made me close to them. I often interacted with them so they trusted me."[14] Abu Rusydan was inducted into the group, when he was 15 years old.[15] He fought in Afghanistan, was a member of JI's central board, and briefly served as interim Amir in the 2000s. Another is Faturrahman al-Ghozi, the perpetrator of the 2000 Rizal Day bombing in Manila that killed 12 people. His father was a member of DI. Al Ghozi and his brother, Ahmad Rofiq Ridho, joined JI. After Al Ghozi's death, Ahmad Rofiq married Al Ghozi's widow.[16]

Another example of joining via the parents is "Hisham," a *da'i* (preacher) with JI. Hisham came from a DI family; his father had been a subordinate of JI's founder, Abdullah Sungkar, before Sungkar established JI. Hisham's parents and all of his siblings and their spouses joined JI. When he was young, he recalls, veterans of the Soviet–Afghan war visited his house, and his father took him to mass religious meetings that Abdullah Sungkar held every weekend. Thus, he was exposed to Salafi-Jihadi ideas starting from a very young age. His parents also sent the boys to Salafi-Jihadi schools affiliated with Sungkar's network, with his elder brother attending Ngruki, Abdullah Sungkar's own *pesantren* (Islamic boarding school), and Hisham being sent to Al-Islam in the early 1990s.[17] Al-Islam represented the second stage in his socialization process not only into JI but also into becoming a *mujahid* (holy warrior). When he graduated in 1997, he took the oath, noting,

> Actually, I had no idea what JI was. I just knew this was a community that fought for Islam through war. I joined them because since I was a kid, my father told me he would like me to die as a martyr and I always dreamed I would.[18]

Hisham's joining process illustrates how family ties and educational ties reinforced one another in constructing a community of like-minded. Like Abu Muslim, whose narrative began this chapter, he was socialized from an extremely young age into the JI community. What stands out to him is not what he learned but, rather, with whom and from whom he learned it. He did not fully understand what he was joining, only that it would enable him to live out the purpose his father had set for him—to die a martyr.[19]

There are also several recent instances in which sons of veterans of the Afghan jihad have gone to join the Syrian jihad, thereby carrying on the family jihadi tradition.[20] The most prominent of these were Umar Abdul Azis, son of Bali bombing mastermind Imam Samudra, who joined ISIS;[21] Rusydan Abdul Hadi, son of Afghan veteran Amir Mahmud, who also joined ISIS;[22] and Ridwan Abdul Hayyie, son of Abu Jibril, who joined a local jihadi group in Syria.[23] In these instances, however, it was not parents intentionally socializing their children into a particular group or sending their children to Syria but, rather, the adult children who made the decision to follow in their fathers' footsteps.

In the Philippines, there are similar multigenerational jihadi families in which fathers brought their sons into the Moro Islamic Liberation Front (MILF), which started training the boys while they were still in their teens. Nine of those interviewed, who went on to join the Maute group, came from MILF families, much as many of those who joined JI had parents in DI. For example, "Abu Islam" shares,

> My father was MILF. When I was young, he fought in battles between the MILF and the military. He would bring me to the MILF camp. I liked going to the MILF camp. We would sleep a lot, eat well, and play volleyball. There were lots of kids in the camp. There, I learned about *jihad fisabililah* [jihad in the way of Allah] and jihad as an individual obligation. We were told we were fighting to raise Islam. The MILF trained me to fight. At 17, I did

my training with Commander Bravo. The training included running and shooting guns like Armalites and M-14 and Carbine RPG.[24]

In these instances, fathers brought their sons, like Abu Islam, to the MILF training camp in their tweens and teens, socialized them into MILF ideology and the Bangsamoro grievance narrative, and in time, the sons came to view the MILF camp as a place where they could learn about Islam and jihad and, also important, have fun. That this was possible at such a young age was because of who their fathers were and because their fathers were MILF members. Unlike in Indonesia, it does not appear that having a parent in MILF expedited the pathway to entry. Yet, it may have created bonds of trust and thick social ties among members as well as a sense of solidarity from a younger age. It may also have created an air of inevitability. There was an expectation that they would eventually become members of the MILF and commit to it. In some instances, fathers, like Abu Hamdan, also brought their sons into the Maute group, in this case during the Butig battles. "I told him this was the right way to go to heaven.... He was 15."[25]

Older brothers also brought younger siblings into Islamist extremist groups without parental approval or encouragement. This functioned in one of two ways. First, older siblings actively recruited younger siblings. Second, younger siblings became acquainted with the older sibling's social circle and gradually won the trust of the group.[26] In both of these instances, sibling affiliation engendered trust. The new recruit was accepted into the community because they were the brother of member "x." For example, Mukhlas, former head of JI's Mantiqi I, brought younger brothers Ali Imron and Amrozi and younger half-brother Ali Fauzi into JI. In fact, Mukhlas had been grooming Ali Imron since Ali Imron was 10 years old. As a result, Ali Imron had an expedited joining process. He did not have to spend years in study sessions. Instead, he took the oath and went to Afghanistan on the strength of Mukhlas' recommendation. As Ali Imron explained,

> I heard from my friends, who studied alongside me in the Afghanistan Mujahidin Military Academy that they joined JI through education first. They were educated by Darul Islam members in their respective areas. They already knew that the study sessions they attended would be different from those organized by [the mainstream organizations] Nahdlatul Ulama and Muhammadiyah. They already knew about Darul Islam, its mission and vision, when they were sent from Indonesia to Malaysia. In contrast, I did not

know. I only knew that Mukhlas had a community or a group or an organization because Mukhlas often talked about it when I was a kid. He told me that he had a community and was an *ustad* [teacher]. I didn't understand the details. Hence when I wanted to join Mukhlas, the only thing I knew and possessed was Mukhlas.... I felt I was the most special. The process was special because it was so fast. I was not from a JI *pesantren*. I spent a very short time [1 month] at Ngruki. I had not been educated [Islamically]. I never joined study sessions.[27]

Ali Imron's experience was somewhat unique among the 25 Indonesian cases of kinship examined. Among the siblings that Mukhlas recruited into JI, only Ali Imron was allowed this expedited trajectory because Mukhlas deemed him ideologically ready for participation in jihad and to become part of the community. His brother, Amrozi, and half-brother, Ali Fauzi, who joined later, after Ali Imron had already left for Afghanistan, were not deemed as "ready." Mukhlas turned away Amrozi initially, not believing his longtime delinquent brother was committed to changing his ways.[28] It was only after he became a devout Muslim that Mukhlas accepted him at Luqmanul Hakim boarding school in Malaysia, allowing him to live in the children's dormitory since he was still a bachelor and to do odd construction jobs around the school.[29] Amrozi and Ali Fauzi both went through courses of indoctrination at Luqmanul Hakim in order to cultivate the correct mindset, devotion, commitment, and temperament.

When siblings joined jihadi groups in Indonesia and the Philippines, rather than being born into them, they typically entered at approximately the same time, or an older sibling, who was already a member, recruited a younger one. For example, according to Abu Hamdan, who was himself a member of the Maute family, "all eight Maute brothers and one Maute sister joined."[30] Among the Indonesians, one pattern tended to be that younger siblings typically did not or were not able to recruit the older ones. Although Mukhlas brought his younger brothers, Amrozi and Ali Imron, into JI, he was not able or did not attempt to recruit his four older siblings. Similarly, the twins Saifuddin and Nurudin, JI and Mujahidin KOMPAK members and Ambon veterans, joined but did not or could not recruit older brother Muinudinillah. Likewise, "Amar" and Arif joined Tim Hisbah and later a pro-ISIS cell affiliated with Bahrum Naim, an Indonesian ISIS recruiter based in Syria, but they did not recruit any of their five other siblings because, according to Amar, "they were not interested in Islamist movements."[31]

Another type of kinship socialization is through an extended family member. Fourteen of those who joined the Maute group in the Philippines were invited by uncles, cousins, or their in-laws.[32] In one instance, "Jabir" moved to Butig with his family in 2013, when he was 13 years old and soon met his uncles, Omar and Abdullah Maute, for the first time. They held a Quran study for kids at that time, and Jabir asked to attend. After 5 months of daily Quran study with his uncles and several other children ages 12–14 years, he was invited to join their trainings. In the morning, they would do physical fitness exercises and martial arts, and in the afternoon, they would study Quran. They groomed him both ideologically and physically, shaving his head "like a skinhead" and instructing him to wear a black garment called a *kimon*.[33] After a year, they showed him how to use guns. He is vague about when exactly he was given the oath—sometime in the second half of that first year. His mother was not living with him at the time; she was selling toys in a nearby province. His father was furious at the change in his son. However, by this time, the Maute brothers had become surrogate fathers. He trusted them. He would live at the camp for 4 years. "My goal was learning to read the Quran. After I could do that, I wanted to be like the big men in the camp. I wanted to emulate them."[34] For those who were recruited by relatives in 2017, however, there was no "pathway" per se. Since battles were ongoing at this time, there was no religious instruction or paramilitary training. One simply joined the fight, often bringing one's own guns from home to the battle.

In Indonesia, recruitment by extended family was less frequent. Of those interviewed, three had been recruited by uncles and one by a cousin. As in the case of parents and siblings, here too familial social ties were used to frame the joining process, as is illustrated by "Abu Azzam," who was systematically and incrementally groomed by his uncle for almost a decade from 2000 to 2009 to join Al Qaeda in the Malay Archipelago led by Noordin M. Top. The grooming of Abu Azzam started when he was still in school:[35]

> [In the beginning] he would often invite me to climb mountains with him. Or go hiking or swimming. [He would then introduce me to people] "Syahrir is from JI. He's good at using weapons." He taught me jihad in a subtle manner. We often had small talks, "about this, what do you think."[36]

When this grooming process came to fruition, Abu Azzam already had a college degree and a steady job. However, his uncle was able to involve him in his cell and in the preparation of an attack on the basis of the depth of their relationship and their emotional connection:

> I studied psychology [at university] but he had a better understanding than me in practicing psychology. We were getting closer. He always called me and asked me where I was. "Could you please take me somewhere? Could you please accompany me?" I only knew afterward that when he asked me to take him somewhere, we were meeting Noordin [M. Top]. I met Noordin several times but I did not know he was Noordin. [I also met] Afham, Soni and Dr. Azahari. He knew I would reject study sessions because I had already studied religion in religious school and felt I no longer needed to attend religious study. Hence, the way he approached me was great. He knew what I liked and what I didn't like.... He was a disciplined person.... He had his cell. He had his network. He was not very open about it. I only knew when I was already on the inside. Suddenly, 10 people visited me. Then he explained who they were. He wanted me to be comfortable. He knew I rejected bombing so he needed to make me love him first. Then, finally, he said, "If someday you are with me, would you participate in a bombing?" He was able to make me say "Yes, I would do it for you."[37]

In this instance, his uncle systematically cultivated him as an asset, built up their relationship, winning his affection, love, and trust, and in doing so caused him to abandon his internal sense of right and wrong and join the terror cell.

Extended family, notably uncles and cousins, also recruited individuals to join ISIS. Reeling from divorce, home foreclosure, and bankruptcy in 2014, "Ari" found himself deeply in debt to the bank. Although his parents gave him moral support, the only person who helped financially was his cousin, who happened to be a follower of ISIS cheerleader, Aman Abdurrahman. His cousin gave him money on several occasions and invited him to Quran study. He was ambivalent about the lessons taught. However, he went to appease his cousin. After 3 months, his cousin began to appeal to him to go to Syria:

> He kept sending me WhatsApp texts. He showed me videos about the situation in Syria. He gave me advice.... He said "life in Syria is better." I would have a free house. I would meet many sexy girls. I would be able to earn a living. I was half-hearted at first. But I concluded after thinking about it that he might be right.[38]

Ari's cousin featured centrally in his narrative. Since his cousin rescued him from financial ruin and was the only family member to really step in to help him, Ari trusted his cousin and depended on him in a way that made Ari vulnerable. He would not have joined Jemaah Ansharud Daulah study circles, joined ISIS, or traveled to Syria without his cousin. Ari was not an ideologue. He had no money for the travel. "My cousin arranged everything, and I was given the money to apply for my visa and my ticket."[39] It was his cousin's promise of a better life in Syria, his connections, and his funds that enabled his travel to Syria.

Within a discussion of kinship, it is also necessary to talk about the role of marriage. Within jihadi groups broadly, marriage has been a way of thickening and solidifying in-group ties by finding a partner from the group, thus ensuring any offspring will be raised to share the group's worldview and, ideally, become members in good standing themselves in time. Within JI and DI, in-group marriage has been commonplace.[40] It would be expected that someone from a JI or DI family would have their marriage arranged to a female member of the group. JI leaders arranged marriages of their sons and daughters to children of other leaders or high-ranking members. For example, Yumna Farahiyang, daughter of JI amir Parawijayanto, was married off to Rusydan Abdul Hadi, the son of JI spiritual leader and former acting amir, Abu Rusydan. Parawijayanto's eldest son, Askari Sibghotulhaq, had his marriage arranged to the daughter of Abu Husna, the former head of JI's education division.[41] For those who joined JI and DI through study sessions, marriage became a way to show commitment to the organization. "Amru," for example, had his marriage arranged while in prison to a member of the JI women's wing in Semarang. Until the 2017 school year, he was sending his children to a JI school in Semarang, thus ensuring they would be raised with the correct Islamic worldview, even though his activities in JI were minimal. His marriage and his connections through marriage to his wife's familyensured that JI would always be part of his larger social network.

Marriage has also played a role in Indonesia's pro-ISIS network. Here, in addition to traditional arranged marriages, there were also "secret marriages" and marriages resulting from "meeting" on Facebook or in a Telegram group, although it should be noted that the first "online marriage" was in Noordin M. Top's network.[42] Although marriages in the pro-ISIS network, DI, and JI all were commitment points, in JI and DI they served to thicken the social bonds within the in-group and loyalty to the network. By contrast, some marriages in the pro-ISIS network in Indonesia—as opposed to those in

Syria—served to underwrite terror attacks. The most prominent of these is that of Dian Yulia Novi, who would have become Indonesia's first female suicide bomber had she not been arrested on her way to attack the presidential palace. According to her deposition, Dian met her husband Muhammad Nur Solikin via an intermediary and married him secretly by proxy, with details arranged online. They only met for the first time 2 days after their marriage in October 2016. In November, on their second meeting, they both took the oath to ISIS leader Abu Bakar al-Baghdadi, and in December, on their third meeting, Dian was to carry out a terror attack.[43]

In summary, kinship is a key pathway to entry into Islamist extremist groups in Indonesia and the Philippines. In both Indonesia and the Philippines, individuals were socialized into extremist groups by parents, siblings, uncles, and extended family members. These relationships were durable and long-standing, with indoctrination often beginning long before actual recruitment took place. Kinship ties offered expedited pathways to entry, in instances in which parents brought children into the extremist group or elder siblings deemed younger siblings "ready" for membership. It solidified commitment and thick in-group bonds in a way that few other pathways could or did, for love, trust, solidarity, and loyalty already existed prior to participating in any activities or taking an oath. In many instances, familial ties were reinforced by educational ties, where children of members were sent to specific radical schools to ensure that they adopted the correct worldview and ideological predilections. In these instances, the constructed kinship of the boarding school could reinforce and even supplant those of the actual family.

## The School/Pesantren Pathway

Indonesia has an extensive Islamic education sector with two main types of schools. *Madrasas* are day schools that adopt the state-mandated curriculum. Various Islamic organizations run *madrasas*, including Muhammadiyah and Al Irsyad. The second type are Islamic boarding schools called *pesantren*, where students live, study, and socialize together. There are officially more than 14,000 registered *pesantren* in Indonesia, 69 percent of which are run by Nahdlatul Ulama and 1.78% by Muhammadiyah.[44] Thus, more than two-thirds of all Islamic boarding schools in Indonesia are run by mainstream Islamic organizations. The number of radical *pesantren*, affiliated with JI or one of its affiliates or splinter groups, is comparatively miniscule; as of 2015, the Institute for the Policy Analysis of Conflict counted 71.[45] The pro-ISIS/JAD network has had comparatively few schools; the most infamous was Ibnu Mas'ud in Bogor, which was affiliated with Aman Abdurrahman. Local police closed the school in 2017, responding to demands from villagers that the school be shuttered.[46]

Of the individuals interviewed for this book, 19 had joined an Islamist extremist group via the schools pathway. Eleven of those came from DI or JI families. Thus, schools and kinship intersected in their trajectory of joining and commitment.

Both DI and JI have their own networks of schools, *madrasas*, and *pesantren*. Many of these were founded by DI members, who went on to join JI and took their school with them. Schools as a means of recruitment have largely been specific to JI and its affiliates. The most notable for jihadi recruitment historically have been Ngruki near Solo, Al-Islam in Lamongan, Al-Muttaqin in Jepara, Darus Syahadah in Boyolali, and the now closed Luqmanul Hakim in Malaysia's Johor state.[47]

The JI school system was and remains completely self-contained, beginning with playgroups to socialize the children in the Salafi-Jihadi tradition before they know any other alternatives.[48] They then move on to kindergartens to study the Quran and, following, to specific elementary schools, which are feeders for JI-affiliated boarding schools.[49] Whether they will make that shift from elementary school to *pesantren* is based largely on the recommendation of their teachers, as well as, of course, the wishes of their parents.[50] The children are socialized to *want* to attend JI boarding schools through field trips to the schools and visits from the teachers.[51] Students can enter and exit at any time; some complete the entire system, whereas others enter this educational system at middle school or high school.

The purpose of these schools has been the cultivation of a network of graduates sympathetic to the Salafi-Jihadi worldview and understanding of Islam. However, a portion who attend the schools are offered the opportunity to participate in the extracurricular religious study groups, which could potentially lead to eventual recruitment.[52] JI parents who send their children to JI schools do so with the intention that their sons will follow fathers into the group while daughters will be educated to become the wives of group members. For example, for "Yasir," a JI member from a multigenerational jihadi family who was involved in the 2000 attack against the Philippine Ambassador's residence, JI schools reinforced the messages he gave his own children about the necessity of jihad and increased the likelihood that his children would have the opportunity to follow in their father's footsteps.[53] However, those on the margins of JI also send their children to JI schools because they view the schools' approach aligning with their personal religious principles. For example, "Amru" sent his school-aged children to a JI-affiliated elementary school because the school separated boys from girls and he deemed the quality of education better compared to other schools in the area.[54]

The experience of attending those schools is powerful. Leaving their families as early as middle school or high school, when they are still in their early teens, their schoolmates become a second family:

> We are in the same classes, same rooms, same activities. We have the same way of thinking. [We develop] a feeling of brotherhood that is greater in the *pesantren* than in any other community because we're together 24/7. We are more than family.[55]

The experience of living and studying together creates extremely thick and sticky social ties. They find connection and community there. They come to trust one another deeply. In some cohorts, almost all students were invited to participate in extracurricular activities such as late night study groups and paramilitary training; as such, attending *pesantren* was about more than just classes.[56] Others were more selective. It was the start of a process of caderization to prepare them to join a movement that they would eventually learn was JI.

M.B., a JI member first recruited into DI while a student at Ngruki *pesantren* in the 1980s, described the assessment metrics that were utilized in recruitment at the school while it was a DI and subsequently a JI school. He contended the screening process began as early as middle school and was undertaken with great care, examining the behavior in religious study outside of formal *pesantren* activities and in one's daily activities. Recruiters observed students in Quran study. Who was diligently participating? They took note of their potential recruit's character: Did they lie? Did they break the rules? Did they dress appropriately? Were they calm? Were they intelligent? Were they clean? etc. They would be visited by the designated recruiters and invited to join Quran study groups and extra classes such as martial arts. They would be observed through these extracurricular activities, and assessed for potential recruitment. Once they reached their second year of senior high school, if they passed that stage, they were then ready for *dauroh* (group internal study sessions) over several evenings where potential members were briefed on the history of DI, on the necessity of continuing the struggle, on intelligence, and on other matters before they ultimately took the *bai'at*.[57]

According to M.B., the process of being recruited at Ngruki into what was DI in the 1980s and the process of being recruited into JI following the split in 1993 was similar, insofar as both targeted the same kind of youth with the same core set of personality characteristics—loyalty, religious fervor, obedience, cleanliness, calmness, and intelligence—and both recruited at the same point, senior high school. He noted, however, that JI was far more cautious in the recruitment process than DI. Only top students from safe family backgrounds were considered for recruitment; it was rare for JI to recruit someone from a military or police family.[58] Moreover, the course of study in the extracurricular study groups differed, as JI study groups followed a specific curriculum.[59] After they had learned the material, they would take a religious course designed to reinforce what they had been learning; this was the final stage prior to induction.[60]

The description by "Hisham" of joining JI via the schools pathway at the Al-Islam *pesantren* in Lamongan following graduation echoed similar themes. Since Hisham came from a JI family, he would have been considered a safe recruit. He took the typical slate of classes, including Arabic, English, and sharia, and likely was observed for his performance. Although Hisham did not discuss being invited into extracurricular study groups, he elaborated on the paramilitary aspects of recruitment. While at Al-Islam, he met JI members who had just returned from training in Mindanao. He learned knowledge of jihad from Ali Imron, and he was taught how to shoot.[61]

Hisham explained that the teacher–student discipleship relationship was among the most powerful social bond to emerge from the schools pathway, notably his experience as a student of Ali Imron. He explains, "When I was at Al-Islam, Ali Imron was my role model in jihad."[62] The bond between the teacher and the student persisted after he graduated. When Hisham wanted to go to Mindanao to fight in a jihad rather than continue to work as a *da'i* (preacher), he reached out to Ali Imron for help.[63] When Ali Imron went on the run following the Bali bombing, he sought out Hisham to accompany him.[64] There was deep respect, trust, and affinity between them. In a 2015 interview, Hisham contended Ali Imron still remained "his" *ustad*, and they conversed weekly via Moto GP, Blackberry Messenger, or WhatsApp chat.[65] He explained the actual joining with almost an air of inevitability. He did his *dauroh* (internal group religious study) with Mukhlas for a week. In either 1996 or 1997, following graduation, members of JI's Surabaya branch appeared, recruited the fresh graduates, and gave them their tasks. He took the oath in 1997.[66]

"Haris" also attended Al-Islam. However, he was a student a decade later than Hisham, between 2004 and 2008. Unlike Hisham, he did not come from a JI family. A teacher told him about Al-Islam at a point in time when he wanted to better himself. He enrolled late, at 17 years old. He described the curriculum and socialization from that curriculum in detail:

> The curriculum was regular but there were add-ons like Sapala (Nature Lovers Islamic Boarding School Student). This was hiking, but also a kind of basic training. For example, crawling, surviving in the forest, camping and exploring materials that can be used to assemble bombs. We were trained to shoot, using airsoft guns. There was also training in how to produce poison, urban war strategy and how to survive in the jungle. This was between 2004 and 2007. The curriculum changed in 2008 because Ali Imron gave instructions to focus on teaching Islam. Lessons on *jihad qital* [battle] decreased. In the past, we learned about jihad every day, namely that jihad is war, jihad is war, jihad is war. Our main reference was Abdullah Azzam.
>
> Most of my teachers were veterans of jihads in Mindanao, Ambon, and Poso. When they came back to the boarding school, they brought their ideology and experience and this made Al-Islam more interesting at the time. At the beginning of my study at Al-Islam, I learned a lot about jihad and application of jihad. However, I also learned about doctrine, including who is un-Islamic; how we look at infidels; how we look at non-Muslims; how we place our loyalty; who are our enemies; who are our friends. I became a student with high jihad spirit. I wanted to join a jihad, but I had no connections.[67]

Unlike Hisham, who came from a JI family and was inducted into JI in the late 1990s, Haris had a more lengthy process of joining, despite attending Al-Islam. He attributed this discrepancy to being at the school in different eras. However, not only did Haris not come from a JI family but also he had been quite secular as a youth. He entered Al-Islam in his last year of high school, in contrast to Hisham, who joined in middle school. Thus, he had less time to prove himself. He was, nevertheless, socialized into Salafi-Jihadi ideology and trained in paramilitary tactics. He became inspired by his teachers, all veterans of various theaters of jihad, and adopted the mental models of a JI member. At that point, he was on his way to becoming a JI sympathizer in good standing.

Haris' recruitment into JI would take a long time, however. He would have to prove himself. "Before we graduated, JI collected all of us. The Head of Al-Islam told us, 'We are going to send you to study here, here, and here.' But there was no *bai'at*."[68] He was given duties as a teacher at a JI *pesantren* in West Nusa Tenggara. He created a paramilitary training program for them. JI monitored him to determine whether he was committed to JI's vision.[69] Did he share their ideology? Did he wear Islamic clothing and grow a beard? Did he fulfill his teaching duties? Did he stay in communication with them? After he finished his duties at the boarding school, he was sent to study the Quran in Solo. However, despite passing the admissions exam, he had begun to have mixed feelings. He wanted to go to college. His parents expressed fear he was becoming a terrorist.[70] He had begun to read more widely.[71] Thus, he left before he was invited to take the *bai'at*.

Why did Haris differ so much from Hisham, even though they attended the same Islamic boarding school? Haris did not come from a JI family. He entered Al-Islam at 17 years of age, compared to Hisham, who began attending in middle school. As a result, his social ties were not as thick. His sense of community and solidarity was not as strong.

Looking at the schools pathway, there are clear commonalities between students who joined DI in the 1980s and those who joined JI in the 1990s and 2000s at Ngruki and Al-Islam. They were carefully selected. They were chosen based on personality characteristics, degree of commitment, and, for JI, having the right family background. As they reached the second year of high school, they were offered the opportunity for extracurricular instruction in Islamic studies that went beyond what was typically on offer at the school as well as instruction in martial arts and sports. To varying degrees, depending on the school, there was also some form of paramilitary training. Either just prior to or following graduation, they would be formally inducted into the group. However, some, like Haris, were given duties to perform to prove their loyalty before they would be invited to take the oath. Together with the family pathway, schools provided a steady stream of members into DI and JI and socialized a wider portion of the population into becoming sympathizers and supporters of those who had formerly been their playmates and peers.

In the pro-ISIS community, Ibnu Mas'ud, which opened in Depok in 2009 before moving to Bogor in 2011, is the most common referent. Founded by Aman Abdurrahman, the school aimed to socialize children as young as 4 years old into takfiri ideology.[72] According to "Abu Ayyas," an ex-militant who was involved in the Aceh training camp in 2010, the school had a dual function: to educate the children of jihadis and to serve as a safe house for fugitive extremists.[73] When Aman Abdurrahman swore *bai'at* to Abu Bakar al Baghdadi, the school became affiliated with the pro-ISIS network. Indeed, as of July 2017, before the local police in the city of Bogor closed the school, eight teachers and four students had gone to fight in Syria or had attempted to go, and another 18 from the school had been arrested or convicted on charges of plotting or carrying out terror attacks.[74] Interestingly, Abu Husna and Jemaah Asharul Khilafa (JAK) have begun opening elementary schools in and around Solo to teach children to read the Quran.[75] Given Abu Husna's JI roots and Abu Husna's long tenure in JI's education sector, such a move would make sense. He is offering a service to the community and, in doing so, currying the favor of that community. This stands in marked contrast to Aman Abdurrahman and Ibnu Mas'ud, where the local community demanded its closure.

## Conclusion

Kinship and schools are two of the most important pathways into Islamist extremist groups in Indonesia and the Philippines. Kinship can provide an expedited pathway to entry into the community, especially in cases in which parents expose their children to the movement from an early age. They meet key players in the group before they are aware of their roles and before they are even aware there is a "group." The members of the group come to trust them due to their family ties. Their social ties become thick and sticky earlier. They are socialized gradually by older relatives and groomed for membership, and some are sent to specific radical schools and later *pesantren* to be exposed and indoctrinated into the correct views, with membership coming later. In some cases, parents and elder siblings can even circumvent the membership process entirely, with children and younger siblings gaining access and entry by virtue of their familial ties. They are already trusted. Kinship ties strengthen commitment by the virtue that one's familial social identity is inextricably tied to the group. It is difficult to refuse a request or an order from one's parents or elder sibling due to the love, respect, trust, and affinity undergirding kinship bonds. Moreover, marriage solidifies that identity and facilitates its passage to the next generation.

In Indonesia especially, schools also represent an important internal pathway. They serve as a point of entry from the community into the network. This is especially true for schools affiliated with JI, its allies, and its splinter factions. However, they can also serve as an entry point for outsiders to have the opportunity to join the community and perhaps eventually the group. In cases in which parents send their children to radical schools to socialize them into the group's mindset, familial ties and educational ties reinforce one another. These are powerful social bonds. Typically, young people are sent to these schools in middle school or high school. They spend formative years away from their family. Thus, the teachers and the peers at the school become a de facto second family. Sometimes, they become even more precious than one's primary family. One finds their mentors at the school. One's life revolves around the school. At these schools, the pathway to entry is explicit. However, most important are the relationships built at various junctures along that pathway. The peer-to-peer relationships and mentor–protege relationships built in these radical boarding schools may continue long after one has graduated. These thick social bonds constitute another form of inviolable trust. One would do most anything for one's mentor or school friends, whom one loves as siblings. It comes to function in terms of strength of social bonds much in the way that actual kinship does.

In cases in which individuals attend these schools and do not become members, one reason may be that they join later and, thus, the social bonds formed are more tenuous than those who began to attend the schools at middle school or the start of high school. They do not displace family in the same way. Also important, someone who attends these schools who does not come from a family with roots in the group or who does not have any other family members in the group, who did not grow up in the community, may not feel as connected to the group as someone with family in the group. They may not feel bound in the same way. This may allow them to consider other pathways and possibilities for their lives more quickly, especially if the begin to feel disillusioned with certain aspects of the group. They may not feel the same binding sense of commitment.

# 3
# External Pathways
## Study Sessions, Conflict, Prison, and Social Media

### Hakim

"Hakim" came from an ordinary family in the province of Aceh, the only province in Indonesia governed under Islamic law. His parents were teachers, and they raised him to value education and respect people with advanced degrees. They sent him to nonreligious schools. When it came time for him to attend university, he chose to attend a college geared toward training civil servants, which would guarantee him a job with the government upon graduation. There, in the months just prior to graduation, he began attending a Salafi study session that was popular on his campus. After 3 months, he graduated and returned home to Aceh to take up his post. It is there that his story begins.

Although he only attended the meetings for a short time, the Salafi study session he attended at his university left an impression. He wanted to find something similar in his hometown. On his campus, the Salafis had sold *As Sunnah Magazine*. Back in his hometown, he found someone selling the same magazine and learned he was a student of Abu Nur, a prominent local cleric in his district. The young man agreed to make introductions for him with Abu Nur. However, there was something Hakim did not yet realize. Abu Nur was not a Salafi as in the study circle on his campus; he was Salafi-Jihadi.

Hakim describes himself as "naive." "I was new to participating in this kind of study session. Thus, I had no filter. I was influenced by all their views. All of it penetrated."[1] Hakim began attending Abu Nur's study sessions, which focused on cultivating Salafi-Jihadi religious views. From Abu Nur, he learned that the government was infidel, un-Islamic, and the most important thing was his faith and his salvation. Hakim wanted to learn more. He respected Abu Nur but also wanted to learn from someone with better credentials. Abu Nur did not have an advanced degree; he did not know Arabic. Abu Nur showed Hakim a video of Halawi Makmun, a takfiri preacher with a master's degree; Hakim had found his teacher. Hakim began consulting with Halawi Makmun over the telephone.[2]

After he began corresponding with Halawi Makmun, Hakim grew increasingly concerned about his soul. He was a government employee. In Abu Nur's study sessions, he had learned that the government was un-Islamic, infidel. However, Abu Nur never would say that someone who worked for the government was also an infidel. He refused to go that far. Halawi Makmun was a takfiri. He had no qualms about declaring individuals or entire groups of people in society as *kafir* (infidel). He informed Hakim that if he continued to work for the government, he too would be an infidel.

Hakim's entire persona began to shift. "After I obtained knowledge from Ustad Halawi, I was no longer interested in matters pertaining to my present surroundings. I was not yet a closed person. However, I didn't care about my job, my family, and my friends." His focus was on his study sessions with Abu Nur and his conversations with Halawi Makmun. That is what mattered. He explains,

> Since high school, my dream was to become a civil servant. I had attained my dreams. Halawi Makmun was able to get rid of my dreams. I was new to Quran study so I was enthusiastic about it. I was also so confused. I had this dream, but I also had my faith. In the end, my faith won and my dream lost. I left the civil service without even submitting a letter of resignation. Why? Because I was afraid of being an infidel. I was scared.[3]

His parents had noticed changes in their son. He had become more serious and inflexible. His father had tried to intervene, saying, "Don't join strange al Quran study sessions." However, it was too late.

When his parents learned he'd quit his job, they were outraged. "My mother was hysterical that I chose to leave the government. My father was very angry."[4] They attempted to discuss it with him using arguments from the Quran, noting that Quran says that children must obey their parents. If he violated their wishes, he'd be sinning. However, "because I knew nothing, I believed the *ustads* rather than my own parents because my parents were not *ustads*. [I was convinced] that these study sessions would salvage my faith and assure my salvation in life and the afterlife."[5] Halawi Makmun's followers thought of themselves like the Prophet and their companions. Thus, like the Prophet, he too would leave his family.

After a brief stint in Makassar to improve his Arabic at the encouragement of Abu Nur, Hakim moved to Jakarta and began attending Halawi Makmun's study sessions in person. This was a special study session, for approximately 20 devoted followers. The focus of these sessions was *tauhid wa'al jihad*. The sessions on *tauhid* focused on who was an infidel, whereas the topic of jihad centered on how to resist the government. He was becoming a different person, what he called "a closed person." After a short time, members of Halawi Makmun's congregation introduced him to an even more extreme takfiri cleric, Aman Abdurrahman, who was then incarcerated in Sukamiskin prison.[6] It was here that his story took darker turn.

In Abu Nur's study session, Hakim had learned the government was infidel. Through Halawi Makmun's study group, Hakim learned to label individuals, groups, and entire segments of society as infidels. He could not work in the government or help the government. However, there were limits. Halawi did not extoll his followers to commit terrorist attacks. According to Hakim, he did not encourage them to hate. The step from labeling the other as *kafir* to hating that other and seeking to harm them, that impetus came from Aman Abdurrahman.[7]

Like many of Halawi's followers, Hakim participated in study sessions with Aman Abdurrahman concurrently. He also read articles online by Aman Abdurrahman. Hakim found Aman Abdurrahman's arguments more detailed and concluded he had a better grasp of Islamic knowledge than Halawi. Thus, he gravitated to Aman Abdurrahman's brand of extremism. He accepted Aman's hatred. He explains,

> It was like I had never existed in my previous life. I was transformed into a new Hakim. Everything was different. My circle of friends, my objectives, my thoughts, everything changed. In the circle of Aman Abdurrahman, I was even asked to hate my own family. My older brother joined a political party. I had to hate him. I felt that I really did hate him.[8]

Hakim moved to Tanjung Barat, a neighborhood in South Jakarta where many of Aman Abdurrahman's followers resided. He joined their activities, lived with them, studied with them, and socialized only with them. In rejecting their own families, the members of the congregation constructed an alternative kinship community based on a narrow understanding of us versus them. Hakim explains, "We are on the right path. We will be safe. People who are not part of our group, they are doomed people. They are on a path that will lead them to destruction."[9] He was now a committed insider. It was at this point, he contends, he stopped smiling.[10]

In short, Hakim migrated from Salafi study sessions to Salafi-Jihadi study sessions to takfiri study sessions, growing progressively (or retrogressively) more isolated. He moved from seeing the government as infidel to labeling government officials as infidels and then to seeing all who did not conform to his group's understanding of Islam as infidel. In the process, he left his job, moved to a different city, distanced himself from outside friends, and broke ties with his family, seeing all of them as doomed. He grew hostile and hateful, loathing his own brother because he had joined a political party. He ultimately moved to a neighborhood populated by members of the group so that he could interact with them. He trusted only them. They were the only family that mattered to him. Together, they constructed a congregation, a community, and a brotherhood of the like-minded. Because everyone outside their group was damned.

Hakim's journey to becoming a committed member of Aman Abdurrahman's community occurred via a common external pathway: the study session. In contrast to internal pathways, where an individual is brought into a group via their family, a mentor, or via multiyear indoctrination in specific radical boarding schools, external pathways are a means in which outsiders can gain entry to an Islamist extremist community. This chapter is the second of two chapters exploring how someone becomes a member of an Islamist extremist group. To that end, this chapter highlights three external pathways and one partial pathway: study sessions, conflict zones, prisons, and social media. It is important to note that study sessions can occur in conflict zones and prisons. As shown in Figure 3.1, in Indonesia, study sessions are the key "free space," the locus of external recruitment and indoctrination. However, people can join an Islamist extremist group in a conflict zone or become socialized into one in a prison without attending study circles, especially if they know someone on the inside. By contrast, among those interviewed in the Philippines, study sessions were seldom the central venue for recruitment. Instead, the key pathway was via conflict. However, the distinction between internal and external pathway was less pronounced in the Philippines, as noted in Chapter 2, because it was often a relative inviting someone to participate in jihad.

This chapter aims to highlight how thick social ties are constructed in instances in which one is not born into the group or living with potential recruits 24 hours per day but, instead, is choosing to participate in group

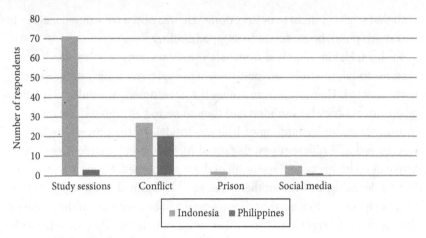

Figure 3.1 External pathways into extremism.

activities when they could just as easily do something else or participate in the activities of a different group. Moreso than internal pathways, joining via external pathways is a two-way street: The individual is actively making a choice to participate in an extremist group, and the group is choosing to accept the individual into its brotherhood of the "saved."

## Study Sessions

Islamic study sessions are the primary free space for indoctrination, socialization, and vetting of outsiders, occurring in a variety of different venues, including mosques, homes, university campuses, Islamic centers, and prisons. They are often held in conflict zones. In Indonesia, 71 respondents stated that they joined extremist groups via the study session pathway, irrespective of which group they joined. Study sessions have multiple functions. They are a mechanism for recruitment and evaluation; a space where members can openly express their radical ideas; a tool for cultivating solidarity, trust, and brotherhood; and, in some circumstances, a means of enforcing a strict worldview.

Study sessions are widespread throughout Indonesia at every point in the religious spectrum. Not only Muslims but also Protestants and Catholics hold religious study groups. Islamic and Islamist groups hold regular study sessions. On any day, one can find progressive study sessions, mainstream traditionalist and modernist study sessions, Islamist study sessions, Salafi circles, and, less widely, Salafi-Jihadi and takfiri study sessions. They are the most common pathway for outsiders seeking entry into Indonesian Islamist extremist groups. This has held constant throughout history, whether one is speaking about joining Darul Islam in the 1980s, Jemaah Islamiyah (JI) or one of its affiliates since 1993, takfiri groups such as Tauhid Wa'al Jihad in the early 2000s, or pro-ISIS groups since 2013. Although the study circle sector is far smaller in the Philippines and the pathways far less intricate, they were also an entry point for recruitment into the Maute group.

People move in and out of study sessions. In some instances, an individual may sample different study sessions offered by different Islamist and Islamist extremist groups until they find the place that fits them socially and ideologically. In other cases, an individual may attend study sessions held by different related extremist groups conterminously, as Hakim did when he attended Halawi Makmun's and Aman Abdurrahman's study circles. In other instances, one may briefly join study sessions held by a particular group only to decide they would rather do something else with their free time.

Not everyone who joins a specific group's study circles will become a member. Some will simply attend study sessions, existing on the margins of a group as a sympathizer. "Zed" is emblematic of this approach:

> I participated in Abdullah Sunata's al Quran study and when Aman Abdurrahman delivered talks, I participated in those too, but I did not become members of their congregations. . . . I attended Jemaah Islamiyah's general study sessions, but I did not want to join their special study sessions. I did not pledge loyalty [to any of them]. I was not so committed to always follow the principle of *sami'na wa'ato'na* [I hear and I obey].[11]

There are several different types of study sessions. There are large mass prayers, which aim to reach out to the broader community in order to spread their message and worldview as well as to survey for possible recruits. Then, there are "special study sessions" that serve as a means of indoctrination in order to prepare prospective members for induction to a specific Islamist group. There are even smaller *halaqoh* (study circles), where one might learn specialized information. These different types of sessions have been crucial for forming new relationships, indoctrinating new members, and ascertaining commitment. The strong social bonds formed in the more exclusive Islamic study sessions ensure loyalty to both one another in that particular study group and the extremist group.

It is important to note that the social relationships built in the study session eventually come to transcend the session itself. Through the study session, the members of the group come to share the same worldview. In doing so, however, through their shared experiences, they come to trust one another and feel a sense of deep affinity and solidarity. If one has a problem, other members of the study session will offer a solution. For example, if someone in the group needed to go home to their village but had no motorcycle, a friend in the group would volunteer theirs.[12] When it came time to marry, a friend in the study session would offer their sister.[13] If a person needed to fix a damaged house, members of the group worked to assist that person.[14]

These friendships transcend education levels and class differences. In time, they may displace ties of friendship with people outside the group and may even come to displace family ties. "Samir," a former member of JI and Jemaah Ansorut Tauhid (JAT), explains the constructing of kinship in the study sessions:

> When I was in the special study sessions, I felt close to the members in it. They felt like family. With our friends in the group, we have our religious faith in a way that friends outside did not. So we feel closest to those inside.[15]

Jemaah Islamiyah's recruitment process through study sessions from its establishment in 1993 until 2002 was a tightly controlled one aimed at establishing a completely reliable and committed membership bound by loyalty not just to the amir but also to their fellow "brothers." From being first "spotted" for potential recruitment in a public study sessions through the different stages of more exclusive study sessions could take anywhere from 18 months to 5 years.[16] The duration of time in the study group depended on the level of commitment shown at the various stages, the frequency of attendance, and relationships built inside.[17] According to Hisham, who ran such study sessions in East Java,

> Leaders determined who deserved to be recruited and allowed to pledge loyalty. There were several stages. First, there were general Quran studies that were open to the public. We would then select people from this stage that had high spirits, for example, 10 people. We would then teach them

about faith, religious service, practice, worship. Then, we would perform another selection. We would check family backgrounds. We would assess whether the candidates were receptive to our teachings. Then, we'd whittle down that number. Ten might become seven. Then, we'd invite them to join special study sessions about jihad, preparations for jihad, right faith and belief. Then, we'd winnow further. These sessions have two purposes. First, to strengthen the ties of brotherhood and friendship among members and second, to strengthen their religious knowledge."[18]

This gradual step-by-step approach of iterated evaluations ensured that by the end, only the most trusted and committed remained.

This rigor and length as well as the formation and reshaping of relationships are illustrated by the example of "Amru," who joined JI via study sessions. Amru developed an interest in Islam as a young adult in the mid-1990s. He was already working when he started attending Islamic study sessions at the Baitul Amin Muhammadiyah Islamic boarding school in Jombang in the evenings. One of the Muhammadiyah teachers, who sympathized with JI, directed Amru and others to attend study session led by a religious teacher from the nearby JI *pesantren*, Darus Syahadah.

After becoming friendly with this religious teacher, Amru started going to his house to learn about Islamic education and *tauhid* (the divine oneness of God). "First I studied Islam then I learnt about jihad. We also discussed the way the regime had treated [JI founders] Abdullah Sungkar and Abu Bakar Ba'asyir."[19] As the Darus Syahadah Islamic study sessions were more intensive than all the others he had attended, he wanted to join this group even though he did not know who they were at the time. Amru then attended what he called special Islamic studies sessions with 20 other young Muslim men for nearly 2 years. These special study sessions were closed to the public and held in private houses.

From there, Amru was invited by a religious teacher from Al-Islam to join an intensive 3-day course, highlighting faith and worship, and a subsequent 3-day paramilitary training, which included hiking, running, camping, and survival skills. Subsequently, it was expected that the members would stop having friends outside the community and would follow the rules of the community, isolating themselves from outsiders and interacting only with in-group friends.

After approximately 6 months of further special study sessions, Amru was invited to attend another 3-day intensive course, which covered *iman* (belief), *hijrah* (migration), and *baiat* (oath of loyalty). It also addressed jihad in narrow military terms as *qital fisabillah* (war in the way of Allah) and considered obligatory.[20] The Islamic studies sessions now shifted from the special study session level to the even more exclusive *halaqoh* (Islamic study circle) level. "In the halaqoh we learned that you don't just join *jamaah Islam* (the Islamic community)but Jemaah Islamiyah. However, I did not properly understand what that meant until the *bai'at*."[21] With his *bai'at* in 1999, he was given a low-risk role, briefly becoming the deputy head for Jombang district; the next year, he was offered the opportunity to train at Camp Abu Bakar in the Philippines in January 2000, thus becoming part of JI's Mindanao generation. At each of these points, his relationship with JI was strengthened.

Amru's exhaustive description of the study session pathway into JI shows that entry into JI as an outsider—as someone not from a jihadi family or JI school—was a painstakingly slow process going from large, public study sessions to increasingly smaller, exclusive, closed, and secretive ones. This gradual process of indoctrination and socialization ensured that only the most committed recruits became members. It enabled the slow development of constructed kinship and the slow building of solidarity and community. It also enabled a careful assessment of the individual's character, and it ensured that by the time he became a member, his circle of friends and mentors had narrowed and become focused on the in-group.

JI's study session pathway gained in importance after the 2002 Bali bombings when JI's schools came under scrutiny. At the same time, however, the joining process became less rigorous and more ad hoc as JI evolved into a "looser" organization following the post-Bali arrest of significant numbers of key JI cadres while the remaining cadres went underground. A second series of arrests hit JI in 2007, which prompted JI to take a step back from jihad in Indonesia but also triggered reorganization followed by a period of consolidation.[22]

The process of joining JI spinoffs and splinter factions such as JAT and Jemaah Anshorusy Syariah (JAS) is faster and more flexible. There is variation in the pathway depending on whether one is an insider, an outsider, or an outsider with inside contacts. Those who have a pre-existing background in jihadi groups—if they had been a member of a different jihadi group and migrated to JAT or JAS—might be invited to attend study circles "a few times."[23] These individuals already have the correct ideological worldview and, if they had been part of a group such as JI, they may already be known in the area. There may already be some sense of brotherhood, solidarity, and community. There may already be thick social ties. They may understand the expectations for morality, belief, and practice. They may already be trusted. Outsiders with a recommendation from a notable inside the group can also have an expedited pathway to entry.[24]

For outsiders with no background in jihadi groups seeking to join JAT or JAS, however, the process was longer. Potential candidates were scouted at mass prayers, which were open to the public, where they would then become acquainted with existing members.[25] If they were deemed suitably enthusiastic, only then would they be invited to attend study sessions for a few months up to 1 year.[26] After they were deemed to be sufficiently disciplined and ideologically ready, they would then participate in a 2- or 3-day training, after which they would be inducted into the group.[27]

With the rise of the internet and social media, study sessions remained a key pathway, as can be seen when examining the pro-ISIS groups in Indonesia. As one jihadi explained, "If you join a Telegram channel or Facebook group you need to be active. Then, after a while, a direct contact would be set up through Facebook or Telegram like an invitation to a study group."[28] Thus, while the entry point was online, the actual process of joining the pro-ISIS community was through personal contact and forming social bonds, which signaled true commitment.

One such pro-ISIS group conducting study sessions was led by Syamsudin Uba, who described his role as "telling people about the concept of al-Baghdadi."[29] He held study sessions for separate groups of men, women, the youth, and the general public "to socialize the caliphate." In the early days, he even held Islamic study sessions on campuses—until he was kicked out. After his public sermons, there would always be a follow-up—for example, through WhatsApp messages—inviting people to join Islamic studies sessions.[30]

As in JI, the study session had different levels. As Uba explained,

> We need to see that they qualify before they go to the next level. This is a process. They need to read the Quran. They need to fast on Mondays and Thursdays. We look at them. We look at the family. Are they just talking or is this truly their belief?[31]

Once an individual has passed through these steps and passed all necessary evaluations, they would come to a point where the next level of commitment would be ascertained. In this case, that meant *hijrah* (migration) to Syria for jihad or to live in the ISIS caliphate. If an individual was deemed to be ready, he would "get instructions via Telegram on how to link up with Bahrumsyah," the Indonesian commander of the ISIS Southeast Asia battalion.[32] Thus, for Indonesian ISIS supporters, true commitment necessitated first establishing new relational ties with other ISIS supporters in Indonesia and then abandoning their entire social network for a new life in Syria.[33] However, this sacrifice may not have seemed so great for "true believers."[34]

In Marawi City, Piagapo, and Butig, in the Philippines, study sessions were present in recruitment and joining but not as a pathway. It was less formal and more ad hoc, dependent on specific notables setting up study sessions or holding Friday prayers at which pro-ISIS views were espoused. Instead of a multistaged pathway with different levels, there were study sessions at specific local mosques that people attended. These mosques served as specific recruiting points for the Maute group. In only three instances did respondents profess to participate in study sessions, and of them, two were related to the person hosting the study session. Study sessions were more important to recruitment in other areas, notably in the case of a pro-ISIS cell that emerged in the city of Cotabato in Central Mindanao.[35] This group was responsible for the bombing of the Davao night market in September 2016. The Cotabato cell relied largely on teacher–student, friendship, and neighborhood ties to bring together the group that would launch the attack. However, study sessions constituted the free space in which the youth gained exposure to ISIS ideology and developed ties of solidarity.[36] Their social ties were thickened by participation in high-risk, high-cost illicit activities, notably a series of carjackings.[37]

In summary, study sessions in Indonesia represent a key pathway into extremism for outsiders. They act as a space for ideological indoctrination, socialization, vetting, and expression. Over time, the social bonds that form inside the groups will thicken and in some instances may displace those on the outside. In-group friends take priority over out-group friends. In some instances, one's constructed family—their brotherhood of faith—may displace their blood family. One comes to count on the group members to help them solve their problems and one feels connected to the in-group by a common worldview, identity, and purpose. This holds true whether one is an outsider joining JI or pro-ISIS groups.

In the Philippines, however, respondents reported that study sessions were rarely part of their experience of joining an extremist group or joining a battle. What study circles existed were short term and ad hoc. Those who attended paramilitary training with the Maute group reported feeling bonded to their fellow participants. However, these ties did not displace kinship ties or the ties one had with nonparticipants. This is likely due to the duration of time one participated and the level of commitment that such participation required over time.

## The Local Conflict Pathway

The second external pathway through which outsiders may come to join Islamist extremist groups is via conflict. This can be communal conflict or insurgency. One typically has to already be a member in good standing to have the opportunity to participate in a jihad experience in a foreign country. However, internal jihads in Ambon, Poso, and Marawi served as entry points for 26 respondents in Indonesia and 20 respondents in the Philippines, respectively. The vast majority of these were people who hailed from the district or province themselves. However, in some cases, individuals who were not yet members of an Islamist extremist group joined specifically in order to participate in a jihad experience in the island of Ambon or the district of Poso. Those who joined in a jihad experience as full members are discussed at length in Chapter 5.

The desire to defend Muslim communities under attack motivated hundreds of Indonesians to go to Afghanistan in the 1980s, to the Philippines in the 1990s, and to Syria between 2013 and 2016. Training or fighting in Afghanistan or the southern Philippines served as a commitment point for those who had already joined an Islamist extremist group and had taken the *bai'at*, whereas the Syria conflict served both as an entry point and commitment point.[38] Between 1998 and 2007, Indonesians also joined local jihads in the context of the communal conflicts, which had erupted in Poso (Central Sulawesi province) in December 1998 and in Ambon (Maluku province) in January 1999.

The experience of joining an Islamist extremist group during a time of conflict is a powerful social experience. First, locals already shared common trauma from the conflict. Their normal routines were disrupted, their families displaced, and their homes and businesses destroyed. They may have witnessed massacres or the aftereffects of massacres. Second, they shared a common desire for revenge against the Christians who perpetrated the violence, and in some instances atrocities, against them. Third, when they attended study sessions held by specific JI and KOMPAK members from

Java, they were indoctrinated in a common understanding of Islam that legitimates that desire for revenge. Fourth, for some, these study sessions were the first time they learned how to pray correctly and how to read the Quran. As a result, participation took on extra significance because this was not only the group legitimating their desire for revenge but also the group that has helped them become a real practicing Muslim. There was a redemptive aspect as well. As a result, the group became a surrogate family and community, after their own families were displaced during the conflict. They shared a common set of norms, worldview, ideology, and a powerful identity, not as a victim but as a *mujahid* (holy warrior). They were bound by a sense of vengeful solidarity, brotherhood, and a common belief that their acts of revenge were justified, even if they occurred long after the conflict has passed.

Before unpacking the conflict pathway, it is important to first take a moment to understand the context in which conflicts took place. The Ambon and Poso conflicts had their roots in economic insecurity and political anxieties in the aftermath of the fall of Suharto's 32-year New Order dictatorship. Although neither conflict was ignited for religious reasons, both soon took on a religious hue, as mosques and churches were common targets. The greatest violent critical junctures on the Muslim side had overt religious links, notably the Bloody Idul Fitri Tragedy[39] in Ambon in January 1999 and the 2000 massacre of at least 100 men and sexual assault of women at a mosque and Islamic boarding school at Walisongo.[40] These attacks and connections to faith, one on a major holiday and another at a mosque and Islamic boarding school, enabled outside forces to politicize a local conflict on religious grounds and call for a jihad to protect Muslims. Weak law enforcement exacerbated the violence,[41] facilitating the creation of a vacuum into which various jihadi groups entered.

The first Javanese to arrive in Ambon in February 1999 came through KOMPAK, the humanitarian aid wing of Dewan Dakwah Islam Indonesia. KOMPAK became the main avenue for Indonesian Muslims seeking to volunteer in Ambon either in a humanitarian or a military capacity. This included members of JI who were frustrated by the initial reluctance of JI to commit fighters. KOMPAK's openness turned the Ambon conflict into a pathway into jihad for anyone who wanted to volunteer as well as a pathway into what became "Mujahidin" KOMPAK. JI, in contrast, remained exclusive; its volunteers were already members, and most of them, like their military commander Zulkarnaen, were Afghan veterans, who already had thick social bonds and had formed a kin-like community within JI. Early KOMPAK volunteers were motivated by feelings of solidarity, by the desire to help Ambon's Muslims "with rebuilding the houses,"[42] and to provide aid to the displaced Muslims.[43] However, in that environment, they soon transitioned from aid workers to fighters.[44]

Like in the Ambon conflict, KOMPAK was the first to enter Poso, followed several months later by JI. Both partnered with local groups. Mujahidin KOMPAK affiliated with local fighters in the Kayamanya neighborhood and JI with the community around Tanah Runtuh. The primary difference between JI's and Mujahidin KOMPAK's recruitment process was that JI instituted a modified version of its study sessions pathway at Tanah Runtuh, whereas Mujahidin KOMPAK ran a 3- or 4-week course that focused on military training, preferring a "learning by doing" approach.[45]

Islamic study sessions were central to the process of becoming a member of Tanah Runtuh, and this differentiated it from Mujahidin Kayamanya as well as the Ambon conflict as a whole. Of the 26 individuals who cited local conflict as key to their joining an Islamist extremist group, 17 attended Islamic study sessions at Tanah Runtuh. They explained that in the weeks following the Walisongo massacre, teachers and trainers from JI began arriving and held public Islamic studies sessions in certain local mosques. For local attendees, the lessons provided a common Islamic lens to legitimate the desire for revenge that was already present.[46]

As "BR," who was in the first batch of volunteers, recalled, "The study sessions took place after the evening prayer in the Bonesompe neighborhood of Poso city. The imam announced it and invited anyone interested to stay. So I decided to stay."[47] Reflecting on what he learned in the study sessions, BR noted he and his peers gained a shared understanding of Islamic brotherhood and how jihad was an obligation from which they could not run.[48] While the youth attendees in Poso were learning to reframe their desire for revenge against the Christians as seeking and obtaining justice, the Javanese *ustads* holding these study sessions were noting regular attendees and checked their background.[49] BR, "after maybe 7 times" attending Islamic studies sessions, was invited to join paramilitary training. The training lasted for a week, and the 30 volunteers were taught "the study of strategy, tactics, warfare, force formation, how to shoot, camouflage, making bombs, and protecting yourself from the enemy."[50]

For the first batch of volunteers, paramilitary training began immediately after the public Islamic studies sessions because fighters were desperately needed and their "instructors were ex-Afghan veterans—11 persons."[51]

Subsequent batches moved to special Islamic studies sessions and only then to *tadrib* (paramilitary training), where their instructors and later their commanders were the star pupils from the first batch like BR. The process was then completed with *dauroh* (group internal Islamic studies), which focused on the Islamic community, the caliphate, and the *bai'at*.[52] The *ustad* determined when one was ready to move on to the next stage, as a result of which "some people from the first batch took their *bai'at* with the third batch."[53] Until the *bai'at*, none of the volunteers were aware that they were being recruited by JI.[54]

The study sessions and training provided the volunteers and later members of Tanah Runtuh and Mujahidin Kayamana with a like-minded peer group, which shared the experiences of the conflict, a sense of vengeful solidarity, an ideological prism to legitimate that desire for revenge, and the experience of induction into their respective organizations. They were taught that if their Muslim brothers were hurt, they would feel it. The thick social bonds formed during the indoctrination process were further reinforced by the shared experience of defending neighbors together and carrying out attacks together against Christians and the security forces. These peer relationships, moreover, developed kinship-like characteristics as the jihadi brethren moved into the space left by their families, which had been killed, dispersed, and displaced to safer areas outside Poso. The new jihadi family strengthened their resolve and motivated members of Tanah Runtuh and Mujahidin Kayamanya in no uncertain terms. One former member of both Mujahidin Kayamanya and Mujahidin Indonesia Timor (MIT) explained:

> We had known each other since we were children in Poso. We loved each other. When we became adults, we learned religion together. We took care of each other. We experienced the good and bad times together in Poso. When one of us was treated unfairly, we also felt the pain. We thought that we were one body. Because we grew up together in Poso.[55]

The thick social bonds formed during the Ambon and Poso conflicts also ensured that enduring and reliable networks existed and persisted after the conflicts ended. MIT has drawn upon these ties to recruit new members. Founding members, Santoso and Daeng Koro, had previously been members of Tanah Runtuh. They had friends and allies in Mujahidin Kayamanya. Three former members of MIT reported that joining was based largely on relationships. "Abu Muslim" explained, "For me, it was easy. Santoso and

I knew each other so it was easy for me to join MIT."[56] "Gungun" spoke more broadly: "People who had been active in Mujahidin Kayamanya were the same people who were active at MIT. They were pretty much the same people. They were all people who had been with the group for a long time."[57] These people had a shortcut to entry because "they understood our journey. They knew about the Poso conflict. It did not take much to make them understand."[58] "Mat" noted, however, that not everyone in Kayamanya study sessions was invited to join MIT. Those who attended regularly, showed due commitment, and participated actively were more likely to be invited than those who attended sporadically.[59]

Those interviewed from MIT repeatedly expressed greater comfort recruiting locals. It is possible that is due to the low number of those interviewed. Only four of those interviewed had joined MIT. However, it cannot be discounted that those in Poso shared a brotherhood rooted in childhood friendships, religious study, shared trauma from war, and their experiences in prior groups together. They knew one another and trusted one another. They saw one another as "blood brothers."[60] They were more than family.[61]

In Marawi, conflict functioned somewhat differently, less as a pathway into extremism than as the general context in which the Marawi siege took place. As noted in the Introduction, there had been an ongoing Muslim insurgency in Mindanao dating back to 1968. As a result, youths in Marawi and other parts of Muslim Mindanao grew up with a common metanarrative of the Bangsamoro struggle, portraying the Bangsamoro as "a 'nation under endless tyranny' that has been repeatedly dispossessed and subjugated by outsiders. [Their] only hope for justice lies in self-government guided by Islamic principles."[62] All interviewed were told by the family members, relatives, or friends who recruited them that this would be their opportunity to "do jihad and go to heaven".[63] When Imam Abilino Dimakaling and other Maute group recruiters extolled them to fight for "Islamic rights" and the "rights of the Bangsamoro people,"[64] they were drawing on these narratives, which resonated with the men who had been primed and who had heard these messages since childhood. Many had seen their fathers and uncles join the Moro Islamic Liberation Front and participate in clashes with the government, and some had been to training camp themselves. They saw themselves bound by brotherhood of shared identity, struggle, clan, and grievance long before the Maute group came into being. The Maute group recruiters deployed these narratives in order to recruit followers and, later, fighters.

The actual "conflict pathway" to the Maute group, thus, was less a specified pathway than a precondition.[65] Since the Moro conflict had been ongoing since 1968 and the grievances were still largely unaddressed, grievances factored in more so than a desire for revenge. Unlike the Poso youths, only two interviewed sought out the Mautes, and they were Maute family members. Typically, individuals were invited to join by relatives, family members, in-laws, and friends, or recruiters came to the mosque where their imam extolled them to join. Thus, the thick social bonds preceded participation rather than developed as a consequence of participation. For example, three, all of whom were relatives of either the Mautes or the Maute recruiter, Imam Abilino Dimakaling, reported attending Quran study. Eight from Piagapo all said they attended Friday prayers regularly at the Tambo mosque where Imam Abilino Dimakaling preached. Thus, there was some basic ideological indoctrination for outsiders and more serious ideological instruction for nephews and son-in-laws.

Those recruited in 2017, either just before the conflict started or just after, received no ideological training or weapons instruction. "Subair" is emblematic of those recruited just prior to the conflict. The same messaging was used, but there was no distinct pathway. Subair said,

> I joined in 2017, just prior to the conflict. I was recruited at the mosque. The men who recruited me promised me 40,000 pesos. They spoke about jihad in the name of Allah and said that when we died, we would go directly to heaven. They spoke about Islamic rights. I wanted to die in jihad so I could go to heaven. They sent me directly to Marawi.[66]

Here, there was no ideological instruction. There was no paramilitary training. However, recruiters drew on the Bangsamoro metanarrative and a simplistic understanding of jihad to encourage them to participate in the fight. They were not trying to create loyal cadres for a lasting group. There was no prioritization of the cultivation of brotherhood. Instead, it was a short-term agenda geared toward convincing as many young men to fight as they could. Almost all respondents were not even told the aims of the jihad—they were not apprised of the plan to take Marawi City. Their dedication was not to the Maute group. There was no caderization. When the fight was over, either the respondents returned to their families or went into hiding.

In summary, conflict was also a pathway into extremist groups, both in Indonesia and, to a lesser extent, in the Philippines. In Indonesia, conflict enticed outsiders to join out of a desire to assist and defend oppressed Muslims. For locals, the conflict radicalized the landscape. Muslim youths sought revenge on Christian paramilitaries for atrocities committed. The conflicts drew in outsiders, who gave them an ideological lens to legitimate that desire for revenge and the training to channel it. Participants in these groups bonded through shared trauma, worldview, and experience until they felt like more than family. These thick bonds proved enduring because MIT used them to recruit when the group formed more than a decade after the formal end of the Poso conflict. In the Philippines, conflict is less a pathway than an enduring contextual condition that cannot be ignored. It tends not to foster new thick social bonds but, rather, builds on old ties—those of shared identity, clan, grievance, and family. However, both remain important to understanding how someone joins Islamist extremist groups.

## Prison

The third external pathway is prison. Between 2010 and 2016, 18 former criminal offenders were involved in terrorism cases in Indonesia. Most of them were radicalized in prison,[67] meaning they adopted extremist views that legitimated the use of violence to achieve political objectives.[68] One argument why prisoners may be susceptible to radicalization asserts that inmates, especially new inmates, may feel fear, disempowerment, and humiliation in their new environment; this renders them vulnerable to an ideology that promises to restore their sense of personal significance.[69] Although there is some truth to this assessment in the Indonesian context, there are also other factors at work, notably the ability to have basic needs met by affiliating with extremists, a desire for redemption from sinful behavior, and the need for protection. Thus, the reality is far more complex.

Prisons in Indonesia are a free space in which Islamist extremist groups can flourish due to a combination of poor prison management, overcrowding, understaffing, and a lack of understanding or perhaps willingness to keep jihadi prisoners separate from the general population.[70] For existing jihadi inmates, time in prison is seen as a time to concentrate on deepening Islamic knowledge.[71] They see the actions that led to their conviction as morally right and their imprisonment as proof the political system is un-Islamic; this can boost their commitment to fight for the cause.[72]

Jihadi prisoners are also often able to congregate together. This enabled jihadi prisoners to not only maintain but also expand their community of believers, some of whom remained with the group after prison and others who became close with group members in order to avail themselves of the protection, better food, and resources that come with affiliation with the jihadis. Of all the pathways, internal or external, the brotherhood formed and fostered in prison has been less likely to be as enduring as that in study circles, conflict, schools, or family, unless the inmate continues association post-release.

This raises three interrelated questions: How do prisons become pathways? Why might prisoners be attracted to jihadi inmates? What are the prison pathways? Due to their religious knowledge, many jihadi prisoners are respected figures. For the first decade of the 21st century, jihadi inmates drew on that respect to secure religious positions inside the prison. Prison authorities would designate jihadi notables as imam in the prison mosque and allow them to lead daily prayers, deliver sermons, and run religious study sessions.[73] At one point, jihadi inmates were even given permission by authorities to create an Islamic school in the notorious Cipinang prison.[74] In most prisons, ordinary prisoners can start in-prison businesses with jihadi prisoners, the jihadi prisoners can move around the visitors hall unencumbered, and they have relative freedom within the prison walls.[75] Pro-ISIS prisoners held loyalty oaths inside prison walls. In some prisons, such as Petobo prison in Palu, as late as 2018, jihadi notables were still holding semi-regular mass prayers.

There are several interrelated reasons why individuals in prison might be attracted to Islamist extremist groups or notables. First, some common criminals sought out Islamist extremist figures out of a desire to find redemption via religion. They wanted to learn to read the Quran or to attend religious study circles, believing it would help them become a better person. Second, Indonesian prisons were notoriously gang ridden. Extremist inmates banded together for their own protection and to pool resources.[76] When fights broke out between gangs, the extremist inmate gangs could often hold their own. Thus, ordinary criminals seeking protection gravitated to the extremists. They began attending Quran study circles and changed their appearance by growing beards and wearing above the ankle pants in order to show they were connected to the jihadists.[77] Third, the jihadi groups often had access to better resources. The food in prisons was horrible. Prison rice often smelled like the sack in which it was stored or it had sand mixed in.[78] Islamic charities such as the Infaq Dakwah Center and Azzam Dakwah Center regularly sent aid to the prisons for jihadi prisoners.[79] Thus, by joining with the Islamist extremists in prison, be they JI or ISIS, prisoners obtained access to better food, money, and even cell phones. Finally, some were looking for community and connection in prison, and they found it among the extremists.

"Khaled," a former member of JI and five other jihadist groups, highlights the interrelationship among these factors, based on his time in prison between 2006 and 2010:

> There were parties that supplied us with food. We bought our own rice. We cooked by ourselves. We bought the food with our own resources. Hence, when we ate together with other inmates, they liked it because the food was different from the food supplied by the prison and more delicious. We made sure our cells and cellblock were clean. We had rules. The situation was different in other parts of the prison, inhumane. We showed we could help other people. When we had leftover food, we gave it to them. If we had a sarong or [a prayer rug], we gave it to them. Some inmates were very poor. They might have only one pair of pants and no sarong. Therefore, we gave them clothes. Then, they participated in our al Quran study and ate with us. They were happy. They became our sympathizers because they felt secure and comfortable with us. After they joined us, no other inmates dared disturb them because they were already our protégés. They had already joined the *ikhwan* [lit. brothers]. No one dared bully them.[80]

In short, he saw the terrorist prisoners as fulfilling basic needs and providing a sense of community. By interacting with the terrorist prisoners, inmates had access to better food, clothing, and protection. However, they also became part of a constructed family. That sense of belonging and affinity is powerful, in part because it comes with the provision of a better prison experience. In time, as in the study circles, the bonds between the men grow, not only because of their common worldview but also because of what they do together outside—they eat together, play football together, and socialize with one another. Moreover, the instrumentality of access to better food and protection may give way to a sense of community in which "they" becomes "we." We assist one another. We protect one another. We are brothers.

It is important to note that inmates recruited in prison seldom became full members, at least of JI. JI considered its informal activities in prison as *dakwah*, Islamic education, and cultivating sympathizers. "Ahmed," incarcerated at Salemba prison between 2014 and 2017, nominally affiliated with JI as well as the pro-ISIS MIT, illustrated JI's gradual ideological socialization process at Salemba prison, highlighting not why people joined but, rather, why so few persisted in becoming true sympathizers:

> Initially, there were some people who studied Quran with us, the terrorist inmates. We taught them how to read the Quran. When they were able to do that, they wanted to memorize the Quran. As time went by, we began teaching them about *tauhid* [the divine oneness of God]. This was done in the prison prayer room. The terrorist inmates then began to deliver materials about hadith and belief. Some of our "students" began to feel the materials were weird and pulled away at this point, but others remained interested. Then, the terrorist inmates began to make demands on the students, whom they recruited, insisting they not participate in state ceremonies, salute the Indonesian flag, or to file a proposal for issuance of conditional release. Many backed down at this point. Others stayed with us until they were released from prison, but after they were freed, they returned to life as usual. Only a few turned out to be loyal followers.[81]

Ahmed highlighted the incremental socialization into Islamic knowledge and group norms. He noted that although some inmates were largely receptive to basic religious instruction in how to read and understand the Quran, when the material shifted toward indoctrination and when they were expected to follow a certain set of rules that might impede early release, far fewer committed. In these instances, their actual community on the outside remained their priority.

The pathway is somewhat different for pro-ISIS groups. Like JI, the pro-ISIS groups also used study sessions. However, unlike JI, pro-ISIS groups held oath-taking ceremonies in prison. Thus, it was possible for individuals to become members of ISIS in prison. ISIS also sought to entice JI and JAT leaders, members, and sympathizers to defect.[82] "When I was in prison, ISIS was at its peak. ISIS people wanted their friends in prison to join ISIS. The recruitment process was intensive. They called for people in the prison to take the oath to ISIS."[83] In some instances, ISIS would attempt to recruit former inmates who had become close to JI post-release. In other cases, recruitment occurred while in prison. For example, ISIS recruiters targeted "big fish" such as Abu Bakar Ba'asyir, co-founder of JI and founder of JAT, and Abu Husna, a founding member of JI and a prominent figure in education and recruitment in the network. In these instances, Aman Abdurrahman, takfiri translator and chief Indonesian cheerleader for ISIS, frequently telephoned Ba'asyir and Abu Husna to engage in discussions about why criticism of ISIS from respected ulama was false.[84] In time, he and his supporters convinced both of them. Study groups were not the medium in these instances. Instead, it was one-on-one conversations and persuasion culminating in the oath of loyalty.

In other instances, ISIS targeted vulnerable prisoners—for example, individuals who never had visitors. In such an instance, the pathway to ISIS, like JI, is via study groups in prison. Inmates may have joined for instrumental reasons at first—better food or protection—but in time, they came to appreciate being part of a brotherhood and they adopted the hard-line views of their fellow members of the group. For those in prison when pro-ISIS groups were holding oath-taking ceremonies in 2014, that they were already participating in the pro-ISIS study groups at the time made it more likely they were going to take the next step and swear the oath.

For example, Hamzah, a convicted murderer, had no family or friends who visited him to bring him food or supplies.[85] As such, he had to rely on prison food. At a certain point in his sentence, he grew tired of the bad food and began attending study groups led by the terrorist prisoners in order to access better resources. They welcomed his participation because they saw him as the ideal recruit, for as a convicted murderer, he clearly had the stomach for violence.[86] By joining the terrorists, he had access to better food and a brotherhood. He became close to Syaiful Anam, a JI member convicted of crimes in Poso.[87] Slowly, he adopted the views of his radical brothers, calling prison officials infidels and refusing to cooperate.[88] When Syaiful Anam and others in his group declared support for ISIS in 2014, Hamzah joined them.[89] He remade himself with a family, social circle, and identity. Soon after, he married a woman who was also connected to the extremist community, and the quasi-familial bonds became thicker.[90]

This was not just the case for vulnerable prisoners. Even those who had regular family visits and were financially stable enough to avoid prison food might find their way into extremism via who they came to know while in prison. Inmates who came to befriend terrorist prisoners or who found their way to their study groups in the prison mosque may adopt the radical views of those study circles. Upon release, those seen as dedicated may have their marriages arranged in order to further embed them within the community.

The use of marriage as a binding agent is a tactic widely employed in jihadi communities, be they pro-ISIS or anti-ISIS like JI. Since one's wife is already part of the group and her community includes the group, it will make it more difficult for the husband to pull away. It thickens social ties. It is more likely, especially in the case of JI and its affiliates, that any children that come from the union will attend JI, JAT, or JAS schools. Moreover, one is more likely to remain in the orbit of the community, if not as a member then at least as a committed supporter or sympathizer.

In short, the third major external pathway into Islamist extremist groups in Indonesia is via prison. As in conflict zones, the prison pathway often makes use of study session. Here, too, social bonds, especially mentor–protege relationships, are important. Ordinary prisoners are attracted to the terrorist prisoners out of a wish to learn more about Islam, a need for protection and better food, a hope for personal redemption, or a desire to belong and find a community and belonging. As ordinary prisoners begin to socialize with and attend study sessions held by extremist notables in prison, they adopt the norms markers of membership, such as growing a beard and wearing pants above the ankle. In time, they may adopt some or all of the radical views espoused. Others may cease activities. If they are associating with members of pro-ISIS groups, they will be given the opportunity to swear the loyalty oath while in prison. JI is more reticent to grant membership. Upon release, to reinforce connections to the jihadi community, those who continue to participate in group activities may have their marriages arranged by their mentors.

## Social Media and the Internet

Social media is widely viewed as a mechanism for recruitment and indoctrination into extremist groups.[91] Bloom, Tiflati, and Horgan emphasize the importance of Telegram for recruitment.[92] Facebook and YouTube have also proved useful, particularly for sharing content and facilitating communication and cohesion.[93] For both ISIS in the West and the right wing extremist ecosystem, social media is a key mechanism for creating sympathizers and identifying and recruiting potential members.[94]

This has not held true in Indonesia or the Philippines. Whereas social media constitutes a pathway into extremism for the extreme right in the United States and for ISIS in Europe, there is no complete "social media pathway" in Indonesia and the Philippines. Very few people join an extremist group or radicalize exclusively through social media. Even in cases in which an individual had professed to have been radicalized via social media, when they shared their full narrative, they typically had friends or family already in or flirting with the movement; social media played a supporting role.

Rather than think of social media as a full external pathway, it is better to consider it as having several possible inflection points in a person's overall trajectory of joining. First, social media can function as a gateway. Extremist content posted on social media may intrigue an individual. In some cases, it may stop there. An individual may passively consume radical content, perhaps join a few Facebook groups, and go on with their life, albeit with views more radical and extreme than before. Second, the individual may find like-minded friends on Facebook or Telegram or may encounter recruiters on Facebook or Telegram and be invited to real-time events. Finally, a person may make direct contact with group members either via attending study sessions or via friends or family, and that is reinforced through internet messaging, texting, Telegram groups, Facebook groups, and WhatsApp communications.[95] In these instances, social media provides a medium for the exchange of ideas among like-minded extremists; the sharing of information, both licit and illicit; and the building of solidarity and community among the already radical and those in the process of radicalizing.[96]

According to the Institute for the Policy Analysis of Conflict, between 1999 and 2009, there was little evidence that significant jihadi recruitment took place online.[97] Recruiting via social media has been quite rare in Indonesia and is often a sign of weakness because groups that must resort to the internet to recruit typically lack deep contacts in the extremist ecosystem and have less practical experience.[98] Even after ISIS came to the fore in 2013, one was still more likely to be recruited by family or friends than by social media alone. Similarly, in the Philippines, among those interviewed, social media played a minor role in actual recruitment, which relied heavily on kinship, extended kinship, and constructed kinship ties.[99]

However, there are examples in which social media played a decisive role in bringing someone on the fringes of extremist movements into the center. For example, Muhammad Fachry, a journalist for Islamist extremist publications, had been a member of Islamist movements while in college and immediately after, particularly Campus Dakwah Activists, one of the permissible campus Islamist groups during the Suharto era, and Hizbut Tahrir Indonesia. In 2004, Fachry became enamored with the British extremist group Al-Muhajiroun after taking part in an online religious discussion, using the video chat forum Paltak, led by Omar Bakri, then the head of

Al-Muhajiroun.[100] The group gave Fachry the green light to set up a branch of Al-Muhajiroun in Indonesia.[101]

During the same period, he started taking part in another online extremist discussion group that counted bombing mastermind, Imam Samudra, as a member.[102] From this latter online forum, he not only made contacts with others in the jihadi community online but also obtained translations of the writings of Islamic Jihad leader Dr. Fadl and Jordanian takfiri cleric Abu Muhammad al Maqdisi.[103] He started a magazine in 2007, which drew him into the orbit of the wider jihadi community.[104] It is at this point that his activism shifts from virtual to real time. In 2007, he joined the team at Arrahmah.com, the largest and most significant jihadi website in Indonesia. He also began attending study sessions at the Al Munawaroh Mosque in Pamulang, Bekasi, led by Abu Jibril and, by 2009, Aman Abdurrahman.

Over time, Fachry gravitated more to the perspective championed by Aman Abdurrahman and parted company with Arrahmah.com, starting his own website Al Mustaqbal. In 2013, he started the Forum of Islamic Law Activists (FAKSI) to raise awareness of the importance of restoring the Caliphate. In November 2014, a month after al-Muhajiroun leader, Omar Bakri, declared support for ISIS, FAKSI, Fachry, and Aman Abdurrahman followed suit.[105] By February 2014, FAKSI began organizing public oaths of loyalty for ISIS.

In this instance, Fachry started out as an activist in conservative Islamist organizations. Via social media, he gained access to online extremist content from the United Kingdom and in Indonesia. This assuredly led to a shift in his ideological perspective. However, his real-time activities, notably the magazine he started, led him into direct in-person contact with jihadi notables, and his participation in Arrahmah.com led to him being accepted in extremist circles. Finally, his attendance at lectures and study sessions run by Aman Abudrrahman led to his embrace of takfiri Islam and the community that supported it. Ultimately, it was his ongoing engagement online with al-Muhajiroun and his real-time activities with Aman Abdurrahman that led him to become a key figure in pro-ISIS circles.

Social media also functioned as a point of entry for women, who were not born into jihadi families. Via the anonymity offered by the internet, women joined jihadi forums on social media, which in turn led to their eventual involvement in extremist communities to varying degrees. One notable example was Dian Yuli Novi, who would go on to participate in the attempted bombing of the Presidential Palace in 2016. While a migrant worker in

Taiwan, Novi spent time surfing Islamic websites and social media and, in doing so, gravitated first toward Salafi Islam and later toward the pro-ISIS online community, where she made several friends.[106] She consumed information about events in Syria and wanted to avenge Muslim deaths. It might have ended there. She might have given to charities supporting jihad in Syria. She might have fantasized about migrating to Syria herself.

However, after learning her father was dying and he had sought assistance from traditional healers, an anathema to her, she decided to sacrifice herself in order to save her father from "hellfire."[107] It just so happened at that time that the ISIS recruiter and terrorism financer, Bahrun Naim, wanted to find a woman to volunteer for a suicide bombing on the Presidential Palace, believing a woman would escape detection. Her Facebook friends in the pro-ISIS community put her in touch with Naim.

In the instances of Muhammad Fachry and Dian Yuli Novi, social media played a decisive role in bringing someone into Islamist extremist circles who might have otherwise stayed on the periphery. However, these are the exceptions rather than the rule. Yet, individuals do find community and connection both online and in real time.

In examining terrorist attacks, there are few instances in which individuals seeking to carry out attacks either found one another online or radicalized themselves through material they found online. In one case, a young man radicalized himself reading jihadi material online, learned how to make a bomb, and attempted to bomb an A & W restaurant. He blew out a few windows.[108] In another instance, a group of young men who met on Facebook plotted to bomb the U.S. embassy in 2012 but were intercepted before they could carry out the attack.[109] More recently, in 2021, Zakiah Aini, a 25-year-old university dropout, opened fire at police headquarters in Jakarta; social media played a role in her radicalization.[110] Successful terrorist attacks such as the 2002 Bali bombing, the 2004 Australian embassy bombing, and the 2009 Marriott and Ritz Carlton bombings were carried out by individuals who knew one another and trusted one another, at least some of whom were properly trained.

It is more common for women and men to initially encounter Islamist extremist activists via study sessions, family, or friends, before they are channeled to jihadi chat forums. In 2008, "Syahadah" joined a study group run by Abu Jibril in Pamulang, Bekasi. Although men and women were separated in the group, she befriended Abu Jibril's sons and other group members via Facebook.[111] His eldest son, who ran Arrahmah.com, hired

Syahadah to administer and write for one of its online forums.[112] With that, she became the only female journalist working for Arrahmah.com, which she did under a male pseudonym until 2011, when she shifted to charity work.[113]

These forums and chats varied in how open they were. Some forums, such as #cafeIslam, were fairly open conversational chats, where men and women could participate. Others, such as Forum Jihad al-Tawbah, were far more careful about who they permitted to join. Only established, long-vetted, committed extremists could join. The point of this latter type of forum was to foster the exchange of ideas among people committed to violent jihad in Indonesia.[114] Still others, such as Forum al Busryo, were a means of spreading ideological indoctrination and disseminating jihadi materials.[115] Via these sites, via Facebook groups, and via Telegram, "individuals could interact with people who shared their thinking and that had the effect of lifting their spirits."[116] One can create their own personal echo chamber of like-minded thinkers. "Arif," a key figure in the Indonesian Islamist extremist online community, explains how this echo chamber developed over time:

> The internet enabled the dissemination of jihad from all over the world to Indonesia. Arrahmah, Al-Taubah and others took videos on jihad from the jihadist forums and disseminated them, aiming to inspire people to understand that there are mujahidin out there fighting against enemies in other parts of the world. That came first.
>
> Then came the thought, the translation of books from Middle Eastern ulama, the thought of Aman Abdurrahman, the translation of books written by Abu Muhammad al Maqdisi that were translated by Aman Abdurrahman. These entered the forums around 2008. These ideas began influencing people. Some of them established real world communities. They would take them and share them with their friends in the real-time communities and use them to justify terrorist attacks.[117]

"Muhammad," a former JI member and former lecturer at Mahad Ali An-Nur, a JI institute for higher education, highlighted the interplay of the online and real-time interactions:

> I worked at an internet café in 1998 and obtained knowledge from the internet that matched what I'd learned from Abdullah Azzam [during the Soviet–Afghan war]. I downloaded these materials and shared them with

my students [at Mahad Ali], who, in turn developed that knowledge and disseminated it widely. I read al Maqdisi. My thinking was closest to al Maqdisi. There were Arabic language forums and I joined them. The internet shaped my thinking during that time, especially regarding the global jihad.[118]

Muhammad was already a member of JI when he joined various Arabic language chats and downloaded these materials for his students. The materials he found reinforced his views, ultimately causing him to defect from JI to help Noordin M. Top and Al Qaeda in the Malay Archipelago because he believed his views better aligned with theirs on the legitimacy of the use of violence. In addition, a trusted friend asked him to defect.

He turned to the internet again when JAS split from JAT in 2014 and he was deciding whether to stay with Abu Bakar Ba'asyir and JAT or defect to JAS:

> I accessed many internet sites that I used as an alternative reference and found that Abu Bakar Ba'asyir and Ustad Afif had a better view. I saw ISIS as the transformation of Al Qaeda. I participated in the declaration in Solo. I tried to go to Syria. I read the propaganda. I watched the videos like the declaration videos. However, that was my mistake. I didn't know reality.[119]

It is important to note that Muhammad did not come into the jihadi movements in Indonesia through the internet. He joined JI because of his affinity for Abdullah Sungkar. He assisted Noordin M. Top, in part, because a friend asked him to do so. He joined JAT because Abu Bakar Ba'asyir offered him a position. The internet and social media play a supporting role in his journey, helping him make choices.

Similarly, Jamal, a former member of the Maute group from the district of Piagapo on the island of Mindanao in the Philippines, says that he attended a study group at the Tambo mosque held by his uncle, Imam Abilino Dimakaling.[120] There, the members watched YouTube videos and Islamic videos.[121] They learned about ISIS on a surface level, linking ISIS into the broader Bangsamoro metanarrative about victory through raising Islam. The online materials helped Jamal become more radical, but it was the direct intervention by his uncle, the imam of the mosque, that facilitated his entry into extremism.

The same holds true for many who chose to migrate to Syria. They were often enticed by family and friends who used social media as a mechanism to communicate from different areas of Indonesia and from Syria. Indonesians who joined ISIS often used WhatsApp and phone communication to persuade family and friends to join them in Syria.[122] According to "Arif,"

> Indonesians in Syria report back to their friends what they do there and this influences their friends. His friends in Indonesia get pictures about what is going on in Syria directly from him, not through the mainstream media. The influence was greater when he asked and provoked his friends back home to join him.[123]

"Farah" shared how her husband convinced 25 members of their family to migrate to Syria. In 2011, his business went bankrupt, and in the next year, she developed a tumor on her neck. Facing a personal multidimensional crisis, they turned to religion, becoming more devout. They followed the Islamic news media, Arrahmah.com and Al Mustaqbal. In time, they learned about the rise of the ISIS Caliphate. They began reading materials her husband had found online by Aman Abdurrahman, and they formed their own internal study session just for themselves and approximately eight other members of the family.[124] Farah and her husband came to believe that it was their duty as Muslims to migrate to Syria. Moreover, it was the answer to their prayers.[125] Farah required surgery, which they could not afford.[126] Her sons were severely autistic. Indonesians with whom they communicated in Syria promised her the best medical care and social services for the children.[127] She followed the Tumblr account, Diary of a Mujahirah, reading it avidly to learn about daily life for women in the Caliphate. She peppered those they already knew in Syria with questions. When the time of departure grew closer, they coordinated through Telegram and WhatsApp with family in Batam who had also decided to go.[128]

Thus, social media served as a powerful force in reinforcing Farah and her husband's decision to migrate to Syria at several critical junctures. Initially, it brought them Aman Abdurrahman's worldview. Then, when they made the decision to go to Syria, social media enabled them to communicate with Indonesians already in Syria to seek answers to their questions and to organize their departure and arrival. However, the key figure in their story was not social media. It was Farah's husband, who downloaded the materials, who organized the family study sessions, and who ultimately persuaded more than two dozen family members to join them. In short, social media was an important part of their pathway—it facilitated indoctrination and information gathering—but it was not the sum total of the pathway.

## Conclusion

For outsiders seeking entry into Islamist extremist groups, there were three pathways (study sessions, conflict, and prison) and one partial pathway (social media). Someone who joined via familial ties or educational ties was socialized into the group from an early age. They felt thick social ties based on kinship or constructed kinship with a group of peers with whom they spend 24 hours a day, 7 days per week. They trusted one another and loved one another. They felt a keen sense of belonging. By contrast, joining via external pathways is a choice. A person is choosing to attend study circles with one movement over another, and they are prioritizing that activity over others. They were not raised in the network. Their parents and siblings are not tied to the network. Instead, through the medium of the study circle, mentor–protege ties in prison, online friends, and friendship ties in conflict, one constructs their own social network, their own alternative family of brothers united in a common worldview. They choose connection within a particular community, and their social ties to that community grow thicker as they study together, assist one another, problem-solve together, and marry into the group. Over time, they may develop trust, affinity, and perhaps even love for one another. This constructed family may come to displace one's own actual kin, especially in conflict situations in which one's family has been forced to flee.

Outsiders make the active choice to participate. They may search until they find the study circle to which they believe they belong ideologically and socially. They may sample multiple circles or attend only intermittently. Some may become committed insiders, adopting the morals, dress, and norms of a group member. Others may simply exist on the margins. Still others may adopt Salafi ways of being to a certain degree in spaces such as prison to secure resources—better food, protection, and cell phones. The ideology only penetrates so far, and the relationships never truly evolve into mentor–protege. For some, social media may reinforce what they learn in study sessions, or it may provide an entry point into a new way of thinking. Those who truly commit do so because they feel connected, not only to the ideas but also to the community. The ideology is the binding agent. The thick social ties, and the feelings of solidarity and belonging they foster, are the forces that compel them to commit.

In the Philippines, among those interviewed, because family was such a driving force in recruitment, study sessions were far less salient. Individuals attended study sessions when it was their uncle or father-in-law holding them. Conflict was an important contextual link because all were raised with the metanarrative of Bangsamoro oppression and the need for jihad in the name of Allah. They learned this from their families; they heard it in Friday prayer sermons at certain mosques. This propelled them to fight. However, it did not necessarily bind them to one another as a group. Their thick social ties predated joining; they were not created by the process of joining. When the conflict was over, they ceased participation in the group and returned to their families.

# 4
# Commitment

Once an individual begins on the path to membership in an extremist group, once they interact with activists, once they gain ideological exposure and build thicker social ties with group members, how do they show commitment? What steps do they take to become a committed insider?[1] Becoming a committed insider is a gradual initiation process in which one slowly begins to adopt norms of identity, shared ritual, sacrifice, and committed action.[2] This deep commitment requires effort on the part of the new/potential member; they have to be willing to demonstrate to the leadership that they have accepted the values, beliefs, and style and are prepared to sacrifice, if necessary.[3] This performing of commitment takes the form of a sort of personal conversion. One feels a strong socioemotional connection, affection, affinity, and belonging to a brotherhood or sisterhood—a community of like-minded.[4] One's identity as a group member takes priority over their identity as an individual, member of a family, or member of other sorts of communities.

This chapter unpacks how candidate members as well as members of extremist groups express commitment to the group. In doing so, it identifies four ways through which this is done: obeying group norms of identity, etiquette, and behavior; conforming to group expectations in how religion should be practiced; following orders; and prioritizing in-group demands and social relationships over those outside. It shows how abiding by these norms and behaviors, in turn, reinforces thick social ties and proves commitment, trust, and loyalty.[5] The chapter also analyzes the variation between expressions of commitment in Indonesia and in the Philippines. In short, Indonesians who joined an Islamist extremist group through the kinship, study sessions, or schools pathway were far more likely to become committed insiders than their counterparts in the Maute group in the Philippines. Indonesians were far more likely to express commitment along all four metrics, whereas members of the Maute group interviewed tended to adopt norms of identity and behavior more so than the other aspects. The Maute group did not require the same level of commitment performance for rank-and-file members because the group was not seeking committed insiders in the latter stages; it was seeking fighters, not members.

## Obeying Group Norms

Perhaps the easiest way to show deep commitment was by obeying group norms. These included adopting the "uniform" of a group member and the rituals, customs, and moral behavior codes of a member in good standing regarding vice, gender, prayer, manner of dress and grooming, and even the naming of children.[6] These shared behavioral norms served to reinforce and consolidate a common identity, which in turn reinforced feelings of connection and community. Abiding by these behavioral norms was necessary for being considered a committed insider and was, in fact, the easiest way to show one's commitment.

These norms held fairly constant across Salafi-Jihadi and takfiri groups in Indonesia. B.R., a former member of Tanah Runtuh, explained, "We were supposed to pray five times a day, stop consuming alcoholic drinks, and stop gambling."[7] Ali Imron, one of the participants in the 2002 Bali bombing and a member of Jemaah Islamiyah (JI), elaborated,

> We had to dress the part. We had to grow a beard. Our pants had to stop at the ankle. We had to eat and drink using only our right hands. We had to respect our seniors. We had to implement all the behaviors taught in Islam.[8]

Norms also affected gender relations. "Haroun," a former member of JI and Tanah Runtuh, explained how his attitude changed when he became a member: "I kept distant from women. I was very careful. I quit smoking and wore pants that stopped at the ankle."[9]

Members also adopted certain norms of speech and interpersonal referents to signal affection, affiliation, and affinity, peppering their speech with specific Arabic terms. They were the *ikhwan* (brothers). They referred to one another as *abu* (father) and *akhi* (brother) and to in-movement women as *ukhti* (sister) and *umm* (mother), as opposed to the gender-neutral Bahasa Indonesia referent, *kakak* (older sibling) and *adik* (younger sibling). They used the Arabic *ustad* to refer to their teachers and seniors, who possessed religious authority, as opposed to the term *kyai*, which was popular on Java and among members of Nadlatul Ulama, the largest Islamic mass organization in the world.

Recruiters evaluated potential candidates based on adherence to these norms, which held constant across Salafi-Jihadi and takfiri groups to a large degree. "BeWe," an ISIS recruiter, would test potential candidates to assess their level of commitment on these norms:

> I would ask someone to meet me before the 4:00 a.m. Subuh prayer to see if he would come. After performing Subuh, we would do physical exercise. If he showed up, that was good. That meant he was committed. Sometimes, I sent a friend. The friend would smoke, wear pants past the ankle and talk about women. What would the [candidate for membership] do?[10]

Syamsuddin Uba, leader of a pro-ISIS study session, concurred with this "testing" approach, noting they also expected members to carry the Quran with them, to fast on Mondays and Thursdays, and to do extra nightly prayers."[11] "Firdaus," who led a study session in Palu for JI and was widely viewed as an elder figure in JI, explained that he looked for candidates who routinely attended his Quran study, who accepted JI's views, and who did not smoke.[12] Likewise, "Badrol" expected potential candidates for JI to "wear a beard, wear pants to the ankle, be disciplined, be loyal, and share the same understanding of Islam."[13]

Women had social norms around dress. Women were expected to adopt a long headscarf that completely covered and enveloped their breasts, possibly a *niqab* (face veil) in certain communities, with arms covered to the wrist and legs to the ankles. Although women were not permitted to take the oath to become members of JI or Darul Islam, it was expected that women in the movement would marry others in the movement, thus ensuring that they would raise the next generation of members. In this way, women were the glue that enabled alliance building, expansion of the network, and the reinforcement of thick relational ties.

It is important to note that many of these norms were not exclusive to Salafi-Jihadi and takfiri groups. Instead, they are Islamic norms of behavior that conservative or Salafi Muslims will adopt in order to mimic the behavior of the prophet and his companions. They are also low-risk, low-cost ways of showing commitment.[14] It is not difficult to dress a certain way, eschew vice, and grow a beard. Salafi Indonesians typically wear ankle-length pants, and even more grow a wispy beard. Devout Muslims tend to eschew alcohol and smoking. Thus, these ways of performing commitment are not perceived widely as signifiers of extremism. However, via adhering to these norms, one can signal to fellow members commitment, affiliation, and affinity while at the same time blending into conservative religious society.

Many of these same norms appeared in accounts from recruits into the Maute group, who attended paramilitary training. They adopted a certain set of behaviors, at least temporarily, while the experience of the camp was still fresh in their minds. When they returned from training, they kept distant from women. They gave up smoking and alcohol. "Jabir," "Abu Islam," and "Jamal" all report being given a black garment, a *kimon*, and a headband that said *la ilaha illallah* (there is no God but Allah).[15] In contrast to the Indonesians, no Maute recruit reported being instructed to grow a beard. This may have been because those interviewed were largely in their teens at the time of their initial involvement and may not have been fully capable of growing one. The Maute group mirrored female social norms regarding dress, which was not surprising because these are conservative Islamic norms. However, they viewed women as having a more expansive role, employing them as fighters and recruiters.[16]

Abu Usama shared how he adopted ways of thinking and knowing from the Maute group after he attended a 4-day seminar and two month-long paramilitary trainings. After the first seminar and paramilitary training, he quit drinking and smoking. He stated,

> After the second training, in 2014, however, I started to think more radically. I kept scolding my girl cousins for not wearing the *hijab* properly. I kept saying, "this is *haram*" and "that is *haram* [forbidden]. You're going to be punished." They responded, "What's up with you?" I didn't tell my family. No one knew I was a member of the group. I changed how I dressed. I didn't wear shorts anymore. I also stopped listening to music around this time.[17]

However, as time away from the Maute group and away from the camp lengthened, he reverted back to type. These norms did not stick to the same degree as they did in Indonesia because he was not participating in regular activities with the group. There were no daily or weekly meetings or events to reinforce solidarity and sustain engagement. As a result, he may not have felt the same degree of connection, community, and commitment as someone who was constantly with members of the group.

The lack of sustained expression of deep commitment by those who were not members of the Maute family may have, in part, been a result of the higher risk associated with continued identification with the Maute group. Those recruited into the Maute group were brought in for a purpose, first to create an Islamic mini-state in the town of Butig and, when that failed, to take over Marawi City. Thus, the adoption of the unique manner of dress may have been about affinity rather than an expression of an enduring community, solidarity, and commitment. Moreover, the *kimon* and headband comprised a distinctive uniform, far more identifiable than the ankle-length trousers and wispy beard of their Indonesian counterparts. Among those interviewed who were recruited into the Maute group, with the exception of members of the Maute family, they reported they were not apprised of the intention to take over parts of Marawi.[18] The takeover and subsequent siege of Marawi resulted in the displacement of hundreds of thousands, including members of their own families. Thus, some may have wanted to take off their *kimon* and headband in order to blend into the larger population and perhaps also to avoid the risk of arrest.

## Correct Practice of Religion

Another important aspect of showing deep commitment was learning, adopting, and embracing the group's understanding and practice of Islam. This was accomplished through active participation over time in religious study sessions and small group religious study as well as, for some, attendance at specific boarding schools affiliated with the extremist group. Thus, it is not simply being good Muslims or practicing Muslims that is necessary for showing commitment. One must learn and subsequently conform their understanding and practice of Islam to the norms of the group, which in turn reinforced community and connection on the basis of common practice and worldview.

Abu Rusydan, the spiritual leader of JI, explained their expectations:

> A good member will be a good Muslim. He will be willing to sacrifice himself in the interests of Islam. He will have a strong and good *aqidah* [creed] and loyalty to Allah SWT. This is very important. People are considered to have good *aqidah* first if they obey the teachings of Islam and sharia. Second, he will be patient toward whatever destiny is stipulated by Allah

SWT. This not only helps Islam's victory by the sword but it also helps Islam through one's *aklak* [ethics and morals]. A person needs to be nurtured for a long time to be ready to be a good warrior for Islam.[19]

This was echoed repeatedly by recruiters from JI as well as by one individual who had started on the path of joining but terminated it prematurely. According to "Hisham," who spent several years as a JI preacher and recruiter, "Good members needed to be obedient in practicing religion and not reject what we convey to them."[20] "Firdaus," an elder JI leader who ran study sessions in Palu, concurred: "Good candidates must routinely attend Quran study. Their views must be the same as ours; they cannot clash. They have to be willing to implement the practice and habits of the Prophet Muhammad and his companions."[21] "Haris," a candidate for JI membership who chose to leave the network prior to taking the oath echoes, "Recruits must share the same ideology. The same views on jihad. The same views on *tauhid* [the divine oneness of God]. Recruits must share those similarities. They must be committed to fight for Islam and kindle the spirit of jihad."[22]

The pro-ISIS community has similar expectations of religious and ritual conformity. New members were expected to learn, adopt, and adhere to ISIS' understanding of the divine oneness of Allah, creed, faith, rejection of democracy, and support for the caliphate of Abu Bakar al Baghdadi.[23] However, ISIS was also searching for individuals who would be ideologically ready to migrate to Syria to fight for them. Deep commitment looked different because it always included the possibility of and desire for relocation. Individuals who joined the pro-ISIS group, who swore the oath of loyalty to al Baghdadi, embraced a grandiose dystopian vision in which they would be gathering together alongside Muslim jihadis from all over the world to fight against enemies of Islam and perhaps even participate in the great battles of the endtimes. They believed they were building a great worldwide Caliphate and were willing to give their lives for it. The risks of arrest, imprisonment, injury, and death were high. The financial, material, and social costs were great. One had to pay their own way to Syria, often leaving their families behind. Thus, if one truly was to become a committed insider, the sacrifice was all-encompassing.

## Prioritizing In-Group Social Relationships

Another way to show deep commitment was by prioritizing in-group social relationships over those outside. In some instances, notably those of Tauhid wa'al Jihad members and other takfiri groups, an individual disassociated from their actual family. "Abu Muslim" noted that after his mother and siblings began following Aman Abdurrahman, they refused to associate with him, his wife, and his child.[24] "Hakim" concurred, noting that he had distanced himself from his parents and brother after following Aman Abdurrahman.[25] For those in JI, its affiliates, and its splinters, it is less a disassociation than prioritizing in-group friends over out-group friends. However, the norm in JI is to view Muslims as potential supporters and sympathizers. Thus, there is not the same pressure to disassociate from family.

One way that members of the ISIS–JAD-Tauhid wa'al Jihad community and the JI–Jemaah Ansharusy Syariah communities showed such commitment was via where they chose to live. They may relocate in order to live together in the same neighborhoods, often close to an affiliated mosque so that they can socialize with one another in their community of like-minded. This is an ultimate expression of commitment because one is physically distancing or disassociating from their previous life in order to fully embrace their current community. Moreover, if one does not come from an extremist family, one is typically prioritizing their in-group constructed kin over their parents, siblings, relatives, and out-group friends—their previous thick social relationships.

When one marries and has children, their children will socialize within the community because that is where they live, thus perpetuating the intergenerational commitment. Their children will not know any other way of being. It is important to note that unlike conforming to religious and social norms, it was not required that an individual relocate in order to prove commitment. However, this was something that members tended to do, gravitating toward the comfort of the community of like-minded.

According to Hakim, Aman Abdurrahman's followers tended to gather in the neighborhood of Tanjung Barat in South Jakarta.[26] Thus, when Hakim joined the community, he too moved to Tanjung Barat. ISIS-umbrella JAD had several such strongholds in Jakarta and Central Java, notably the towns of Cilacap, Banyumas, and Sukohardjo, as well as the neighborhood of Tanjung Barat.[27] The same held true for JI, which, according to "Amru," has a presence in Magetan, Solo, Malang, East Jombang, Lamongan, and Jepara.[28] Members tended to congregate together in specific neighborhoods or towns so that they could socialize with one another and maintain the quasi-familial networks of mutual aid. Despite being "inactive Jemaah Islamiyah," Amru explained that he still lives in a neighborhood of Semarang near other members because

JI people like to live near other JI people. We farm together. We go to the market together. Our kids go to school together. We go to the same mosques. When we marry, we select a person from that area.[29]

He also noted that "it's easier to socialize the kids into the community if they live near one another. If there are around 50 JI families that live in a particular area, Jemaah Islamiyah will build a school for them."[30] This ensures that group cohesion, a powerful sense of brotherhood, and solidarity remain strong as all aspects of one's life come to revolve around the group, from major life events to ordinary everyday activities. One's most trusted friends and constructed family will be there.

Marriage is also an expression of deep commitment to the group. Marriage acts as a bonding agent, thickening and reinforcing social ties, cementing alliances, and ensuring that the social norms of these groups are passed down to the next generation through the creation of multigenerational jihadi families. For someone on the fringes of the group, marriage to a woman from a good JI or pro-ISIS family is a means of ensuring that they hold true to the group's basic religious and ideological principles.

The agency of the women may vary. In some instances, fathers cajole their daughters into accepting a suitor in order to create or solidify bonds between communities. However, women also have agency of their own and may seek out the opportunity to marry a *mujahid* (holy warrior), even in defiance of their fathers. For example, in Poso, "Munira"'s father, a prominent local extremist imam, pressured her into terminating her studies prematurely in order to marry the head of JI-Poso and cement an alliance between his group, Tanah Runtuh, and JI.[31] In another instance, "Umm Farish" sought out the opportunity to become the second wife of an imprisoned member of JI because "I wanted to marry a *mujahid* and he was a *mujahid*."[32] In the latter case, Umm Farish, then a member of a women's study circle at Tanah Runtuh, used her decision to marry and her choice of a partner in marriage as an expression of commitment to a group and a cause.[33] She made that choice over the objections of her father, prioritizing in-group devotion over the Quran's dictates that children should obey their parents.[34]

## Following Orders

Another common way individuals prove deep commitment to an extremist group is through committed actions, notably via following orders.[35]

Members are assigned duties and are expected to fulfill those duties in order to prove loyalty and trustworthiness.[36] They are expected to do as they were told, without question, and to prioritize the group's interests over their own personal interests.[37] Moreover, they are expected to comply with tasks, even over personal misgivings and objections. Similarly, both candidates for membership and committed members are expected to participate dutifully, regularly, and enthusiastically in all group activities and group meetings.

According to "Maresh," a former member of JI who headed up its branch in the city of Palu,

> I showed I was a good member by listening and obeying in all things requested and in all things they prohibited me from doing. I implemented my duties that they gave me as best as I could. When I was ordered to go [somewhere], I would go there. When I was requested to retreat, I would retreat. If I was ordered to keep guard, I would do so. When I was ordered to assist people who come and go, I would help them because that is my duty.[38]

"Joko," a former member of Al Qaeda in the Malay Archipelago (AQMA), explained,

> I always tried to be successful in doing what I was asked to do. If I was asked to provide a meeting venue, I did. If I was asked to make donations, I did so. I showed my commitment by following them.[39]

"Khaled," a member of JI's pro-bombing wing and later AQMA, shared a similar sentiment:

> Because I was young in comparison to them, I did my best in serving them. I tried to provide all the things they needed. I provided the rental house. When they arrived, I made tea for them. I washed their clothes if they had no time to wash their clothes. I showed, as a young person, that I served my elders. When they asked me to participate in activities, I did my best.[40]

Among those interviewed, following orders and doing whatever was asked of them without question was the most common way of proving loyalty, trustworthiness, and commitment. This was irrespective of which group someone joined and whether the individual participated in a terrorist attack or not. This expectation to follow orders led individuals to put aside personal misgivings about a particular terrorist attack and carry out the task assigned to them.

This following of orders was not simply a phenomenon restricted to JI, its affiliates, and its splinter factions. "Zed," a former participant in pro-ISIS study sessions run by Aman Abdurrahman and Abdullah Sunata, said that although he never became an official member, and although he never took an oath to either figure, he felt a subtle pressure to follow orders: "I didn't want to disappoint them. I felt I had to obey and follow."[41] Two former members of the pro-ISIS Mujahidin Indonesia Timor (MIT) echoed this view. "I was always ready when I got the call. Whatever was needed, I was always ready."[42] "I did what I was ordered to do."[43]

Following orders could be something as innocuous as agreeing to return to school after paramilitary training, when one really wanted to do anything else. Alternatively, following orders could also require participating in illicit activities, irrespective of personal reservations. One subordinated their personal preferences and concerns to the directives of their seniors and to the "good" of the movement. By following orders, one showed one was committed through one's actions.

For example, "Reza," had been ordered by his superior in Mujahidin KOMPAK, Abdullah Sunata, to assassinate a prominent figure in Nahdlatul Ulama, an Islamic mass organization with approximately 50 million members.[44] As a child of Muhammadiyah, a rival Islamic mass organization, Reza feared that assassinating the individual could hold significant consequences. He felt deeply troubled. However, he felt bound by his oath to Sunata and bound by his status as a committed member.[45] It was only luck that he was arrested for his participation in the Australian embassy bombing before he had been able to carry out the assassination.[46] Likewise, when Ali Imron learned about the plan for the 2002 Bali bombing, he argued against it:

> I asked whether this bombing was true jihad. [My brother] Mukhlas said that "according to us, it is." I asked whether the brothers of JI had agreed to this sort of jihad. Mukhlas replied, "That is not your concern; it is my concern." Ali Imron repeatedly tried to appeal to Mukhlas. "I was trying to warn him about whether our bombing plan was a real jihad or based on selfish aspirations."[47]

However, when he could not convince his brother and the others to abandon the plan, he followed orders. He helped his brother, Amrozi, prepare the car. He surveyed the tourist areas to determine which had the largest number of followers. He tried a second time to convince his siblings that this attack was ill advised. However, he asserts, "I was a junior member and also a younger brother. At the time, I did not win the argument with them, so I had to follow them.... I followed because I trusted my seniors in JI."[48]

It is expected that committed insiders will follow orders, irrespective of the risk to one's person, their personal belief about whether an action is wise or justified, or the consequences. Those who do not wish to follow orders can and do still stay within the broader jihadi movement. They may be viewed as a sympathizer and not be fully trusted. They may choose to migrate to another group in the broader Salafi-Jihadi ecosystem that better suits their needs. Had Ali Imron walked away, it is possible he would have alienated his beloved older brother, something he would later do in the aftermath of the bombings when he chose to cooperate with the authorities and publicly apologized to the victims for his actions in return for a life sentence. At that point, however, he was not ready to do so.

Takfiri groups shun and excommunicate members and their families for defiance of even basic orders. They sever connection and ties to the community. Hakim shared an example from his time in prison:

> Some inmates needed to use the "biological rooms" for conjugal visits with their spouses. The government provided these rooms; inmates just had to pay for using them. Aman Abdurrahman said that if his followers used the conjugal rooms, it would damage our faith. He said those who used the rooms were infidels. Once, one of his followers used a biological room with his wife. His wife lived in [the city of] Medan [on the island of Sumatra], and when she went to Jakarta to visit her husband [in prison], she stayed at Aman Abdurrahman's *pesantren*. When Aman found out he and his wife had used the biological room for a conjugal visit, he ordered his subordinates at the *pesantren* to tell the wife she could not stay there any longer. She was in limbo for several days until someone helped her find a place to stay.[49]

Such was the demand for conformity in following all orders and adhering to all norms within the takfiri groups associated with Aman Abdurrahman. Something as simple as a single conjugal visit in prison with one's spouse could be grounds for expulsion and the end of that person's place in the community. The act of excommunication came with profound social consequences. If a member was expelled, their in-group family and friends would no longer associate with them. They would be considered an "infidel."

Wives would be divorced from husbands and "remarried" to members in good standing, even while legally remaining married to their original now "infidel" husband.[50] The exiled member could lose access to his children. The group would dehumanize the excommunicated member. The individual would no longer be trusted; they would be viewed as beyond redemption, an infidel, an apostate. In fact, in this line of thinking, if a member murdered the excommunicated person, because that person was an infidel or an apostate, the murder would not be viewed as a sin.

## Types of Commitment

To this point, this chapter has addressed how individuals seeking to become members express commitment, what attitudes recruiters look for in a committed member, and how members sustain commitment. There are three manifestations of commitment. A person can become a committed insider of a particular jihadi group and remain an active member of that group over decades. Eventually, the individual might decide to "go inactive," meaning they no longer accept duties from the organization and the organization no longer gives them formal responsibilities as a member. However, they still consider themselves a member of the group; this is a core component of their identity. They may also live near other members and utilize group resources like a network of *pesantren*.

Second, a person may migrate among organizations and groups that exist in the same extremist ecosystem. Third, a person may join a group and commit for the short term. Alternatively, some individuals participated in activities or even terrorist attacks but never became members of any group. They were recruited for a particular operation because they were related to a member of the cell.

Indonesian respondents who joined via kinship and schools were more likely to commit to one group in the long term or, alternatively, to initially commit to one group and after a few years migrate to splinter or affiliate groups in the same Salafi-Jihadi ecosystem. These individuals tended to join JI. They were far less likely to join and commit in the short term compared to those who joined via study sessions, conflict, prison, and social media (Figure 4.1). The reason for this lies in the nature the commitment. When one joins via internal pathways, they are either propelled by family or the constructed kinship ties that come from the boarding school experience. Thus, it is more likely they are either going to be committed insiders in a particular group or members of the Salafi-Jihadi community in good standing. Since kinship and constructed kinship ties exist prior to membership, it makes it highly likely an individual will remain in the group or migrate to a related group within the same jihadi ecosystem. If they become disillusioned, they may choose to go inactive rather than leave. Very few committed in the short term.

Some Indonesian respondents who joined via study sessions also committed long term. Note that the high numbers in Figure 4.1 are simply a reflection of the sample—more in the sample joined via study circles than via other mechanisms. Migration took place at levels similar to the levels for those who joined via kinship and schools. However, of those who joined via study sessions, more committed in the short term compared to those who joined via internal pathways. Respondents who joined via conflict were far more likely to commit in the short term. This makes sense, especially given that the majority of the sample who joined via conflict were locals. When they left prison, after serving time for participating in terrorist attacks against Christians in the aftermath of the Poso conflict, they found their city rebuilding. Although some joined MIT and continued the struggle, the majority chose to cease participation in acts of violence and dedicate themselves to their families and to helping their city recover. The same held true for interviewees who joined the Maute group in the Philippines. However, in the Philippines, conflict was the guiding environmental condition rather than an explicit pathway. Much like 23 out of 26 jihadis in Poso, all committed for the short term.

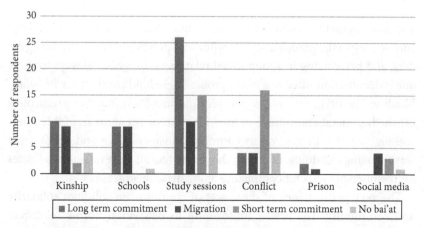

Figure 4.1 Commitment type by pathway to entry.

In summary, Indonesians who join via internal pathways are more likely to become committed insiders in the long term than those who join propelled by conflict. They were more likely to stay in the group longer, develop thick and enduring social ties, and, if they left, migrate to another related group in the Indonesian Salafi-Jihadi ecosystem. By contrast, those who joined via the conflict did not have family already in the group. They did not grow up socialized into the group or go to schools where they and their constructed kin joined together. They joined because they sought a mechanism to exact revenge against Christian militia for the Walisongo massacre and because the ideology taught to them legitimated that desire for revenge. Although some might have known one another prior to joining, the social ties they built together were simply not as thick, given there was an instrumentality to their joining that did not exist for those who joined via study circles or internal pathways. Moreover, the 2007 Densus raids on the Tanah Runtuh compound and the arrests that followed crippled Tanah Runtuh as an organization.

When the arrested were released from prison, they found their city in the process of rebuilding; society had moved on. The conflict was long over. They could acclimate to this new normal or they could continue to fight a war without the support of the residents of their city. Therefore, although they still may have identified with Tanah Runtuh in spirit and felt a sense of sincere camaraderie toward one another, they were no longer committed to the group.

## Conclusion

The four elements discussed in this chapter—adopting in-group norms, conforming to the group's understanding and practice of Islam, following orders, and prioritizing in-group social relations—are essential ways to show one is deeply committed to a jihadi group. These hold constant across Salafi-Jihadi and takfiri groups, across pro-ISIS and anti-ISIS groups, and regardless of whether members commit in the long term or the short term. Members seeking to prove themselves as committed insiders learn and adopt these ways of being and doing. Likewise, those who recruit and evaluate candidates for membership look for compliance along these measures as well.

The very performance of these acts of commitment solidifies solidarity and community. The act of conforming to behavioral norms reinforces the sense that all are bound together with a common moral code. The act of participating in regular group religious activities and conforming to the group's understanding of religion deepens social relationships, for group members are partaking of a common worldview. The act of following orders bonds a propective member to their seniors, for doing so proves a candidate's trustworthiness. The act of relocation is the penultimate expression of community and solidarity in prioritizing in-group over out-group. Taken together, performing these acts over time transforms a candidate for membership into a committed insider.

This chapter also showed how individuals commit to extremist groups on differing time horizons that are shaped, at least in part, by the pathway in which they entered. Those who join via internal pathways (kinship and schools) are more likely to commit in the long term or, alternatively, to migrate between groups in the same Salafi-Jihadi ecosystem. They have a greater sense of community and connection that fuels their commitment. Those who join via the conflict or prison pathways tend to commit only in the short term; their commitment has an instrumental component that is absent from those who join via internal pathways or even study sessions.

# 5
# Jihadi Activism

To this point, this book has explored why individuals become members of Islamist extremist groups, how they become members of Islamist extremist groups, and how they express commitment. This chapter unpacks what happens after a person becomes accepted as a member. In some cases, this means they have taken a *bai'at* (loyalty oath). In other instances, they are simply treated as a member. What sorts of activities occupy their time? Drawing primarily on the case of Indonesia, the chapter makes the case that most activities in which one engages inside an Islamist extremist group are quite mundane, low-risk activities. An individual may be assigned to preach or teach. The person may attend, organize, or run study sessions; set up websites or run online chat rooms; or teach at an extremist boarding school. Others will be tasked to engage in moderate risk activities: recruiting, logistics, or armaments. Some, but not all, will be offered the opportunity to join in high-risk activities such as jihad experiences and paramilitary training. Some may be invited or persuaded to participate in terrorist attacks.

Figure 5.1 details the roles and responsibilities assigned to the Indonesian interviewees. The most commonly cited activities were ordinary, low-risk religious activities that both members and recruits attend several times a week. Ninety-seven attended religious study sessions, either larger *pengajian* (study sessions) or smaller *taklim* (study circles). Seventy participated in *dakwah* (Islamic propagation). They preached either formally or informally to other Muslims. Religious study sessions and *dakwah* activities are the gateway for recruitment of "outsiders," those who do not come from jihadi families or attend affiliated schools. As noted in Chapter 3, these study sessions and *dakwah* activities take place in jihadi free spaces—specific affiliated mosques, homes, prison spaces, online spaces, and in conflict zones. Smaller numbers of individuals were given tasks in media (7) or as educators/educational administrators (12). Collectively, these jobs can be classified as "low risk"[1] insofar as the anticipated dangers to one physically, mentally, socially, financially, and legally are fairly minimal.

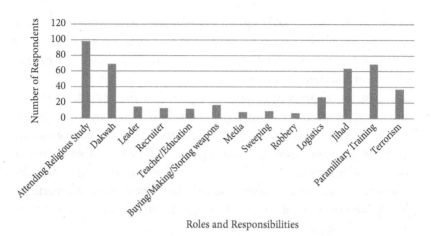

Figure 5.1 Forms of Jihadi Activism.

At the other side of the spectrum, more than half of those interviewed participated in jihad experiences (63) and/or paramilitary training (69). Most commonly, individuals received paramilitary training prior to deployment in a legitimate field of battle. Indonesians joined jihads in Afghanistan, Mindanao, and Syria abroad and domestically on the island of Ambon and in the district of Poso. In a small handful of cases, individuals participated in paramilitary training without the subsequent opportunity to join an active jihad. This was typically not due to a lack of desire or willingness to join a jihad but, rather, the lack of an actual jihad front in Indonesia. Thirty-seven of those interviewed participated directly or indirectly in acts of terrorism. They built bombs, set bombs, conducted survey operations, selected targets, or gathered teams together. In this last instance, not all were sworn members of a particular group. Some were siblings or nephews of members who were thereby trusted by virtue of their relations. These activities are classified as high-risk activism[2] because a person could be arrested, injured, killed, imprisoned, tortured, or estranged from their family as a result of high-risk activism.

Other assignments carried a moderate level of risk. Fourteen were leaders and thirteen recruiters, roles that can be considered "moderate" risk due to likelihood of arrest. Other moderate-risk jobs existed on the periphery of violent actions, enabling the participation of others in those activities. For example, interviewees tasked with logistics (27) were charged with arranging travel of individuals to jihad fronts or training camps. Likewise,

16 interviewees were tasked to purchase, smuggle, collect, store, or fabricate guns, typically for jihad actions. Comparably smaller numbers of young men participated in robbery operations (8) to gather funds for jihad or for the establishment and maintenance of training camps. Another 6 took part in fights and destruction of property (e.g.: sweeping) in the name of eradicating vice.

It is important to note that members of Indonesian jihadi groups interviewed typically held several of these roles over the course of their lifetime in extremist groups. Some engaged in multiple activities concurrently. Members, irrespective of role, may still attend study sessions. Many preachers also recruited. Leaders also preached. Someone with expertise in logistics, who set up a training camp or helped their fellow members leave for jihad, also stored guns.

In his book, *Membongkar Jemaah Islamiyah*, Nasir Abas, the former commander of the JI training region, Mantiqi III, shared that after returning to Malaysia following the Soviet–Afghan war, he was then assigned to go to Mindanao to create JI Camp Hudaibiyah, administer it, and train fighters there.[3] When he returned to Malaysia at the start of 1997, he was then tasked to teach Arabic at JI's Luqmanul Hakim boarding school. A month later, Abu Tholut, then the head of Mantiqi III, promoted him to the deputy head of Mantiqi III based in Sabah, Malaysia, with the duty to arrange entry and exit of members to and from the Southern Philippines.[4] Thus, during the 1990s, Abbas' roles spanned leadership, administration, logistics, education, paramilitary training, and jihad.[5]

Individuals migrated from violent to nonviolent roles and remained in nonviolent roles or moved back and forth as the group needs demanded. Moreover, Indonesians often moved between and among jihadi groups. There was no certainty that a person working in logistics for one group would be tasked with that responsibility in another.

This chapter shows that most activities that members undertake in jihadi groups are low risk and banal. In order to participate in some moderate-risk activities (gun procurement, recruitment, and logistics) or high-risk activism (paramilitary training, jihad, and terrorism), one must know the right people and be trusted by those people. This trust may come from actual kinship ties or from constructed kinship ties. The individual may be family. They may be the protégé or sibling of a trusted member. Alternatively, they may be alumni of the same boarding school or fellow members of the same study session.

Participation in high-risk activities such as jihad experiences, paramilitary training, and terrorist attacks thickens and reinforces the social ties among the participants, which can lead, in turn, to further opportunities for participation among the same subgroup of people, thus perpetuating high-risk activities.

It is important to note at the outset that many members of Indonesian Islamist extremist groups will never join a jihad experience, a terror cell, or participate in a paramilitary training. They are simply members in good standing, joining in the kind of relatively innocuous activism that keeps an organization thriving: teaching, preaching, recruiting, fundraising, and media. Many will have day jobs. Their activism will not be a full-time affair. That they may not be full-time activists should not be taken to mean they lack devotion to the cause. That they were not tasked with participation in jihad experiences, terrorist attacks, or paramilitary training does not imply they were less committed. Someone who is an especially good teacher, recruiter, or preacher may be seen as best serving the group through their continuation in that role. Even for those who are recruited to participate in a jihad experience, a paramilitary training, or a terrorist attack, high-risk activism is never a full-time job. This chapter shows how membership in a jihadi group is mostly composed of mundane tasks that can be, but are not always, punctuated by periods of high-risk, high-cost activity. The exception to this, of course, is in zones of active conflict.

This chapter unpacks eight different forms of jihadi activism: three low risk (religious study sessions, Islamic propagation, and education), two moderate risk (armaments and recruitment), and three high risk (jihad, paramilitary training, and terrorism).

## Study Sessions, Dakwah, and Education

Study sessions are ubiquitous activities. Even after one becomes a member, one continues to attend study sessions. In JI, new members attend study sessions twice weekly, whereas individuals who have been members for a long time may only attend once per week.[6] Once per month, members attend larger sessions bringing together individuals from multiple sectors.[7] "Amru" explains, "This is an obligation. [It's a way of expressing] loyalty."[8]

When one is a member, there may be more opportunities to attend sessions with specialized topics such as "why robbery in the name of Islam (*fai*) is legitimate."[9] After becoming a member of Jemaah Anshorut Tauhid (JAT), Ahmed Junaidi reported,

> The doctrine we learned [in the study sessions] included jihad, *dakwah* (Islamic propagation), *idad* (preparations for jihad), *tadrib* (paramilitary training), and the need to launch actions to the extent capable in order to attack the *kafir* who do not follow Allah's law. On jihad, they covered battle, preparations for battle and terrorist attacks. There were also routine activities where a larger group of people gathered together to discuss books.[10]

Discussions of topics such as jihad, paramilitary training, and preparations for jihad may become more explicit and detailed once one is a member. Because loyalty and trust are established, the *da'i* and *ustads* share information that would otherwise remain internal.

High-profile group leaders give study sessions, but ordinary members lead them as well. The members who ran study sessions as their primary duty were called *da'i*, and their primary job was *dakwah* (Islamic propagation). In JI circles, it was fairly common for graduates of JI-affiliated *pesantren* to be assigned as *da'i*, following their graduation, either prior to induction, as a test of loyalty and devotion, or post-*bai'at* as their first official responsibility.[11]

Attending study sessions and preaching are a key means of showing loyalty to the group. They are also low-risk, low-cost activities and duties, irrespective of group, and are unlikely to lead to arrest. They are a means of assessing potential and new members to determine who is trustworthy and to what extent. The *da'i* are the leaders of those sessions, both large and small. As such, they are responsible for that community building.

Another duty that is fairly commonplace, especially among graduates of JI and JAT *pesantren*, is a stint teaching either at an affiliated *pesantren* within the same network or at the one in which they graduated. For some, this is a first assignment, immediately after graduation. Others are assigned to teach after returning from a jihad experience or training camp or, conversely, they are instructed to go to a special academy for further study. Teaching and preaching may be viewed as rather mundane assignments, if one is a young man between ages 18 and 30 years, yet they are important. Jihadi groups cannot function without teachers, preachers, and study sessions. These roles, in certain cases, can also be gateway assignments. If someone is a regular attendee at study sessions or proves themselves a capable teacher, in time, they may be afforded the opportunity to participate in more desirable activities such as jihad experiences and paramilitary training.

## Recruitment

Recruitment is a task vitally important to the survival of any Islamist extremist group. This is a high-trust position insofar as recruiters must be members in good standing who can be counted on to identify, screen, and evaluate potential candidates for membership.[12] It tends to be a moderate-risk position insofar as one is unlikely to face physical, social, or financial consequences for taking on that role, yet the risk of arrest is higher than that for a teacher or preacher, especially if one is recruiting for Syria. Moreover, it is a dangerous position because if the recruiter mistakenly allows an informant in, the whole organization could be compromised.[13]

Hegghammer, in his study of Al Qaeda recruiters in Saudi Arabia, contends that recruiters look for signs of trustworthiness in potential recruits—signs that are typically too costly to fake and that are context-specific.[14] To do so, they go through three phases to identify potential members and weed out those who may prove problematic: initial evaluation, probing, and induction.[15] These stages also hold true for the Maute group in the Philippines. In Indonesia, however, one would add a stage between probing and induction: indoctrination.

Recruitment is often a fluid assignment. Some groups have designated recruiters. However, individuals may recruit in their capacities as preachers, teachers, or media or loosely by approaching susceptible out-group friends and acquaintances. Within JI circles, all members were tasked to look for new followers.[16] In short, they were expected to do that initial evaluation and perhaps a bit of probing. Then, there were specific individuals assigned to shepherd candidates through indoctrination, assessment, and vetting to induction.

Irrespective of group affiliation and irrespective of role, all looked for individuals who were loyal and obedient. Recruiters tended to approach people they already knew or people who had credibility due to prior membership in other Islamist extremist groups in the area, in conservative Islamist groups such as Hizbut Tahrir, or in Islamist militia groups such as the Islamic Defenders Front. For example, recruiters from the pro-ISIS umbrella, Jemaah Ansharud Daulah (JAD), preferred individuals who had long attended study sessions held by JI, Darul Islam, or JAT to common persons.[17] Such individuals already held prior knowledge about behavioral, religious, cultural, and relational norms and expectations of closed religious movements. Within JAD, there was also the expectation the individuals who became members would recognize and swear loyalty to the ISIS Caliphate.[18]

"Hakim," a former member of Tauhid wa'al Jihad, was not tasked to recruit for the community. However, upon returning to his home province of Aceh in 2008, he began recruiting for them anyway:

> I asked friends who shared a similar worldview to me; they were Salafi. It was easier for me to ask people who already had emotional ties with me. I would give them books or writings or videos and tell them, "You need to read this. You need to watch this." When they were interested, we would discuss it further. Then, I would introduce that person to Ustad Kamal. He had gone to Aceh at that time to recruit for Aman Abdurrahman's network.[19]

Thus, Hakim's first selection rule in recruitment was to look for people who already knew him, with whom he already had an emotional bond, and whom he already trusted. His second selection rule was that these potential recruits should already follow Salafi Islam. Since Aman Abdurrahman was takfiri, it would have been highly unlikely a secular Muslim would have accepted his approach. In fact, Hakim himself, as mentioned in Chapter 3, migrated slowly from Salafi to Salafi-Jihadi to takfiri Islam. Thus, his approach to recruitment makes sense in light of his personal experience. Since this was not his assigned task, he did that initial assessment of who might be susceptible to joining and made the initial approach. However, then he turned his findings over to Ustad Kamal, the designated recruiter for the area.

"Gungun" was assigned to recruit and do logistics for the Poso-based MIT, the first Indonesian jihadi organization to swear loyalty to ISIS. He had been a long-trusted member in good standing, having migrated from Mujahidin Kayamanya during the conflict era to the Poso branch of JAT and finally to MIT upon its establishment. Its leaders, Santoso and Daeng Koro, trusted him. He regarded them as brothers. Like Hakim, Gungun also recruited from friends. MIT especially favored individuals who had previously been members of Mujahidin KOMPAK, during the Poso conflict:

> They understood our journey. They had already learned from the Poso conflict. So when we asked them, it only took a little effort. There were many who volunteered to help. But we were very selective. We looked for the individuals who already understood the objectives of our organization.[20]

Among the former members of the Maute group, recruitment was more fluid than it was in the Indonesian jihadi ecosystem. Selection rules varied more widely. Some recruiters approached persons they trusted, whereas others recruited on a more ad hoc basis. Maute family members recruited their relatives. Commanders such as Abu Dar recruited at sympathetic area mosques, and Imam Abilino Dimakaling, a Maute sympathizer, approached his extended family and attendees at his mosque in the district of Piagapo. On the other hand, two teenage women interviewed also were tasked with recruiting. Aisyah explains,

> I was told to recruit teenagers, girls, and men, telling them that they would have the opportunity to do jihad to raise Marawi City as a truly Islamic city. For those who were poor, I was also instructed to offer them money."[21]

Aisyah detailed her strategy for identifying potential recruits:

> I tried to befriend men and women and talk to them. We would exchange details about our lives. I would tell my story, how I came from a family so poor that sometimes, we could only eat rice, salt, and river vegetables. They would share their story. If I felt their status in life was ok, I would not recruit them because they would not have agreed to be recruited. However, if I found someone who was poor and vulnerable, in a similar situation to me, I would try to recruit them.[22]

In contrast to the Mautes, Gungun, and Hakim, Aisyah did not target people she knew. Instead, she sought to recruit people she deemed vulnerable, in similar economic circumstances, who could benefit from the extra income. Neither Gungun nor Hakim would have taken such a risk. As trusted members and committed insiders, they recruited those whom they trusted. The Maute group was recruiting individuals not to become members of a group but, rather, to fight in a jihad to take Marawi City. Thus, their aims, goals, and time horizons differed. For the Mautes, as time to the takeover of Marawi neared, it mattered less if recruits were reliable or not.

## Armaments

A second moderate-risk, high-trust activity concerns the procurement, smuggling, hiding, and fabrication of bullets and guns. This is an important activity for extremist movements in that it is necessary for both paramilitary training and terrorism. It is a moderate-risk activity because it is a clandestine, illicit activity that can result in arrest and imprisonment. Thus, there are consequences to this activity that are not seen in teaching, preaching, or attending study sessions.

It is a high-trust activity insofar as individuals must have thick ties to the networks, and the best fabricators and smugglers may even have overlapping ties to multiple networks. One must have the network to obtain the materials to fabricate weapons as well as purchase, smuggle, and distribute them. This is not a task given to new members. One has to prove their loyalty and commitment in order to be trusted with such an assignment, critical for productive paramilitary training and crucial for jihad actions.

In some instances, gun runners and fabricators were committed members of a particular group; in other cases, they moved among organizations, supplying weapons to various groups. Regardless, they were respected, trusted, and well-known entities in those communities. Often, those procuring guns had other jobs as well, such as logistics or teaching.

As a clandestine organization, JI took steps to ensure that those tasked with procuring, smuggling, hiding, and fabricating guns were committed insiders. They had proven themselves in jihad theaters. They had shown that they would carry out tasks set forth before them, irrespective of whether they were assigned to teach, support and sustain logistical operations, participate in jihads, or run guns.

Other gun runners set themselves at the intersection points of different organizations. They may have been a member of one specific group, but they were trusted, either due to their preexisting relationships or due to their prior jihad experiences, by multiple groups. For example, Abu Ayyas was not a member of any specific jihadi group. However, he had been well known in those circles for some time. He had been one of the key people behind a plan to set up a training camp for multiple jihadi groups in the province of Aceh. One role he took on was gun procurement: "Between March and April 2009, I sent bullets and weapons to Aceh. The Aceh program materialized in October 2009. I served as military trainer, main supplier of weapons and ammunitions, and also an ideologist."[23] This was not the first time Abu Ayyas had procured weapons for extremist groups. When he was a policeman, he had had easy access to guns. During that time, he says he sent weapons to members of a group called the Indonesian Islamic State[1] (NII) fighting

---

[1] Indonesian Islamic State (NII) is unaffiliated with the Islamic State of Iraq and Syria (ISIS) and predated it by decades.

during the Ambon conflict.[24] Abu Ayyas was willing to take the risk. Groups trusted him because he had made the acquaintance of key people and won their trust. It was on the basis of those relationships rather than group affiliation that enabled him to take on that role.

In some instances, those tasked to procure guns had participated in jihads in the past. Thus, they had preexisting thick bonds of trust. Ali Imron, a member of JI who participated in the 2000 Christmas Eve bombing and the 2002 Bali bombing, explains how he was asked to gather weapons while also teaching at JI's Al-Islam *pesantren*:

> Besides teaching at Al-Islam School, I had also a meeting in 1998 facilitated by Zulkarnaen who had returned to Indonesia. I was [to be] part of special team of Jamaah Islamiyah. The task was collecting ammunition, weapons and other materials. This was only for preparation. It turned out to be true that in 1999, Christians attacked and killed Muslims [on the island of] Ambon on [the holiday of] Idul Fitri. What we imagined was coming true. The materials we collected were really useful.[25]

M.B., another JI member and teacher at Al-Islam, shared that at approximately the same time, "I was assigned to buy weapons. I knew the routes. I knew the seller. . . . I brought thousands of dollars, exchanged them for pesos, we purchased the weapons, collected them, and brought them into Indonesia."[26] Both Ali Imron and M.B. were recruited into Zulkarnaen's *Laskar Khos*, the paramilitary wing within JI. Both were Afghan veterans and as such trusted by the other Afghan veterans. Both went on to fight in the local jihad on the island of Ambon and participate in the same terrorist attacks. M.B. was trusted to smuggle weapons from the Philippines because he had participated in jihad and training in the Philippines.

The late Pepen was also an Afghan veteran who participated in the Ambon conflict. He had been tasked with logistics for people traveling to Ambon and Poso and to fabricate weapons. "I produced weapons, AK-47s. I had a molding device. The materials were abundant; you could even find them in a junkyard."[27] Umar Patek had participated in jihads in Afghanistan and on the island of Mindanao. He too was trusted by Zulkarnaen and was thus assigned first to work as a trainer of Moro National Liberation Front (MILF) members and subsequently in the weapons lab at MILF Camp Abu Bakar making RPG-2s and explosives for use by JI and the MILF.[28]

Around 2012, JI's strategy for gathering weapons changed. As it became more difficult for JI to buy weapons on the black market or smuggle weapons in from the Philippines, JI built its own weapons shop. The goal was to make weapons and ammunition[29] and to modify airsoft guns and pellet guns to fire real bullets.[30]

Although JI's tactics may have shifted, its approach to staffing had not. The leaders of Proyek Bengkel (the Workshop Project) had been members of JI in good standing. They were veterans of the conflicts in Ambon and Mindanao. They were trusted; they were proven. Jimi, the leader of the workshop, as well as several other participants had worked in the weapons lab at MILF Camp Abu Bakar.[31] Others were recruited for their background in welding and metallurgy.[32] Then amir, Parawijayanto, saw the gun workshop as important for building group strength and skill.[33] As such, he recruited the key figures for the gun workshop himself.[34]

## Jihad

Some members in good standing may also have the opportunity to participate in jihad experiences varying from a few months to several years. This was highly desired because according to Salafi-Jihadis, participation in a jihad is an individual obligation incumbent on every able-bodied Muslim. Indonesian jihadis have participated in three international major theaters of jihad: the Afghan jihad (1979–1993), the conflict in the southern Philippines (1994–2006), and Syria (2013–2016). In addition, there were two local jihad arenas: communal violence on the island of Ambon in the Moluccan islands (1999–2002) and in the district of Poso (1999–2001) in the province of Central Sulawesi.

Different groups had different selection parameters. JI, for example, had fairly rigid metrics, favoring those showing due commitment, fluency in the ideology of the group, and, if possible, prior jihad experience. Other groups, such as Mujahidin KOMPAK, had more flexible decision rules. This led certain members of JI to either migrate to Mujihidin KOMPAK or participate in both, utilizing KOMPAK as a means to travel and participate in jihad in Ambon. "Anas," a JI member in good standing, bypassed his direct mentor, Abdul Haris, after Haris told Anas he could not join the Ambon jihad.[35] Anas then approached Zulkarnaen, head of JI's *Laskar Khos*, who connected him to Aris Munandar, another JI member who was coordinating aid for

KOMPAK.³⁶ With Zulkarnaen vouching for him and via his relationship with Aris Munandar, Anas fought in Ambon with Mujahidin KOMPAK.³⁷ "Hisham," another member of JI's *dakwah* wing, also bypassed the wishes of his direct superiors and joined the Ambon conflict due to his close ties with Zulkarnaen. He also went to Ambon with KOMPAK:

> About a year after I graduated [from Al-Islam], I requested to be sent to Moro—the Philippines, but the request was turned down. Then, when the event broke out in Ambon, I asked our leader to allow me to be sent [to Ambon]. I was still not sent. Because I really wanted to participate, I left JI Surabaya. I contacted Ali Imron. . . . I told [him] that I was prevented from leaving for Moro and Ambon. I was asked to do *dakwah* in Surabaya. Ali Imron told me to travel to Solo to see Zulkarnaen. Thank God, Pak Zul considered me as just like his adopted child. Thank God, Praise God. That person [is great]. Then, I traveled to Ambon with KOMPAK people.³⁸

In both of these instances, JI members, who wanted to do jihad but were disallowed because their role was in preaching and because they were not veterans of a prior conflict, relied on personal relationships to enable their participation in jihad. Zulkaraen, the head of the *Laskar Khos*, and Aris Munandar, head of KOMPAK, had no problem allowing eager new members in good standing to join the jihad in Ambon. Without those relationships, however, neither youth would have had the opportunity to participate.

Since KOMPAK was first and foremost a humanitarian aid organization, it was possible for individuals to travel to Ambon via KOMPAK without any social ties to Islamist extremists groups. KOMPAK was the humanitarian aid wing of Dewan Dakwah Islamiyah Indonesia, a conservative Islamist organization with a nationwide reach. When the Ambon conflict erupted, KOMPAK was the first humanitarian organization on the ground in Ambon, providing aid and documenting the violence against Muslims in order to raise awareness.³⁹ Individuals with no ties to JI but who wanted to assist and defend their Muslim brothers in Ambon could join KOMPAK. What started out as simple delivery of aid became militarized once the volunteers witnessed the brutality of the Ambon conflict and as KOMPAK became the primary conduit for JI members impatient with the slow pace of JI's decision-making in sending its members to Ambon. According to Aput, one KOMPAK volunteer,

I went to Waihoang bringing with me medicines and food for KOMPAK. Then, I went to distribute the humanitarian aid.... I was sent to deliver aid to Seram [a large island next to Ambon Island]. On the way, we were shot at and I felt scared. When we arrived in Seram, there was a five year old child who had just been found killed.[40]

When he returned from delivering the aid to Seram, Abdullah Sunata, who ran the office in Waihaong, "asked us whether we wanted to return to Java as our mission was competed or whether we would like to join the military training and help defend Muslims."[41] Aput joined the training.[42] Dozens of young men like Aput, who initially went to deliver aid, joined trainings and subsequently participated in clashes. In doing so, they made connections with other jihadists from JI.

Local fighters in Poso also did not need to rely on prior relationships, schooling, or familial ties to join the local jihad in the area. They were in the correct place at the correct time. Many of them knew each other and came from the same neighborhoods: Kayamanya, Tanah Runtuh, Bonesompe, and Gebang Rejo, among others. When Mujahidin KOMPAK and JI arrived, they went looking for young men and chose those who attended their study sessions repeatedly and showed an interest, a susceptibility to the material, and a desire to exact revenge against Christian militiamen for the May 2000 Walisongo massacre.

The shared experience of participation strengthened social relationships, thus leading to more opportunities for joining in paramilitary training, future jihad experiences, and even terrorism. "Haroun" attributed the strong feelings of brotherhood to the experience of being "united against a common enemy. Brotherhood feelings are stronger when there is an enemy."[43] However, jihad was also a bonding experience that connected former participants long after the experience has ended. They shared the common experience of jihad as something profoundly religious. "The angels were smiling down on us. God was taking note of our actions."[44] They experienced the same physical and emotional hardships and the adrenaline rush of being in a theater of conflict. When they told stories, their fellow participants understood their references. They recognized the unique tells that only someone who had been in that jihad would know: the frigid temperatures of Afghanistan winters, the homesickness mixed with exaltation, the feeling right before they went into battle, the unique type of happiness they felt, and their fervent wish to die on the field of battle.

Hisham addressed these feelings when he discussed his participation in the Ambon jihad:

> The spiritual experience was top. It's hard to explain if you haven't been through it but I really enjoyed it. Only those who understand war would understand the feeling. It was amazing.... My dream was to participate in jihad in order to die as a martyr. Then, I went on jihad. So you can imagine my feeling. We were scared. It was hard at first. But after you hear the gunshot, we were just like horses released from the ropes. As if the gunshots were the sound of music. Indeed, we looked for the moment. We will always enjoy the moment.... All people are scared of death, if they have not collected enough good deeds. We are not looking for death. We're looking for the best death. Dying as a martyr is the best death.[45]

Ali Fauzi, a former trainer for both JI and Mujahidin KOMPAK, concurred with Hisham's recollection, when he shared,

> As soon as I finished [my training] at the military academy, I was [assigned to] a sentry post there. I had my first fire exchange with the enemy. We were really in a race. I had an extraordinary willingness to die without thinking about what would happen to my family at home. How my mother ... how ... I imagined I would get shot and die. I enjoyed it at the time. I moved forward on the basis of ideology, with a conviction that I was doing what was righteous and that if I died on this path, I would get my compensation in heaven, nothing else.[46]

This was something that the ordinary civilian would not understand. Existing friends became brothers after jihad experiences. Actual brothers also grew closer, bonded by shared experiences in jihad. Ali Fauzi warmly recollected how he and his half-siblings, Ali Imron and Mukhlas, all persons with prior experience in training camps and fields of battle, gave their brother Amrozi a crash course in guns and bomb-making while all were deployed in Ambon:

> At the time, we were four: Amrozi, Ali Imron, Ali Gufron [Mukhlas] and me. Rozi [sic] did not have a military background. He learned the knowledge from me and Ali Imron. How to use weapons. Ingredients in bomb-making. We taught him all in a room in a house. We went camping for 4 days and brought weapons and bomb-making ingredients."[47]

This was a bonding moment for all the brothers, who were finally able to share their *askari* (military) knowledge with their formerly wayward sibling. All of them had prior jihad experience in either Afghanistan or Mindanao; Ambon would be Amrozi's first jihad.

Much like with military veterans, these relationships endure long after the actual battle experience has passed. When it came time for the next jihad, veterans of the prior jihad called upon and enabled their old friends and partners in war to join the next one. They trusted one another.

## Paramilitary Training

There have been five large-scale opportunities for paramilitary training for Indonesians and a handful of smaller ones. All have enabled the formation, reinforcement, and consolidation of both in-group and cross-group social bonds. These include in Pakistan at As Saada and in Afghanistan at Torkham (1985–1994); Afghanistan at Al Qaeda Camp al Faruq (1999–2001); the Philippines at MILF Camp Abu Bakar and JI Camp Hudaibiyah (1994–1999), JI Camp Jabal Quba (2000–2003), and Pawas (2003–2005); Central Sulawesi (2011–2013) on the Blue Mountain; and in Syria (2013–2016). There were also smaller paramilitary training sessions at Waimorat on Buru island in Maluku in 1999 and 2000; in Central Sulawesi at Pendolo on the shores of Lake Poso and in Luwu, North Luwu, and Tangkura in 2001; and in Aceh between October 2009 and March 2010.[48,49]

Those invited or allowed to participate in paramilitary training typically fell into one of four categories: They came from jihadi families, they attended an affiliated boarding school, they had fought in prior jihads together, or they simply knew the right people. "Yasir," explains,

> I was chosen to go to Afghanistan because I was the son of a Darul Islam member. My father was one of the screeners. Individuals could go to Afghanistan [via Darul Islam] if they were (1) involved in the study sessions; (2) children of Darul Islam fighters; or (3) graduates of the Ngruki pesantren. The head screener, A. S. Broto, came to my house; he was my father's former subordinate. When Darul Islam was going to approach a candidate [to go to Afghanistan], they needed a reference [from an existing member]. In my case, my father was my reference. They talked. He said, "I wish your son would go to Afghanistan."[50]

Rashid was given the opportunity to train at Al Qaeda's Camp Al Faruq in large part because he had a close relationship with Mukhlas and because he was fluent in Arabic.[51] He also came from a good JI family. Not only were his parents members of JI but also they had married their daughter to a rising star in the Malaysia wing, Noordin M. Top, who would go on to become the director of Luqmanul Hakim boarding school and eventually be the mastermind of the 2004 Australian embassy bombing, the 2005 Bali bombing, and the 2009 Marriott and Ritz Carlton bombings. It was Rashid's thick social ties to key members of the JI community and the trust he inspired in those individuals due to his lineage and commitment that led him to have this golden opportunity.

Those sent to JI Camp Hudaibiyah also went by virtue of their connections. However, there were also prerequisites every trainee had to meet. They had to be a member of JI in good standing for at least 1 year, a bachelor between ages 18 and 23 years, physically fit, and conversant in English.[52] They also had to be prepared to go to war; to stay in the field, if required; and to die a martyr.[53] The selection criteria for JI members who trained in Syria was even more rigorous than for Hudaibiyah. Potential candidates for Syria were typically chosen from among the best graduates of JI *pesantren*.[54] After the initial selection stage, they were sent for 6 months of training at one of 12 sites in Indonesia, where they were taught close fighting combat methods, basic physical training, and basic medical treatment, among other skills.[55] According to Parawijayanto, who was amir when the program was active, to qualify for the training program, one had to be a JI member or the child of a member, at least 19 years of age, and committed to following the program until it was complete. Candidates also had to pass physical fitness assessments, accept the risks that come with participation, and adhere to the principle of "I hear and I obey."[56] The best graduates of the 6-month course were sent to Syria.

The experience of participating in paramilitary training is also socially significant because it creates bonds of brotherhood based on shared understandings that often supersede bonds from schools and study circles. "Umar" attended two JI-affiliated *pesantren* as a youth: Ngruki for middle school and Darus Syahadah for high school. He extolled the brotherhood built in *pesantren*, where students become "*more* than family" because "they're together 24 hours a day. They are in classes together. They share the same rooms, activities and the same way of thinking."[57] However, he admitted that

> I felt closer to the guys I trained with [in Mindanao] than my fellow students in *pesantren* that I had spent so many years with. That is because military training is hard and those who do it do so in heavy conditions. It's difficult. It's exhausting. We lived together under difficult conditions.[58]

Umar was only in Mindanao training at JI's Camp Hudaibiyah for 3 or 4 months. Yet, he felt closer to and more bonded with those with whom he trained than those with whom he lived and studied for 8 years. This feeling of being tied to someone by shared hardships can lay the foundation for being pulled into other opportunities: training camps, jihad experiences, and even terrorist attacks. After training, one has proven themself. They now have skills. They have proven their commitment to militancy.

For Abu Usama, who joined the Maute group early on, motivated by a desire for redemption, the brotherhood he found in the training camp left an indelible impression. It was far more intense than the friendships he had in the past with Karate buddies, drinking pals, or friends at university. "We were united in our submission to God."[59] He noted that the social bonds were not only shaped by their common experiences in training but also, and perhaps more important, by what they would do in their free time together: "When we weren't training, we would bond. We'd massage each other. We would tell stories. The stories of our lives."[60]

Abu Usama echoes many of the points raised by the Indonesians. Participating in paramilitary training is not only a religious or physical experience but also a social experience. One's peers in the camp understand the full measure of what one has been through: the physical exhaustion, the thrill of learning to fire weapons, and the sense of religious rebirth. They help one another and, in doing so, come to know one another. Those thick social bonds remain, for most of them, long after the training has ended.[61] These ties created a reservoir of trusted persons from which to draw, if one wanted to carry out a training or a terrorist attack; gave participants a community after release from prison; and provided a refuge if one needed to hide.[62] This was true of even the smaller camps. "Many of the relationships established in Poso between late 2000 and early 2002 were reactivated in the interests of ISIS after being dormant in some cases for more than a decade."[63] Whatever social ties they had going in, when they finished the training together, those ties had become enduring—they were brothers. That, in turn, reinforced commitment, engagement, and increased the likelihood of participation in high-risk activism.

## Terrorism

Terrorism is a high-risk, high-trust form of activism. It is high risk because a person committing a terrorist attack may die in the process. They may also be arrested, imprisoned, and executed. They may become estranged from family members who are horrified at what they did, lose jobs, and be stigmatized for participation in an attack that cost lives of innocent civilians. Terrorism is a high-trust form of activism because one must trust the members of the cell to keep their actions secret and not betray them to authorities. In Indonesia, terror cells are typically composed of some combination of family members, former classmates from particular radical *pesantren*, alumni of the same jihad experience or training camp, mentors and protégés, or friends from the same neighborhood. Less frequently, individuals from the same study session may join together in an attack.

Terrorism is one arena of activity in which one does not have to be a member of a group to participate. In many instances, the individuals involved in a terror cell came from the same group, yet there are notable cases in which nonmembers were pulled in, typically because they were related to a member of the cell. This flexibility exists because the group itself may not support the commission of acts of terrorism and the cells are bypassing the group's leadership to carry out attacks, even in open defiance of the leadership. Participants may not all be devoted members of a particular organization, but they will all be committed members of their cell, even if they have misgivings about the operation.

For group members, terrorism is an assignment. One is tasked to gather chemicals, study bomb-making, or make bombs. One is given the duty to set a bomb. In many cases, one may even be pulled into a terrorist attack without being fully aware; one is given an assignment to rent a car, procure a house, bring a tube to someone, or allow a deposit into their bank account. They are not fully apprised of why. They follow orders either because they are a committed insider, and it is a senior giving the order or, as often happens, they have thick social ties to the person giving the order through kinship, constructed kinship, and shared experiences. They trust the person asking and vice-versa. In some instances, terror cells required that members of the core team and those working in support roles temporarily sever ties with their families while they planned and carried out attacks.[64] This was true for members of Al Qaeda in the Malay Archipelago (AQMA) and Mantiqi 1 of JI.[65]

However, it is also important to note that no one is a full-time terrorist. An individual may have other responsibilities within the network; one may be a teacher, preacher, trainer, leader, recruiter, or work in media, logistics, or guns. One may even have a job outside the network. Anas, who built circuits for the 2002 Bali bombing and procured dynamite for the 2004 Australian embassy bombing, was a university student. So too were several members of the Cotabato cell, which detonated a bomb in the Roxas Night Market on September 2, 2016, killing 15 and injuring 40 in the city of Davao in the Philippines.[66] Nur Rochman, a Tim Hisbah member who detonated himself in 2017 outside a police post in Solo, was the head of his neighborhood, a local civil servant in charge of procuring letters of support for ID cards and birth certificates as well as organizing events such as neighborhood cleanups.[67]

In Indonesia, terrorist cells have often included family members of one of the masterminds. The most infamous case is the near simultaneous suicide bombing by one single family of six, composed of Dita Oepriarto, his wife Puji Kuswati, their teenage sons, aged 18 and 15 years, and two young daughters, aged 12 and 9 years.[68] They targeted three churches—the Santa Maria Catholic Church, the Surabaya Center Pentecostal Church, and the Diponegoro Indonesian Christian Church—killing 13 persons, including the 6 members of the Oepriarto family, and wounding 41.[69]

The next day, on May 14, another family detonated two motorbike bombs at the entrance of police headquarters in Surabaya, killing four of the attackers, three police officers, and three civilians.[70] The 8-year-old daughter of the suicide bombers survived only because her parents had not strapped her with her own suicide vest, and she was flung from the bike at the last minute.[71] There would have been a third bombing had bomb-maker Anton Febrianto been more competent. His bomb blew up prematurely at home in Sukoharjo, a suburb of Surabaya, killing his wife, Puspitasari, and eldest son and injuring his two younger children and himself. He was later shot dead by police. The families, all part of the same JAD study circle led by Oepriarto, believed that the end of the world was immanent and the only way they could ensure they would secure their place in heaven was to martyr themselves together.[72]

This was not the only time attack planners brought family into the operation, although it was the first bombing in Indonesia that used children. In the 2002 Bali bombing, Mukhlas convinced his younger brothers, Amrozi and Ali Imron, to participate. Abdul Jabar was recruited to participate in the bombing of the Philippine ambassador's residence by friends of his older brother, Farihin Ahmad; other members of the cell trusted him implicitly because he was Farihin's brother. Noordin M. Top recruited his brother-in-law, "Rashid", for the 2003 Marriott bombing. The 2009 Marriott and Ritz Carlton bombings included relatives of Saifuddin Zuhri, including his nephew, "Abu Azzam" (see Chapter 2).[73] In some of these instances, older family members intentionally groom younger family members, playing on attachments and bonds of love and deep trust in order to secure their relative's participation in the attack. Who knows someone better than their parents or their revered elder brother or favorite uncle? They know what buttons to push to mute disagreement and ensure compliance.

Terror cells have also been composed in part of friends from the same *pesantren*. For example, the best known JI bombers, including Hambali, Mukhlas, Amrozi, Ali Imron, Fathurrahman al-Ghozi, Dulmatin, Imam Samudra, Dr. Azhari Husin, and Noordin M. Top, taught, worked at, or studied at Luqmanul Hakim boarding school.[74] The core team for the JW Marriott bombing included five alumni from Luqmanul Hakim and six from Ngruki.[75] Two of the core team were alumni of both schools.[76] As noted in Chapter 2, the social bonds formed at *pesantren* are extremely thick and sticky because students spend 24 hours a day together 7 days per week, living together, studying together, and playing together. The bond between teacher and student can also be quite thick. If a teacher asks their student or a former student to assist them with illicit activity—for example, hiding them from authorities—the student may not believe they can refuse due to the loyalty they feel toward that individual.[77]

Terror cells can also consist of individuals from the same neighborhood or the same study session, who are organized into an operational cell by a key radical leader. Several of the members of the Cotabato cell, who carried out the Roxas Night Market bombing in the city of Davao in the Philippines, were from the same neighborhood, Rosary Heights, in the city of Cotabato.[78] They attended religious study sessions led by pro-ISIS teacher Fakhrudin Dilangalen at the Salaf Mosque in Sousa, Cotobato; Dilangalen organized them into a cell and liaised with Ansharul Khilafa Philippines in order to arrange paramilitary training for them.[79] These were not Sageman's "bunch of guys," a group of young men who *find* each other in mosques and develop a shared identity.[80] Most were friends, fellow students, and business associates who lived in the community in which they had grown up,[81] who knew one another, and who possibly even trusted one another prior to becoming part of an actual terror cell. However, "the process of attending those religious discussion groups and sympathizing with the victims in ISIS videos solidified their commitment to wage war at home."[82] The social bonds existed prior to attending the study sessions and prior to the establishment of the cell. The study sessions were a catalyzing agent that led to their involvement in terrorism.

Finally, terror cells can also be composed in part of friends, particularly in the case of long-standing friendships dating back to childhood. Trusted friends know each other's hopes and dreams. They may share a common history and have similar reference points, organizational affiliations, and a similar worldview. When ISIS recruiter Bahrun Naim wanted to enlist a small group of young men to learn to make bombs, he turned to Ibadurrahman, a friend from childhood, who grew up in the same village.[83] Naim was already in Syria when he reached out to Ibadurrahman via Facebook, claiming that this action would serve as preparation for eventual migration to Syria to join Khatibah Nusantara, the Southeast Asian division within ISIS, something Ibadurrahman greatly desired.[84] Ibadurrahman, in turn, recruited five of his close friends, all of whom were members of a pro-ISIS group in Solo, Tim Hisbah, and some of whom knew Naim.[85] Naim and Ibadurrahman set up a virtual study center so that the members of the cell could learn to make bombs, launder money, make online purchases with stolen credit cards, and choose the right vehicles for car bombings.[86] By July 2015, Naim was encouraging members to launch terrorist attacks. The cell settled on three places: a police post, a church in Solo,[87] and a Buddhist temple.[88] However, police disrupted the plot before the cell could carry out its attacks.[89]

Cells are often composed of not one but multiple types of thick social ties. The 2003 JW Marriott bombing drew on individuals from the same family and alumni of the same boarding schools. The core team and extended network that planned the 2002 Bali bombing brought together (1) individuals from the same family—Mukhlas, Ali Imron, and Amrozi; (2) specific alumni and teachers from Luqmanul Hakim and Ngruki; and (3) fellow veterans of the training camps in Pakistan during the Soviet–Afghan War. The 2018 Surabaya bombings drew on ties of family and friendship. The 2016 Davao night market bombing drew on friendship and neighborliness reinforced by membership in the same religious study group.

Irrespective of how one comes to join a terror cell, ideology often functions as a binding agent. The three families that were part of Dita Oepriarto's terror cell carried out their attacks on the churches and police station in Surabaya because they were convinced that the world was about to end. That conviction came from their cursory understanding of jihadi eschatology on the endtimes. Ibadurrahman and Bahrun Naim recruited friends from Tim Hisbah not only because they knew them but also because they all shared a similar pro-ISIS ideology. Occasionally, due to the love, loyalty, and trust one feels toward one's family members, kinship ties are sufficient to catalyze a person to participate in a terrorist attack.

## Conclusion

Once one becomes a member of a jihadi group, one is typically given assignments that one must fulfill in order to remain a member in good standing. Many of these are low-risk duties. All members may be required to attend religious study sessions once or twice per week or to lead them. One may be tasked to preach in an affiliated mosque, teach in an affiliated *pesantren*, or study in an affiliated institute. These assignments can be given early in one's tenure in a jihadi group. They are neither exciting nor adventurous. They are serious roles in which one is teaching, preaching, or learning. In these roles, one proves themself and shows their degree of commitment. For many members of extremist groups, their involvement will never go beyond these roles, irrespective of duration in group. They may be tasked with administrative roles—local leadership positions, perhaps—but their involvement will remain in the licit sphere.

A subset of committed members may be tasked with moderate-risk, high-trust assignments such as procurement and fabricating of weapons, logistics, and recruitment. These assignments are moderate risk because they carry an increased likelihood of arrest if discovered. In Indonesia, all were considered high-trust assignments. Recruiters were the front lines for vetting new members. Gun runners and fabricators had to be at the center of networks in order to secure necessary weaponry. Logisticians were responsible for ensuring individuals could successfully travel to jihad fronts. These were the middle managers that made organizational continuity (in the case of recruiters) and high-risk activism (in the case of gun runners and logisticians) possible.

A subset of members in good standing may be afforded the opportunity to participate in high-risk, high-trust assignments that can be a few months to a few years in duration: jihad and paramilitary training. Individuals chosen for these roles typically have connections. They have family members in the group; they have participated in prior jihads; they come from affiliated schools; they are close to those individuals in charge of selection; or, less frequently, they have shown themselves committed members of study sessions and to their roles. They are known and trusted entities within the group. Their participation reinforces and thickens existing social bonds, enables them to build new ones, and enables them to develop and strengthen interpersonal trust within the group. The relationships they build in training camps and during jihads endure long after the actual experience has ended and often provide the foundation for future high-risk activism, notably terrorist attacks and subsequent jihad experiences.

Finally, a small number of members and even some outsiders who are related to existing members are recruited to participate directly or indirectly in terrorist operations. Since the actions are so high risk due to their illegality and the likelihood of death cum martyrdom or execution, the most important priority in selecting members of terror cells is interpersonal trust. A review of the terrorist attacks conducted in Indonesia indicates that the cells tend to feature a combination of individuals from the same family; alumni of the same handful of radical *pesantren*; friends from prior jihad and training experiences; long-standing friends; and, less frequently, individuals from the same study sessions. To participate in a terrorist attack either directly or indirectly, one of the core team members must vouch for that person. They must be known by at least one if not multiple parties involved. In short, as activities increase in risk, so too does the need for trust. Absolute loyalty becomes a necessity, and who can one count on most if not their family and their brothers from shared experiences, who have become even more important than family.

# Conclusion

## Arif Tuban

Arif was born into a Muhammadiyah family, but he did not attend Muhammadiyah schools. His formal religious education began in middle school. His parents sent him to *pesantren* affiliated with the renowned Islamic modernist school, Pondok Modern Gontor, for the first year of middle school. However, in 1996, they transferred him to Al-Islam. There, he took classes in Arabic, English, and math; he participated in martial arts and rock climbing as extracurriculars; and in the school's mosque, he learned about jihad. It was there his journey began. Arif stayed at Al-Islam for only 2 years because he fell sick so often that his parents thought it better he live closer to home. Upon moving back home, he joined a Quran study group run by an *ustad* who was a friend of his teachers at Al-Islam, a graduate of another Jemaah Islamiyah (JI)-affiliated pesantren, al Muttaqien, in the city of Jepara. Thus, he stayed in the broad JI community. Arif enjoyed socializing with people from various groups in the Islamist and Islamist extremist ecosystems in Indonesia. "I participated in events organized by the Prosperous Justice Party, Jamaat Tabligh, and Hizbut Tahrir, when I studied at vocational high school, and I joined all of them."[1] JI members would rebuke him, "Why did you join them?" He responded, "to broaden my insights. I'm still young. I still have time. Why should I join one organization only?"[2] Perhaps because of his youth, he was still permitted to join in JI activities while he participated in other groups' events. He continued to attend JI's special study sessions regularly. He met alumni from Al-Islam and Ngruki. This went on for 3 years until late 2001 or early 2002. Then, his seniors in JI pressured him to cut ties with the other groups. "I was admonished. They said, 'So, which one do you chose? Don't join them [anymore]!'"[3] He chose JI.

However, soon after making this decision, the 2002 Bali bombing occurred. JI ceased activities temporarily in his area, and he distanced himself from JI for a few years, fearing guilt by association. Several of his teachers from Al-Islam had been involved in the Bali bombing. In 2005, he again began to participate in activities, slowly this time. He visited some of his former teachers, who had been imprisoned for their role in the Bali bombing. Often, he was not the only person visiting the terrorist prisoners; he was impressed by the sheer number of sympathizers.

He came to a decision. He would marry into this circle, thereby thickening and consolidating his social ties. He asked one of the imprisoned teachers, "Ustad, please find me a wife."[4] His teacher procured a suitable candidate; they married and soon had a child. When the child was 1 year old, Arif got a job working at the canteen of the JI girls' *pesantren* al Ikhlas and began interacting "more intensely" with other JI members.[5]

To this point, Arif had been on the fringes of JI for more than a decade. He had attended Al-Islam briefly. He attended JI study sessions for 3 years. However, because he had been young, in middle school and high school, he still sampled other groups. During this period, he interacted with activists across groups and gained ideological exposure to both Islamist and Salafi-Jihadi thought. It was not until he began to visit his former teachers in prison, he shares, that Salafi-Jihadi ideology took root. He gained more exposure to arguments supporting the September 11, 2001, attacks and the Bali bombings. He came to sympathize with those arguments. However, ideology was not the proximate driver of his engagement; social bonds were.

> "When I visited them in prison, my ties to them grew. When they helped me to marry, my ties grew stronger. When they gave me a job, my relationship with them became even stronger. That's the process."[6]

His social ties grew thicker the more links he made—social, personal, then professional. When he attended the funeral for Mukhlas and Amrozi, two of the Bali bombers who were executed by the government, he saw the thousands of people in attendance and felt awed by how many supporters were present. He felt further connected to the community. However, he bonded not with "structural" JI, which eschewed violence outside of designated zones of jihad, but to those in the Indonesian Salafi-Jihadi ecosystem that supported terrorist attacks:

> Seeing thousands of people at Amrozi's funeral in 2008 strengthen my interest to follow the jihad path. After that, I sought friends who had the same thoughts as me [more actively than before]. I sought them out through the internet. By 2009, internet forums had been created. I came across people who shared my thinking but we had not yet met in the real

world. I developed contacts in Medan [on the island of Sumatra]. In 2009, I was given [my first] assignment: I was to look for people to participate in a training near Medan. That began my career in the jihadist world as a networker.[7]

Arif was never given the oath to JI. He did not sufficiently conform to JI norms and expectations. His thickest ties were with people like him, alumni of Al-Islam or former members or sympathizers with JI who had since migrated to groups more willing to take violent action. He drifted among these groups in the Indonesian Salafi-Jihadi ecosystem. He was trusted by people across organizations due to his Al-Islam pedigree, his networking skills, his marriage to a woman from a good JI family, and his extensive thick social ties. Thus, he was given low- to moderate-risk roles, including recruiting for jihadi groups in Medan, purchasing weapons for Mujahidin Indonesia Timor in Poso, hiding fugitives, and running a jihad website and chat.

As young men continue to join extremist groups, it is important to understand the processes and pathways via which individuals become members of such groups, what propels them to join, how they express commitment, and how they become involved in moderate- and high-risk activism. Understanding these interrelated processes is critical for designing effective counter-radicalization and disengagement efforts.

There are several takeaway messages from this book that can help with these efforts. These messages highlight the variations in the joining process, the importance of social ties at *every juncture* in the process of becoming a member of an extremist group, and the key emotions that underpin joining.

## Understand the Variation in the Process of Joining

This book found that joining is a process that varies deeply depending on the group one joins, the time in which one joins that group, and the contextual environment in which one finds themself drawn into the group. First, this book enumerated six pathways via which individuals joined extremist groups: two internal pathways (kinship and schools), three external pathways (study sessions, conflict, and prison), and one partial external pathway (social media). It found that a person may join via one pathway or a combination of pathways. For example, an individual who was born into an extremist family and sent to an affiliated boarding school would join via two pathways: kinship and schools. Likewise, an individual recruited by an uncle, a brother, or a relative during a time of conflict would join via two pathways: kinship and conflict. In Indonesia, study sessions were the key free space that often constituted a singular route in itself, although details and duration varied from group to group. However, because study sessions existed in conflict zones and in prisons, one can also see them feature in those pathways as well.

Second, the time it takes to become a member varies depending on group and pathway. Some groups have longer time horizons for joining in order to ensure that any potential member is socialized into the various aspects of Salafi-Jihadi ideology, from discussions of faith, belief, and practice to those about *jihad fisabililah* (jihad in the way of Allah) and the need for an Islamic state. Other groups have comparatively shorter time horizons. If one joins a group during a period of communal conflict or political violence, the pathway to entry may be expedited due to the need to quickly train fighters. For example, those who joined the Maute group in 2017 received no training or vetting. The Maute group needed fighters and whether one was an imam, a methamphetamine addict, a hit man, or a farmer, all who were willing to join the jihad were welcome to participate.[8] By contrast, joining JI took years, as one attended study sessions in order to become socialized into the Salafi-Jihadi worldview and show due commitment. The joining process also moved more slowly or more quickly depending on whether one joined via internal pathways or external pathways. Insiders, those who joined via internal pathways, had family in the movement or had attended affiliated schools. They were already known and were at least in part socialized into the group's worldview. Outsiders who joined via external pathways typically had a lengthier time horizon for joining because they had to go through a heavy indoctrination, socialization, and vetting process and prove commitment.

Another point of variation is commitment. This book found that commitment tended to vary by pathway to entry. Those who joined via internal pathways—kinship and schools—or study circles were more likely to either commit in the long term or migrate among groups in the Salafi-Jihadi ecosystem due to the social and emotional investments that bonded them to their fellow group members. When members of one's immediate family—parents and siblings—are members of a movement, exiting it is quite difficult because one's proximate social ties are all within the group. One has grown up in the group. However, individuals who join an extremist group in a time of conflict or communal violence tended to join for the short term, committing for the conflict itself and the years immediately following the conflict. Over time, they might drift away from the group, seeking a "normal life."

In summary, in working to combat violent extremism, it is important to assess individuals according to these varied parameters: why they join, how they join, how they prove commitment, and the duration of time during which they express that commitment. Knowing that someone recruited in a conflict zone may not be as committed as someone who grew up in the movement offers promise for developing disengagement and reintegration programs in those regions. Likewise, recognizing when someone shifts from a clandestine illicit movement or an extremist group that carries out terrorist attacks to a nonviolent group within the Salafi-Jihadi community also offers opportunities for interventions to assist with their chosen pathway to disengagement.

## Joining and Commitment Are Fundamentally Social Experiences

If we are going to devise effective strategies to prevent and counter violent extremism, we have to fully understand the importance of social ties in the processes of joining and commitment. People join extremist groups for a variety of reasons, many of which are the same reasons why people join mainstream social movements: They have family and friends in the movement, they want to make the world a better place, or they are seeking to improve themselves. However, what makes them stay, commit, and participate in high-risk activities is the solidarity and brotherhood they find in the group. Regardless of who they are, what traumas they may or may not have experienced in their lives, their social class, their education level, or their personal ambitions, they find connection and community in these groups.

Although it is important to note the variation in how one can join an extremist group, social relationships are the basic commonality that exists across groups. Figure C.1 denotes a broad picture of motivation, pathway, commitment, and role assignment in Indonesia, highlighting these common cross-group social elements.

Figure C.1 illustrates how social bonds are paramount at each juncture in the processes of joining, commitment, and role assignment. They thicken at each step during the process. If one looks at motivating forces, social relationships are a key component. One joins based on an intersection of two

## 154 CONCLUSION

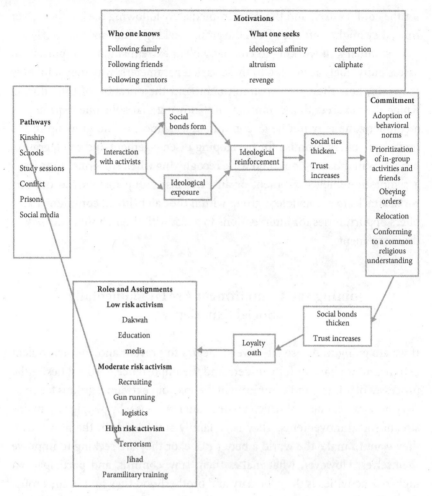

**Figure C.1** Joining and commitment in Indonesia.

factors in Indonesia: whom they know (following family, friends, or mentors into the group) and what they seek (joining fulfills a need or a purpose—a desire to learn more about jihad, to make lives better for Muslims, redemption, or revenge). Without that social bond to existing group members, one would most likely not have had a point of entry into the extremist group in the first place.

Regardless of why someone joins and the pathway via which someone joins, there are certain commonalities in how one does join. They interact with activists. They gain exposure to the group's ideology and form ties to other group members. If they join via internal pathways—that is, kinship or schools—these relationships will likely thicken and become stickier at an earlier point in their trajectory of joining. They will come to love one another and trust one another at an earlier point, in the former instance because they are actual family and in the latter because they spend so much time together through the *pesantren* experience that they come to perceive one another as family. If they join via external pathways, the study circle will serve as the free space via which individuals come to interact with activists, gain ideological exposure, and make fast friends. In time, those ties will thicken further as ideology becomes a binding agent. They become united by a common worldview and a common purpose, and that makes the sense of connection, community, and brotherhood they feel all the more potent.

Regardless of whether one joins via internal or external pathways, should one move along the pathway, they will come to exhibit signs of commitment. They will conform to the norms of the group—behaviorally and religiously. This will further bind them to fellow members of the group. They will tend to prioritize in-group friends over out-group friends and to obey orders given to them by their seniors. They may even relocate to live closer to other members of the group. They may marry the siblings and children of group members. These indicators of behavioral and religious conformity and social cohesion tend to remain the same regardless of which pathway via which one joined and of which group one became a member. Indonesians who joined via the study circle pathway, the kinship pathway, and the conflict pathway all expressed commitment in a similar manner.

Typically after induction, but sometimes before, individuals are assigned roles. These roles can be high risk, moderate risk, and low risk. In some groups, individuals can be assigned low-risk roles as a way of proving commitment, for example, to teach or preach. This may occur before induction. However, as one comes into moderate-risk and high-risk roles, trust and thick social ties become more necessary and apparent. One must have the right connections to be trusted in such roles. This is especially the case for participating in paramilitary training or jihad experiences. Thus, one is more likely to have taken an oath prior to such assignments.

Perhaps interestingly, however, this book found that one does not need to be a member in good standing of an extremist group to be pulled into a cell plotting a terrorist attack. One may be invited to join a terrorist cell if they are related to existing cell members. This research found instances of siblings and nephews being pulled into a terror cell for a specific action. Key at all of these junctures are (1) knowing the right people and (2) being trusted by those people.

The process diverged among Maute group members in the Philippines, but social bonds were no less important. Social bonds were key to joining the Maute group, irrespective of the timing of recruitment. The key actors recruited extensively from their extended families, especially nephews; second, third, and fourth cousins; and in-laws. As a result, many of those who joined already had thick social bonds and already trusted those inviting them. They were accepted into the group not only because it needed fighters but also because their actual relatives were vouching for them. Connection and community preceded entry. Thus, in contrast to Indonesia, where kinship was one of many pathways into a group and trust was built over time, in all but the most exceptional of circumstances, in the Philippines, trust tended to predate entry. Brotherhood often predated entry. A summary of how joining worked in the Maute group is shown in Figure C.2.

In the Philippines, among those interviewed from the Maute group, the paramilitary training experience did not thicken social bonds as much as it expanded them. One came to know more people through paramilitary training who were having the same experience. They prayed together. They ate together. They trained with guns together and did calisthenics together. In their off times, they shared stories of their lives and massaged each other. In so doing, they came to know more members of the community. Why didn't it result in thickening social ties? As in Indonesia, the experience of participating in paramilitary training is difficult. Why didn't it result in the

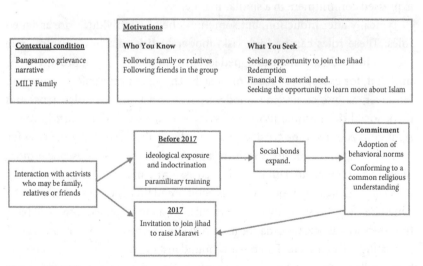

Figure C.2 Joining, commitment, and action among Maute group members in the Philippines.

same bond? When Maute group members returned home from training, they largely went back to their lives. There were no weekly meetings or study sessions. For those assigned to recruit, after initial instruction, there were no daily or weekly meet-ups. As a result, one's thickest social ties were with the people who brought them in—typically family members and relatives.

This book also found that preexisting social ties are not a necessary condition for entry into conservative Islamist movements and Islamist paramilitary groups. Individuals can choose to join these groups without being invited by a friend or following a family member into the group. Assuredly, many will join because they know someone already in the group. However, it is not a prerequisite, as it is for Islamist extremists. In joining conservative Islamist movements and Islamist paramilitaries, it is possible that one may be motivated less by whom they know and far more by what they seek, much as Amar and his brother initially sought a licit group through which to work for sharia and to clean up their neighborhood. Social bonds will come to play a role in the later stages, as one's commitment to the group increases.

In summary, individuals join and commit to Islamist extremist groups in large part on the basis of social ties. They may form connections and communities based on revenge, redemption, a desire to do good, or religious affinity. Each of the pathways into extremist groups is a process of building that connection and consolidating that community—of building and consolidating thick social ties. If they were born into the Indonesian Salafi-Jihadi ecosystem and/or attended an affiliated school, this may have been their community and point of connection before they knew of any other viable alternatives. Their social ties to the community have long been thick. The narratives in this book tell of a journey of becoming a member of a brotherhood and a constructed family of like-minded—a family they would do anything for, even if it means skirting or breaking the law. The ways of exhibiting commitment are part of signaling that one is part of this community—through how they dress, the behaviors they adopt, the orders they obey, the religious understanding to which they adhere, and where they choose to live.

## There Are Deep Emotions Involved in Joining, Commitment, and High-Risk Activism

A third takeaway of this book concerns the emotional component of becoming a member of an extremist group. This book found that primary emotions that propelled joining, commitment, and participation in high-risk activism were often positive emotions: Love, trust, respect, affinity, and validation featured prominently in narratives of joining, commitment, and role assignment.

Negative emotions—notably revenge, fear, and hatred of the other—also featured, but these tended to largely be confined to specific communities, notably the Poso-based youth that sought revenge for the Walisongo massacre. Those who joined takfiri groups such as Tauhid wa'al Jihad as well as others affiliated with Aman Abdurrahman spoke of being taught to hate as well as to fear excommunication.

The core emotion at the root of all in-group relations across groups irrespective of whether one resided in Indonesia or the Philippines, whether one joined a Salafi-Jihadi or takfiri group, was trust. Trust was the emotion underpinning the decision to follow a friend, family member, or mentor into an Islamist extremist group, and it was also the basis on which the group determined who to invite to become members. Individuals who join via the kinship pathway may have an expedited pathway to entry precisely because they are already trusted based on having a parent, sibling, or uncle vouching for them. Potential members from jihadi families also trust those family members and family friends recruiting them. They have grown up socialized in the movement. Individuals recruit family members into extremist groups because they know they can trust those individuals to remain loyal. If one is going to participate in an act of terrorism, who better to trust than one's own family? The loyalty is unmatched, and the likelihood of betrayal is exceedingly slim.

Individuals who join via the schools pathway trust their peers as if they are family. Some youth, especially those who began studying at *pesantren* early in middle school, may consider their classmates and teachers as closer to them than their actual blood family. They spent their formative years living, studying, socializing, eating, and playing together, and through years of doing so they came to trust one another deeply. That preexisting trust is reinforced through socialization into the movement and the eventual *bai'at*. All are now members of the same community.

The process of joining via study sessions is the process of building trust, affinity, and loyalty out of a group of individuals who did not have prior thick social ties due to kinship or schools. The iterated steps and levels of activity and engagement are a means of building social cohesion and a common sense of connection and community. Members of study sessions were encouraged to view their fellow members as brothers and to help one another solve their problems. Those iterated experiences of helping one another and seeking refuge in the comfort of having that connection and community also helped build and reinforce affinity and trust. Even among takfiri groups, the view that they were the only ones living correctly and all outsiders were infidels was also a means of building trust and social cohesion among members, based on a sense of common righteousness in a damned world.

The process of proving commitment also reinforced feelings of trust among group members, between potential members and the leadership, and among people in the same Salafi-Jihadi/takfiri ecosystems. The process of adopting the same social norms, manner of dress, and approach to religion reinforced in-group social cohesion, trust, and loyalty. Obeying orders given by in-group seniors signaled to leaders that an individual was trustworthy. Why were specific individuals given moderate-risk or high-risk roles in the network? They were deemed by their seniors to be loyal and trustworthy. Likewise, certain members were given opportunities to participate in paramilitary training and jihad experiences because their seniors trusted them due to their proven commitment to the community.

Similarly, trust was a core component in the composition of terrorist cells from the point of view of both those joining the operation and those composing the cells. The members of the cell must trust one another. They must trust in their seniors in the cell and their justification for the operation. Trust is also an element of cell composition. Members of a cell must trust that the other members will not betray them to the authorities. Thus, cell leaders may pull in individuals from the same family and same school networks, who already have that preexisting trust.

Affinity was another positive emotion that members of Islamist extremist groups shared, regardless of whether they joined via internal pathways or external pathways and whether their group was Salafi-Jihadi or takfiri, based in Indonesia or the Philippines. Individuals migrated between extremist groups in the Salafi-Jihadi and takfiri ecosystem in Indonesia seeking ideological affinity—the view closest to theirs. The experience of participating in study sessions was designed to foster a common sense of personal and performative affinity based on a common worldview, goal, and community. In the Philippines, among Maute group members, the training camp experience fostered affinity ties, albeit weaker ones, based on the same points. Jihadists in Poso felt a closeness to one another based on common trauma and desire for revenge. Members of Tauhid wa'al Jihad felt that same closeness for one another based on a common hatred of the other and a view that only they were worth saving. Several of the performative aspects of commitment—conforming to social and religious norms, prioritizing in-group friends, and relocation—are designed to signal affinity. The experiences of participating in training camps and jihad experiences also reinforce the feelings of affinity and create new affinity-based ties based on common experience. Affinity and trust are the emotions undergirding those thick, sticky social bonds.

Love was also an emotion important for understanding why individuals joined Islamist extremist groups and participated in acts of terrorism. This was especially notable for those who joined via the kinship and schools pathways. One followed parents or siblings into a group often out of love. Youth, displaced from their families of origin studying in Islamic boarding school, come to feel love for their peers and teachers, their surrogate brothers and parents. For those who join via external pathways, the process of indoctrination is designed to cultivate love and loyalty toward one's fellow Muslims. Love can also extend to reasons undergirding involvement in terrorism. Several respondents professed to have participated in an act of terrorism, despite internal misgivings, out of a sense of love for a sibling, parents, or an uncle. Parents brought their children into terrorist attacks because they hoped all of them would go to heaven together as martyrs.

Individuals who joined takfiri groups were not seeking hate. Either they joined seeking ideological affinity or the leaders of their group became enamored with Aman Abdurrahman's teachings and the entire group went takfiri. However, the binary in which Aman Abdurrahman insisted his followers operate between the righteous and the *kafir* made hatred very much a part of the emotional underpinnings of being a member of groups that subscribed to Aman Abdurrahman's thought—for example, Jemaah Ansharud Daulah (JAD) and Tauhid wa'al Jihad. Likewise, threat of expulsion for the smallest violation of in-group norms meant that members also lived in fear for their livelihood, their core relationships, and their very souls. Parents severed ties with their children; wives divorced their husbands; and brothers hated their siblings who became involved with politics and the "infidel" state. Hatred and fear did not propel an individual to join JAD or Tauhid wa'al Jihad, but once one was already inside, those were core emotional components of in-group affinity. Conversely, feelings of revenge, following the 2001 Walisongo massacre, were the key that propelled Posonese Muslims to join Mujahidin Kayamanya, Tanah Runtuh, and, later, Mujahidin

Indonesia Timor. The affinity they felt was bound up in that desire for revenge.

In summary, negative, reactive emotions were less prominent in the joining process, although they certainly played a role in specific groups, notably the pro-ISIS groups and the Poso-based groups. People tended to join due to the vitalizing and reciprocal feelings that being a member of the group incurred. They felt loved. They trusted their fellow members and seniors in the group and felt trusted. They felt a deep affinity for their fellow members. They felt a sense of solidarity with their fellow members and pride in what they were accomplishing. Those feelings only deepened as members performed acts of commitment and as their active participation increased. Jihad experiences and paramilitary training increased feelings of affinity and trust among members. One participated in terrorist attacks because one believed in the cause; trusted the people setting the targets; and felt affinity and, in some cases, even love—especially if they were related to the other cell members—for their fellow members of the cell.

# Notes

## Introduction

1. Interview with Umar Patek, Afghan veteran, Moro veteran, July 2018, Porong Prison, Surabaya, Indonesia.
2. Mukhlas is an alias of Huda Bin Abdul Haq (also known as Ali Gufron), one of the masterminds of the first Bali bombing. He taught at Ngruki pesantren in Solo and was among the founders of Luqmanul Hakim boarding school in Malaysia. Mukhlas fought in the Soviet–Afghan war at the Battle of Jaji with Osama Bin Laden. He took over for Hambali as head of Mantiqi 1, the Jemaah Islamiyah fundraising region. He recruited his younger brothers, Ali Imron and Amrozi, and half-brother, Ali Fauzi, into Jemaah Islamiyah and recruited Amrozi and Ali Imron into the team for the first Bali bombing in October 2002.
3. Interview with Umar Patek, Afghan veteran, Moro veteran, July 2018, Porong Prison, Surabaya, Indonesia.
4. Interview with Umar Patek, Afghan veteran, Moro veteran, July 2018, Porong Prison, Surabaya, Indonesia.
5. Interview with Umar Patek, Afghan veteran, Moro veteran, July 2018, Porong Prison, Surabaya, Indonesia.
6. Interview with Umar Patek, Afghan veteran, Moro veteran, July 2018, Porong Prison, Surabaya, Indonesia.
7. Interview with Umar Patek, Afghan veteran, Moro veteran, July 2018, Porong Prison, Surabaya, Indonesia.
8. Interview with Umar Patek, Afghan veteran, Moro veteran, July 2018, Porong Prison, Surabaya, Indonesia.
9. Interview with Nasir Abas, Patek's boss at Abu Bakar/Hudaibiyah in the Philippines, via Zoom, July 24, 2022.
10. Interview with Umar Patek, Afghan veteran, Moro veteran, July 2018, Porong Prison, Surabaya, Indonesia.
11. Interview with Umar Patek, Afghan veteran, Moro veteran, July 2018, Porong Prison, Surabaya, Indonesia.
12. Interview with Umar Patek, Afghan veteran, Moro veteran, July 2018, Porong Prison, Surabaya, Indonesia.
13. "Bali Bomb Maker Umar Patek Jailed for 20 Years." BBC. June 12, 2012. https://www.bbc.com/news/world-asia-18529829.
14. Institute for Policy Analysis of Conflict (IPAC), "Killing Marwan in Mindanao," report no. 17 (2015, March 5), 6.
15. IPAC, "Killing Marwan in Mindanao," 6.

16. For a discussion of "thick" and "thin" levels of trust, see Florencia Torche and Eduardo Valenzuela, "Trust and Reciprocity: A Theoretical Distinction of the Sources of Social Capital," *European Journal of Social Theory* 14, no. 2 (2011): 181–198for a discussion of thick and thin relationships, see for a discussion of thick ties in networked communities, see Andrea Kavanaugh, Debbie Denise Reese, John M. Carroll, and Mary Beth Rosson, "Weak Ties in Networked Communities," *The Information Society* 21, no. 2 (2005): 119–131.
17. John Horgan, "From Profiles to Pathways and Roots to Routes: Perspectives from Psychology on Radicalization into Terrorism," *Annals of the American Academy of Political Science*, 618 (2008): 80–94, 89.
18. Daniel Koehler, *Understanding Deradicalization* (London: Routledge, 2017): 74.
19. Randy Borum, "Radicalization into Violent Extremism: A Review of Social Science Theories," *Journal of Strategic Security* 4, no. 4 (2011):7–36, 15
20. Christian Picciolini, *Breaking Hate* (New York: Hachette, 2020), xxxiii.
21. Doug McAdam, "Recruitment to High Risk Activism: The Case of Freedom Summer," *American Journal of Sociology* 92, no. 1 (1986): 64–90, 66.
22. McAdam, "Recruitment to High Risk Activism," 66.
23. Clark McCauley and Mary Segal, "Terrorist Individuals and Terrorist Groups," In *Series of Psychobiology. Terrorism: Psychological Perspectives*, ed. J. Groebel and J. H. Goldstein (Seville, Spain: Publicasiones de La Universidad de Sevilla, 1989), 55.
24. Pete Simi and Robert Futrell, *American Swastika* (New York: Rowman & Littlefield, 2015), xiv.
25. Interview with M.B., Jemaah Islamiyah member, January 2012, Jakarta, Indonesia.
26. Interview with Anas, former member of Jemaah Islamiyah, January 2012, Jakarta, Indonesia.
27. John Morrison, "Trust in Me: Allegiance Choices in a Post-Split Terrorist Movement," *Aggression and Violent Behavior* 28 (2016): 47–56.
28. Clarke McCauley, "Testing Theories of Radicalization in Polls of US Muslims," *Analysis of Social Issues and Public Policy* 12, no. 1 (2012): 296–311; John Horgan, *The Psychology of Terrorism* (London: Routledge, 2009), 96.
29. See the May 2018 Surabaya church bombings and the 2009 Marriott and Ritz Carlton bombings.
30. Greg Fealy and Aldo Borgu, *Local Jihad*: Radical Islam and Terrorism in Indonesia (Barton, Australia: Australian Strategic Policy Institute, 2005).
31. Fealy and Borgu, *Local Jihad*; Gilles Kepel, *Jihad: The Trail of Political Islam* (Cambridge, MA: Harvard University Press, 2002), 220.
32. Quinton Wiktorowicz, "Anatomy of the Salafi Movement," *Studies in Conflict and Terrorism* 29, no. 3 (2006): 207–239, 217.
33. Greg Fealy and Virginia Hooker, *Voices of Islam in Southeast Asia: A Contemporary Sourcebook* (Singapore: ISEAS, 2006), 362.
34. Fealy and Borgu, *Local Jihad*.
35. Fealy and Borgu, *Local Jihad*.
36. Abd Al-Salam Faraj, "Jihad: The Neglected Duty," in *Princeton Readings in Islamic Thought*, ed. Roxanne Euben and Muhammad Qasim Zaman (Princeton, NJ: Princeton University Press, 2009), 341.

37. Abdullah Azzam, "Defense of Muslim Lands: The First Obligation After Iman," 7–8.
38. Mukhlas, "Jihad Bomb Bali: Sebuah Pembelaan Operasi Peledakan Bom Legian dan Renon," *Bali District Police Jail, Denpasar* (2003, March 25), 35, quoted in Fealy and Hooker, *Voices of Islam in Southeast Asia*, 378.
39. Mukhlas, "Jihad Bomb Bali," 35, quoted in Fealy and Hooker, *Voices of Islam in Southeast Asia*, 384.
40. Kepel, *Jihad*, 31.
41. See Horgan, *Psychology of Terrorism*; Randy Borum, "Understanding the Terrorist Mindset," *FBI Law Enforcement Bulletin* (2003, July); Quintan Wiktorowicz, *Radical Islam Rising* (Oxford, UK: Rowman & Littlefield, 2005); Marc Sageman, *Leaderless Jihad* (Philadelphia: University of Pennsylvania Press, 2008); Marc Sageman, *Turning to Political Violence* (Philadelphia: University of Pennsylvania Press, 2017); Max Taylor and John Horgan, "A Conceptual Framework for Addressing Psychological Process in the Development of the Terrorist," *Terrorism and Political Violence* 18, no. 4 (2006): 585–601; Andrew Silke, "Becoming a Terrorist," in *Terrorists, Victims and Society*, ed. Andrew Silke (London: Wiley, 2003): 29–53; Arie Kruglanski, Michelle Gelfand, Jocelyn Belanger, Anna Sheveland, Malkanthi Hetiarachchi, and Rohan Gunaratna, "The Psychology of Radicalization and Deradicalization: How Significance Quest Impacts Violent Extremism," *Advances in Political Psychology* 35, no. 1 (2014), 69–93; Kumar Ramakrishna, *Radical Pathways: Understanding Muslim Radicalization in Indonesia* (London: Praeger, 2009).
42. Kruglanski et al., "The Psychology of Radicalization and Deradicalization."
43. See Borum, "Radicalization into Violent Extremism," 8; Donatella Della Porta and Gary La Free, "Guest Editorial: Processes of Radicalization and Deradicalization," *International Journal of Conflict and Violence* 6, no. 1 (2012): 7; Horgan, "From Profiles to Pathways and Roots to Routes"; John Horgan, *Walking Away from Terrorism* (London: Routledge, 2009); Sageman, *Turning to Political Violence*, 9.
44. Clarke McCauley and Sophia Moskalenko, *Friction: How Conflict Radicalizes Them and Us* (London: Oxford University Press, 2016), 19; John Horgan and Kurt Braddock, "Rehabilitating the Terrorists? Challenges in Assessing the Effectiveness of Deradicalization Programs," *Terrorism and Political Violence* 22 (2010): 267–291, 279.
45. Anna Halafoff and David Wright-Neville, "A Missing Peace? The Role of Religious Actors in Countering Terrorism," *Studies in Conflict and Terrorism* 32, no. 11 (2009): 921–932.
46. Kruglanski et al., "The Psychology of Radicalization and Deradicalization" ; Ramakrishna, *Radical Pathways*, 31.
47. Alex Schmid and Eric Price, "Selected Literature on Radicalization and Deradicalization of Terrorists," *Crime Law Social Change* 55 (2011): 337–348.
48. Pete Simi, Bryan Bubolz, and Anne Hardman, "Military Experience, Identity Discrepancies and Far Right Terrorism: An Exploratory Analysis," *Studies in Conflict and Terrorism* 36 (2013): 657.
49. Sageman, *Turning to Political Violence*, 9; Andrew Silke, "Holy Warriors: Exploring the Psychological Processes of Jihadi Radicalization," *European Journal of Criminology* 5, no. 1 (2008): 99–123, 109.
50. Ramakrishna, *Radical Pathways*, 33.

51. Silke, "Holy Warriors," 112.
52. Marc Sageman, *Understanding Terror Networks* (Philadelphia: University of Pennsylvania Press, 2004); Sageman, *Leaderless Jihad*; Silke, "Holy Warriors," 111.
53. Mia Bloom. *Bombshell: Women and Terrorism.* (Philadelphia: University of Pennsylvania Press, 2012)
54. Sulastri Osman, "Jemaah Islamiyah: Of Kin and Kind," *Journal of Current Southeast Asian Affairs* 29, no. 2 (2010): 157–175; Mohammed Hafez, "The Ties That Bind: How Terrorists Exploit Family Bonds," *CTC Sentinel* 9, no. 2 (2016): 15–17; Julie Chernov Hwang, "Relatives, Redemption and Rice: Motivations for Joining the Maute Group," *CTC Sentinel* 12, no. 8 (2019): 23–27; Kirsten Schulze, "The Surabaya Bombings and the Evolution of the Jihadi Threat to Indonesia," *CTC Sentinel* 11, no. 6 (2018): 1–7; Julie Chernov Hwang and Kirsten Schulze, "Why They Join: Pathways into Indonesian Jihadist Organizations," *Terrorism and Political Violence* 30, no. 6 (2018): 911–932.
55. Ken Ballen, *Terrorists in Love.* (New York: Free Press, 2011)
56. Neil J. Kressel, *To the Extreme: When Faith Becomes Fanaticism* (New York: Prometheus, 2007).
57. Kruglanski et al., "The Psychology of Radicalization and Deradicalization."
58. Jessica Stern, *Terror in the Name of God* (New York: Ecco, 2003).
59. William Rosenau, Ralph Espach, Roman Ortiz, and Natalie Herrera, "Why They Join, Why They Fight, and Why They Leave: Learning from Colombia's Database of Demobilized Militants," *Terrorism and Political Violence* 26, no. 2 (2014): 277–285.
60. Silke, "Becoming a Terrorist."
61. Guilian Denoeux and Lynn Carter, *Guide to the Drivers of Violent Extremism* (Washington, DC: U.S. Agency for International Development, 2009).
62. J. M. Berger, *Extremism* (Boston: MIT Press, 2018), 124–125.
63. Wiktorowicz, *Radical Islam Rising*, 77–78.
64. Wiktorowicz, *Radical Islam Rising*, 90.
65. Wiktorowicz, *Radical Islam Rising*, 90.
66. Wiktorowicz, *Radical Islam Rising*, 99.
67. Mohammed Hafez and Creighton Mullins, "The Radicalization Puzzle: A Theoretical Synthesis of Empirical Approaches to Homegrown Extremism," *Studies in Conflict and Terrorism* 38, no. 11 (2015): 958–975
68. Sageman, *Leaderless Jihad.*
69. Taylor and Horgan, "A Conceptual Framework," 586.
70. Taylor and Horgan, "A Conceptual Framework," 590–591.
71. McCauley and Moskalenko, *Friction*, 91.
72. McCauley and Moskalenko, *Friction*, 91.
73. Simi and Futrell, *American Swastika*, 4.
74. Simi and Futrell, *American Swastika*, 4.
75. Simi and Futrell, *American Swastika*, 4.
76. Mary Beth Altier, Christian Thoroughgood, and John Horgan, "Turning Away from Terrorism: Lessons from Psychology, Sociology and Criminology," *Journal of Peace Research* 51, no. 5 (2014): 647–661, 650.
77. Altier et al., "Turning Away from Terrorism," 650.

78. Altier et al., "Turning Away from Terrorism," 650.
79. Altier et al., "Turning Away from Terrorism," 650.
80. Donatella Della Porta, "Recruitment Processes in Clandestine Political Organizations," *International Social Movements Research* 4 (1992): 158–160; Osman, "Jemaah Islamiyah"; Hafez, "The Ties That Bind"; Horgan, "From Profiles to Pathways and Roots to Routes"; Horgan, *Walking Away from Terrorism*.
81. Rosenau et al., "Why They Join, Why They Fight, and Why They Leave"; Rodney Stark and William Sims Banbridge, "Networks of Faith," *American Journal of Sociology* 85, no. 6 (1980); John Lofland, *Doomsday Cult* (Hoboken, NJ: Prentice Hall, 1966); Andrew Papachristos, David Hureau, and Anthony Braga, "The Corner and the Crew," *American Sociological Review* 78, no. 3 (2013): 417–447; Jessica Stern, "Mind over Martyr," *Foreign Affairs* 89, no. 1 (2010): 95–108.
82. Osman, "Jemaah Islamiyah"; Sidney Jones, "Inherited Jihadism: Like Father, Like Son," *Australian Financial Review* (2007, July 4); Navhat Nuraniyah, "More than a Fanclub," *Inside Indonesia* (2015); Chernov Hwang, "Relatives, Redemption and Rice"; Navhat Nuraniyah, "How ISIS Charmed a New Generation of Militants," Middle East Institute (2015, January 9); Sidney Jones, "Radicalisation in the Philippines: The Cotobato Cell and the 'East Asia Wilayah,'" *Terrorism and Political Violence* 30, no. 6 (2018): 933–943; Chernov Hwang and Schulze, "Why They Join."
83. Sageman, *Understanding Terror Networks*.
84. Sageman, *Leaderless Jihad*.
85. Sageman, *Understanding Terror Networks*, 110, 120–121.
86. Sageman, *Leaderless Jihad*, 67.
87. See Osman, "Jemaah Islamiyah"; Jones, "Inherited Jihadism"; Nuraniyah, "How ISIS Charmed a New Generation of Militants"; Chernov Hwang and Schulze, "Why They Join"; Nava Nuraniyah, "Not Just Brainwashed: Understanding the Radicalization of Indonesian Female Supporters of the Islamic State," *Terrorism and Political Violence* 30, no. 6 (2018): 890–910; Kirsten E. Schulze, "The Surabaya Bombing and the Evolution of the Jihadi Threat in Indonesia," *CTC Sentinel* (2018, June 22); Kirsten Schulze and Julie Chernov Hwang, "From Afghanistan to Syria: How the Global Remains Local for Islamist Militants," in *Exporting Global Jihad*, ed. Tom Smith and Kirsten Schulze (New York: IB Taurus, 2020), 15–37, 29–30. Ramakrishna, *Radical Pathways*.
88. Sageman, *Turning to Political Violence*, 8–9.
89. Sageman, *Turning to Political Violence*, 8–9.
90. Julie Chernov Hwang. *Why Terrorists Quit: The Disengagement of Indonesian Jihadists* (Ithaca, NY: Cornell, 2018); Julie Chernov Hwang, "The Disengagement of Indonesian Jihadists: Understanding the Pathways," *Terrorism and Political Violence* 29, no. 2 (2017): 277–295; Julie Chernov Hwang, Rizal Panggabean, and Ihsan Ali Fauzi, "When We Were Separated, We Began to Think for Ourselves Again: The Disengagement of Jihadists in Poso, Indonesia," *Asian Survey* 53, no. 4 (2013): 754–777; Nuraniyah, "Not Just Brainwashed"; Osman, "Jemaah Islamiyah"; Jones, "Inherited Jihadism"; Nuraniyah, "How ISIS Charmed a New Generation of Militants"; Chernov Hwang and Schulze, "Why They Join"; Tom Smith and Kirsten

Schulze, "Introduction: Examining the Global Linkages of Asian and North American Jihadis," in *Exporting Global Jihad*, ed. Tom Smith and Kirsten Schulze (New York: IB Taurus, 2020), 1; Schulze, "The Surabaya Bombing"; Schulze and Chernov Hwang, "From Afghanistan to Syria," 29–30; David Duriesmith, "Militarized Masculinities Beyond Methodological Nationalism: Charting the Multiple Masculinities of an Indonesian Jihadi," *International Theory*. 11, no. 2 (2019): 139–159; Kiriloi Ingram, "Revising Marawi: Women and the Struggle Against the Islamic State in the Philippines," *Lawfare* (2019, August 4); Ramkrishna, *Radical Pathways*; Quinton Temby, *Terrorism in Indonesia After "Islamic State,"* Issue 3 (Singapore: ISEAS Yusof Ishak Institute, 2020); Jones, "Radicalisation in the Philippines".

91. Chernov Hwang and Schulze, "Why They Join"; Nuraniyah, "Not Just Brainwashed"; Jones, "Radicalisation in the Philippines."
92. Osman, "Jemaah Islamiyah"; Jones, "Inherited Jihadism."
93. Nuraniyah, "Not Just Brainwashed."
94. Noor Huda Ismail," Indonesian Foreign Fighters, Hegemonic Masculinity and Globalization," PhD thesis, Monash University. (2019, February 6).
95. Ramakrishna, *Radical Pathways*.
96. Jones, "Radicalisation in the Philippines."
97. Chernov Hwang, "Relatives, Redemption and Rice"; Ingram, "Revising Marawi".
98. See Sohahuddin, *The Roots of Terrorism in Indonesia* (Ithaca, NY: Corrnell University Press, 2013); Ioana Emy Matesan, *The Violence Pendulum* (Oxford, UK: Oxford University Press, 2020); Ioana Emy Matesan, "Organizational Dynamics, Public Condemnation, and the Impetus to Disengage from Violence," *Terrorism and Political Violence* 32, no. 5 (2020): 949–969; Julie Chernov Hwang, "Dakwah Before Jihad: Understanding the Behavior of Jemaah Islamiyah," *Contemporary Southeast Asia* 41, no. 1 (2019): 14–34; Gilian Oak, "Jemaah Islamiyah's Fifth Phase: The Many Faces of a Terrorist Group," *Studies in Conflict and Terrorism* 33, no. 11 (2010): 989–1018; Nasir Abas, *Inside Jemaah Islamiyah* (Jakarta: Grafindo, 2011); Greg Barton, *Jemaah Islamiyah* (Singapore: Ridge Books, 2005); Dirk Thomsa, "Jemaah Islamiyah After the Recent Wave of Arrests: How Much Danger Remains," *Sudostasien Aktuell* 26(2007): 73–84; Sidney Jones, "Radicalization in the Philippines"; Quinton Temby, "Cells, Factions and Suicide Operatives," *Contemporary Southeast Asia* 41, no. 1 (2019): 114–137; Joseph Franco, "Confronting the Threat of an ISIS Province in Mindanao," in *Learning from Violent Extremist Attacks*, ed. Khader Majeed, Neo Loo Sang, Jethro Tang, Damien Cheong, and Jeffrey Chin (Singapore: World Scientific, 2019): 21–34; Zachary Abuza, "The Moro Islamic Liberation Front at 20," *Studies in Conflict and Terrorism* 28, no. 6 (2005): 453–479; Kirsten E. Schulze, "From Ambon to Poso: Comparative and Evolutionary Aspects of Local Jihad in Indonesia," *Contemporary Southeast Asia*, 41, no. 1 (2019): 35–62; Schulze, "The Jihadi Threat to Indonesia."
99. Schulze and Chernov Hwang, "From Afghanistan to Syria"; Tom Smith and Joseph Franco, "Mujahidin in Marawi: How Local Jihadism in the Philippines Tried to Go Global," in *Exporting Jihad*, ed. Tom Smith and Kirsten E. Schulze (London: IB Taurus, 2020), 37–55; Aida Arosoaie and Joseph Chinyong Liow, "Contextualizing

the Appeal of ISIS in Malaysia," in *Exporting Jihad*, ed. Tom Smith and Kirsten E Schulze (London: IB Taurus, 2020): 55–72; Kirsten Schulze and Joseph Liow, "Making Jihadis, Waging Jihad: Transnational and Local Dimensions of the ISIS Phenomenon in Indonesia and Malaysia," *Asian Security* 15, no. 2 (2019): 122–139;

100. See Sohahuddin, *The Roots of Terrorism in Indonesia*.
101. Matesan, *The Violence Pendulum*; Matesan, "Organizational Dynamics, Public Condemnation."
102. Chernov Hwang. "Dakwah Before Jihad."
103. Ken Ward, "Indonesian Terrorism: From Jihad to Dakwah," in *Expressing Islam*, ed. Greg Fealy and Sally White (Singapore: ISEAS, 2008), 211–228.
104. Schulze, "From Ambon to Poso."
105. Temby, "Terrorism in Indonesia After 'Islamic State.'"
106. Quinton Temby, "Cells, Factions, Suicide Operations: The Fragmentation of Militant Islam in Post-Marawi, Philippines," *Contemporary Southeast Asia* 41, no. 1 (2019): 114–137.
107. See Quinton Temby, "Jihadists Assemble: The Rise of Militant Islam in Southeast Asia," PhD thesis, Australian National University (2017); Rohan Gunaratna, *Inside Al Qaeda* (New Delhi: Roli Books, 2002); Zachard Abuza, *Political Islam and Violence in Indonesia* (London: Routledge, 2007); Maria Ressa, *Seeds of Terror: An Eyewitness Account of Al Qaeda's Newest Operations in Southeast Asia* (New York: Free Press, 2004); Ken Conboy, *The Second Front: Inside Asia's Most Dangerous Terrorist Network* (Jakarta: Eqinox, 2005); Kumar Ramakrishna, "The 'East Asia Wilaya' of ISIS: Long Time in the Making," Institute for Autonomy and Governance {2017, October 14); Rohan Gunaratna, "Global Threat Forecast," *Counter Terrorist Trends and Analysis* 10, no. 1 (2018): 1–6; Joseph Franco, "Assessing the Feasibility of a 'Wilaya Mindanao,'" *Perspectives on Terrorism* 11, no. 4 (2017): 29–38; Joseph Franco, "The Maute Group: New Vanguard of IS in Southeast Asia," *RSIS Commentaries*, No. 107 (2017).
108. Temby, "Jihadists Assemble."
109. See Amitav Acharya and Arabinda Acharya, "The Myth of the Second Front," *Washington Quarterly* 30, no. 4 (2007): 75–90; Conboy, *The Second Front*; John Gershman, "Is Southeast Asia the Second Front?" *Foreign Affairs 81*, no. 4 (2002); Andrew Tan, "Southeast Asia as the Second Front in the War Against Terrorism," *Terrorism and Political Violence* 15, no. 2 (2003): 112–138.
110. There is considerable disagreement over exactly how many Moros were executed.
111. Initially, the camp was located in Pabbi, Pakistan, but it moved to Saada in 1987. Solahudin, *Roots of Indonesian Terrorism* (Ithaca, NY: Cornell University Press, 2013), 141.
112. Chernov Hwang, *Why Terrorists Quit*, 27.
113. Solahudin, *Roots of Indonesian Terrorism*, 126.
114. Solahudin, *Roots of Indonesian Terrorism*, 126; Nasir Abas, *Membongkar Jemaah Islamiyah* (Jakarta: Grafindo, 2005), 66–67. Abas stipulates names and numbers for batches from 1992 and 1993.
115. Solahudin, *Roots of Indonesian Terrorism*, 141.

116. See Sageman, *Understanding Terror Networks*; Chernov Hwang and Schulze, "Why They Join"; Jones, "Radicalisation in the Philippines"; Nuraniyah, "Not Just Brainwashed"; Chernov Hwang, "Relatives, Redemption and Rice."
117. Chernov Hwang. *Why Terrorists Quit*, 23.
118. Solahudin, *Roots of Indonesian Terrorism*, 63, 69, 122–123.
119. IPAC, "The Decline of ISIS in Indonesia and the Emergence of New Cells," report no. 69 (2021, January 21), 36.
120. Management Systems International, "Indonesian and Malaysian Support for the Islamic State" (Washington, DC: U.S. Agency for International Development, 2015), 15.
121. Kirsten Schulze, "The Jihadi Threat to Indonesia."
122. Management Systems International, "Indonesian and Malaysian Support for the Islamic State," 18.
123. IPAC, "Extremists in Bandung: Darul Islam to ISIS—And Back Again?" report no. 42 (2018, February), 8.
124. IPAC, "The Decline of ISIS in Indonesia," 5.
125. IPAC, "Extremists in Bandung," 8.
126. Quoted in IPAC, "Extremists in Bandung," 8.
127. IPAC, "The Decline of ISIS in Indonesia," 5.
128. IPAC, "The Decline of ISIS in Indonesia," 6.
129. IPAC, "The Decline of ISIS in Indonesia," 6–7.
130. IPAC, "Support for the Islamic State in Indonesian Prisons," report no. 15 (2015, January 25), 5.
131. IPAC, "The Decline of ISIS in Indonesia," 27–28.
132. IPAC, "The Decline of ISIS in Indonesia," 23.
133. IPAC, "The Decline of ISIS in Indonesia," 23.
134. IPAC, "The Decline of ISIS in Indonesia," 23.
135. Kirsten Schulze, "The Jihad Threat to Indonesia," *CTC Sentinel* 11, no. 6 (2018), 3.
136. Joseph Chinyong Liow, Muslim Resistance in Southern Thailand and the Southern Philippines: Religion, Ideology and Politics (Washington, DC: East–West Center, 2006), 7–9.
137. International Crisis Group, "Philippines: Addressing Muslim Militancy After the Battle of Marawi" (2018, July 17).
138. International Crisis Group, "The Philippines: Militancy and the New Bangsamoro" (2019, June 27), 16.
139. International Crisis Group, "The Philippines: Militancy and the New Bangsamoro," 14.
140. Institute for the Policy Analysis of Conflict, "Marawi: The 'East Asia Wilayah' and Indonesia" (2017), 2.
141. Institute for the Policy Analysis of Conflict, "Marawi: The 'East Asia Wilayah' and Indonesia," 2.
142. Institute for the Policy Analysis of Conflict, "Marawi: The 'East Asia Wilayah' and Indonesia," 3.
143. Chernov Hwang, "Relatives, Redemption and Rice."
144. Raju Gopalkrishnan and Manuel Mogato, "The Mautes of the Philippines: From Monied Family to Islamic State," Reuters (2017, June 22).

145. "'Articulate, Educated, Idealistic' Maute Brothers Who Brought Islamic State's Brand of Terror to Southern Philippine City," *South China Morning Post* (2017, June 12).
146. Chernov Hwang, "Relatives, Redemption and Rice."
147. Author correspondence with a Southeast Asia security analyst, May 2019.
148. Chernov Hwang, "Relatives, Redemption and Rice."
149. Temby, "Cells, Factions, and Suicide Operatives," 116.
150. Amnesty International, "The Battle for Marawi: Death and Destruction in the Philippines" (2017, November 17), 13, 16.
151. I chose not to include those who went to Syria, not to fight but to live, as well as women who took on roles. This accounts for five missing.
152. In calculations of education, 12 individuals were either not asked or did not disclose educational background. These were typically individuals from the Salafi paramilitary militia Laskar Jihad, or they were group interviews conducted with more than one person in 2010 in Poso.

# Chapter 1

1. See Ana Arjona and Stathis Kalyvas, "Recruitment into Armed Groups in Colombia: A Survey of Demobilized Fighters," in *Mobilizing for Violence*, ed. Yvan Guichaoua (New York: Palgrave, 2011), 143–171; Mohammed Hafez and Creighton Mullins, "The Radicalization Puzzle: A Theoretical Synthesis of Empirical Approaches to Homegrown Extremism," *Studies in Conflict and Terrorism* 38, no. 11 (2015): 958–975; John Horgan, *Psychology of Terrorism* (London: Routledge, 2014); John Horgan, "From Profiles to Pathways and from Roots to Routes: Perspectives from Psychology on Radicalization into Terrorism," *Annals of the American Academy of Political and Social Science* 618 (2008): 80–94; Julie Chernov Hwang and Kirsten Schulze, "Why They Join: Pathways into Indonesian Jihadist Organizations," *Terrorism and Political Violence* 30, no. 6 (2018), 911–932, https://doi.org/10.1080/09546553.2018.1481309; Sidney Jones, "Radicalisation in the Philippines: The Cotobato Cell of the 'East Asia Wilayah,'" *Terrorism and Political Violence* 30, no. 6 (2018): 933–943, https://doi.org/10.1080/09546553.2018.1481190; Clarke McCauley and Sophia Moskalenko, *Friction: How Conflict Radicalizes Them and Us* (London: Oxford University Press, 2017); Fathali Moghaddam, "The Staircase to Terrorism: A Psychological Explanation," *American Psychologist* 60, no. 2 (2005): 161–169; John Morrison, "Trust in Me: Allegiance Choices in a Post-Split Terrorist Movement," *Aggression and Violent Behavior* 28 (2016): 47–56; Nava Nuraniyah, "Not Just Brainwashed: Understanding the Radicalization of Indonesian Female Supporters of the Islamic State," *Terrorism and Political Violence* 30, no. 6 (2018): 890–910, https://doi.org/10.1080/09546553.2018.1481269; Marc Sageman, *Leaderless Jihad* (Philadelphia: University of Pennsylvania Press, 2008); Andrew Silke, *Terrorists, Victims, Society* (London: Wiley, 2010); Ali Riaz and Saimum Parvez, "Bangladeshi Militants: What Do We Know?" *Terrorism and Political Violence* 30, no. 6 (2018): 944–961, https://doi.org/10.1080/09546553.2018.1481

312; Max Taylor and John Horgan, "A Conceptual Framework for Addressing Psychological Processes in the Development of a Terrorist," *Terrorism and Political Violence* 18, no. 4 (2006): 585–601; Francisco Guttierez Sanin and Elisabeth Jean Wood, "Ideology in Civil War," *Journal of Peace Research* 51, no. 2 (2014): 213–226, https://doi.org/10.1177%2F0022343313514073; Macartan Humphreys and Jeremy Weinstein, "Who Fights? The Determinants of Participation in Civil War," *American Journal of Political Science* 52, no. 2 (2008): 436–455, https://doi.org/10.1111/j.1540-5907.2008.00322.x.
2. Silke, *Terrorists, Victims, Society*, 37.
3. McCauley and Moskalenko, *Friction*; Taylor and Horgan, "A Conceptual Framework"; Sageman. *Leaderless Jihad*; Chernov Hwang and Schulze, "Why They Join"; Jones, "Radicalisation in the Philippines."
4. Andrew Silke, *Terrorists, Victims, Society*, 37.
5. Silke, *Terrorists, Victims, Society*, 37.
6. Silke, *Terrorists, Victims, Society*, 37.
7. McCauley and Moskalenko, *Friction*.
8. For an explanation, see Tore Bjorgo, "Process of Disengagement from Violent Groups on the Extreme Right," in *Leaving Terrorism Behind*, ed. Tore Bjorgo and John Horgan (London: Routledge, 2009), 36–40.
9. *Perjalanan Spiritual*, an unfinished draft autobiography of Muhammad Rais, 1.
10. *Perjalanan Spiritual*, 1.
11. *Perjalanan Spiritual*, 1.
12. Interview with Rashid, former member of Jemaah Islamiyah, July 2017, Pekanbaru, Indonesia.
13. Interview with Rashid, former member of Jemaah Islamiyah, July 2017, Pekanbaru, Indonesia.
14. Interview with Rashid, former member of Jemaah Islamiyah, July 2017, Pekanbaru, Indonesia.
15. Interview with Rashid, former member of Jemaah Islamiyah, July 2017, Pekanbaru, Indonesia.
16. Interview with the late Sam, member of Ring Banten, ISIS, January 2012, Serpong, Indonesia.
17. Interview with the late Sam, member of Ring Banten, ISIS, January 2012, Serpong, Indonesia.
18. Kirsten Schulze, "The Surabaya Bombings and the Evolution of the Jihadi Threat in Indonesia," *CTC Sentinel* 11, no. 6 (2018), 1–2.
19. Greg Fealy, "Apocalyptic Thought, Conspiracism, and Jihad in Indonesia," *Contemporary Southeast Asia* 41, no. 1 (2019), 63–85.
20. Sidney Jones, "The Surabaya Bombings and the Future of ISIS in Indonesia," Institute for Policy Analysis of Conflict report no. 51 (2018), 6.
21. Fieldwork notes, three interviews with former members of Mujahidin Indonesia Timor (MIT), August 2018, Poso and Solo, Indonesia.
22. Fieldwork notes, three interviews with former members of Mujahidin Indonesia Timor (MIT), August 2018, Poso and Solo, Indonesia.

23. Deposition of Ahmed Junaidi, Berita Acara Pemeriksaan (BAP) Ahmed Junaidi alias Abu Salman alias Jun alias Ju, 11, May 2015, 3–4.
24. Nava Nuraniyah, "How ISIS Charmed a New Generation of Militants," Middle East Institute (2015, January 9).
25. Fieldwork notes, interviews in Semarang and Malang, 2018 and 2019, respectively.
26. BAP for Ahmed Junaidi, 11–12.
27. BAP for Ahmed Junaidi, 11–12.
28. BAP for Ahmed Junaidi, 11–12.
29. Interview with Abu Tsabita, former member of JI, MMI, JAT, and current member of JAS, July 2019, Semarang, Indonesia.
30. Interview with Jamal, former member of the Maute group, February 2019, Marwai, Philippines.
31. Interview with Ryan, former member of the Maute group, February 2019, Marawi, Philippines.
32. Interview with Ryan, former member of the Maute group, February 2019, Marawi, Philippines.
33. Interview with Ryan, former member of the Maute group, February 2019, Marawi, Philippines.
34. Mohammed Hafez, "The Ties that Bind: How Terrorists Exploit Family Bonds," *CTC Sentinel* 9, no. 2 (2016), 15–17, 16.
35. Hafez, "The Ties that Bind," 16.
36. Interview with Abu Ayyas, former lead member of the Aceh training camp, July 2015, Jakarta, Indonesia.
37. Interview with Abu Ayyas, former lead member of the Aceh training camp, July 2015, Jakarta, Indonesia.
38. Interview with Abu Ayyas, former lead member of the Aceh training camp, July 2015, Jakarta, Indonesia.
39. Interview with Abu Ayyas, former lead member of the Aceh training camp, July 2015, Jakarta, Indonesia.
40. International Crisis Group, "Indonesia: Jihadi Surprise in Aceh," no. 189 (2010, April 20).
41. "Indonesia: Jihadi Surprise in Aceh."
42. Interview with Abu Ayyas, former lead member of the Aceh training camp, July 2015, Jakarta, Indonesia.
43. "Indonesia: Jihadi Surprise in Aceh."
44. "Indonesia, Jihadi Surprise in Aceh."
45. "Indonesia, Jihadi Surprise in Aceh."
46. Interview with Hajir, former member of the Subur Cell in Semarang, July 2012, Semarang, Indonesia.
47. Interview with Hajir, former member of the Subur Cell in Semarang, July 2012, Semarang, Indonesia.
48. Interview with Hajir, former member of the Subur Cell in Semarang, July 2012, Semarang, Indonesia.

49. Interview with Anas, former member of Jemaah Islamiyah and Mujahidin KOMPAK, July 2010, Jakarta, Indonesia.
50. Interview with former member of Tauhid wa'al Jihad, July 2015, Jakarta, Indonesia.
51. Interview with former member of Tauhid wa'al Jihad, July 2015, Jakarta, Indonesia.
52. Interview with former members of the Maute group, Nabi, Naga, and Omar, February 2019 and July 2019, Butig and Marawi, Philippines.
53. Mark Woodward, Mariani Yahya, Inayah Rohmaniyah, Diana Coleman, Chris Lundry, and Ali Amin, "The Islamic Defenders Front: Demonization, Violence and the State in Indonesia," *Contemporary Islam* 8 (2014): 153–171, 159.
54. Interview with Amar, former member of FPI and Tim Hisbah, July 2019, Solo, Indonesia.
55. Interview with Amar, former member of FPI and Tim Hisbah, July 2019, Solo, Indonesia.
56. Interview with Amar, former member of FPI and Tim Hisbah, July 2019, Solo, Indonesia.
57. Institute for Policy Analysis of Conflict (IPAC), "The Failed Solo Suicide Bombing and Bahrun Naim's Network," report no. 30 (2016, July 29), 3.
58. Interview with Amar, former member of FPI and Tim Hisbah, July 2019, Solo, Indonesia.
59. Interview with Amar, former member of FPI and Tim Hisbah, July 2019, Solo, Indonesia.
60. IPAC, "The Failed Solo Suicide Bombing," 8.
61. IPAC, "The Failed Solo Suicide Bombing," 8.
62. Interview with Amar, former member of FPI and Tim Hisbah, July 2019, Solo, Indonesia.
63. Interview with Amar, former member of FPI and Tim Hisbah, July 2019, Solo, Indonesia.
64. Interview with Amar, former member of FPI and Tim Hisbah, July 2019, Solo, Indonesia.
65. Interview with Amar, former member of FPI and Tim Hisbah, July 2019, Solo, Indonesia.
66. Interview with Reza, former member of Mujahidin KOMPAK, July 2015, Salemba prison, Jakarta, Indonesia.
67. Interview with "Joko," former member of Jemaah Islamiyah, Mujahidin KOMPAK, JAT, and JAD and current member of JAS, July 2016, Solo, Indonesia.
68. International Crisis Group, "Weakening Indonesia's Mujahidin Networks: Lessons from Maluku and Poso," report no. 103 (2005, October 13), 7.
69. International Crisis Group, "Weakening Indonesia's Mujahidin Networks," 7.
70. Interview with Agus, former member of Mujahidin KOMPAK, July 2012, Porong Prison, outside Surabaya.
71. Tim Hisbah first went by the name Laskar Arafah, in connection with the Arafah mosque.
72. Interview with Khoirul, former member of Tim Hisbah, July 2019, Solo, Indonesia.

NOTES 175

73. Interview with Faisal, former member of the Maute group, July 2019, Marawi, Philippines.
74. Interview with Abu Islam, former member of the Maute group, February 2019, Marawi, Philippines.
75. Fieldwork interviews in Butig, Marawi, and Piagapo, February and July 2019, Philippines.
76. Interview with Fauzan, former member of Tanah Runtuh, July 2011, Petobo Prison, Palu, Indonesia.
77. Interview with Fauzan, former member of Tanah Runtuh, July 2011, Petobo Prison, Palu, Indonesia.
78. Interview with Fauzan, former member of Tanah Runtuh, July 2011, Petobo Prison, Palu, Indonesia.
79. Interview with Fauzan, former member of Tanah Runtuh, July 2011, Petobo Prison, Palu, Indonesia.
80. Interview with Fauzan, former member of Tanah Runtuh, July 2011, Petobo Prison, Palu, Indonesia.
81. Interview with Fauzan, former member of Tanah Runtuh, July 2011, Petobo Prison, Palu, Indonesia.
82. Interview with Fauzan, former member of Tanah Runtuh, July 2011, Petobo Prison, Palu, Indonesia.
83. Julie Chernov Hwang, *Why Terrorists Quit: The Disengagement of Indonesian Jihadists* (Ithaca, NY: Cornell University Press, 2018), 37.
84. Dave McRae, *A Few Poorly Organized Men: Interreligious Violence in Poso, Indonesia* (Sydney, Australia: Brill, 2013),96, cites 100; Haji Adnan Arsal, head of the Tanah Runtuh community, cites 300; Interview Haji Adnan Arsal, June 2010, Poso, Indonesia.
85. Julie Chernov Hwang, *Why Terrorists Quit*, 38–39.
86. Julie Chernov Hwang, Rizal Panggabean, and Ihsan Ali Fauzi, "When We Were Separated, We Began to Think for Ourselves Again: The Disengagement of Jihadists in Poso, Indonesia," *Asian Survey* 53, no. 4 (2013), 754–777.
87. Chernov Hwang et al., "When We Were Separated," 763.
88. Interview with "Gungun," member of Mujahidin Indonesia Timor, July 2019, Poso, Indonesia.
89. Interview with "Salman," member of Mujahidin Indonesia Timor, July 2019, Poso, Indonesia.
90. Interview with Abu Usama, former member of the Maute group, February 2019, Marawi, Philippines.
91. Interview with Abu Usama, former member of the Maute group, February 2019, Marawi, Philippines.
92. Interview with Abu Usama, former member of the Maute group, February 2019, Marawi, Philippines.
93. Interview with Abu Usama, former member of the Maute group, February 2019, Marawi, Philippines.

94. Interview with Abu Usama, former member of the Maute group, February 2019, Marawi, Philippines.
95. Interview with Abu Usama, former member of the Maute group, February 2019, Marawi, Philippines.
96. Interview with Abu Usama, former member of the Maute group, February 2019, Marawi, Philippines.
97. Interview with Abu Usama, former member of the Maute group, February 2019, Marawi, Philippines.
98. Interview with Abu Usama, former member of the Maute group, February 2019, Marawi, Philippines.
99. Interview with Abu Usama, former member of the Maute group, February 2019, Marawi, Philippines.
100. Interview with Abu Usama, former member of the Maute group, February 2019, Marawi, Philippines.
101. Nuraniyah, "Not Just Brainwashed," 898.
102. Interview with Ivan, former member of the Maute group, February 2019, Marawi, Philippines.
103. Interview with Ivan, former member of the Maute group, February 2019, Marawi, Philippines.
104. Interview with Abu Hamdan, former member of the Maute group, February 2019, Marawi, Philippines.
105. Christian Picciolini, *Breaking Hate* (New York: Hachette, 2020), xxxii.
106. Nuraniyah, "Not Just Brainwashed," 899.
107. Nuraniyah, "Not Just Brainwashed," 899.
108. Nuraniyah, "Not Just Brainwashed," 899.
109. Nuraniyah, "Not Just Brainwashed," 899.
110. Interview with Aisha, former recruiter for the Maute group, February 2019, Marawi, Philippines.
111. Interview with Aisha, former recruiter for the Maute group, February 2019, Marawi, Philippines.
112. Interview with Aisha, former recruiter for the Maute group, February 2019, Marawi, Philippines.
113. Interview with Aisha, former recruiter for the Maute group, February 2019, Marawi, Philippines.
114. Interview with Aisha, former recruiter for the Maute group, February 2019, Marawi, Philippines.
115. Fieldwork notes, February 2019 and July 2019 trips to Marawi, Philippines.
116. Interview with Abu Islam, former member of the Maute group, close to Abu Dar, February 2019, Marawi, Philippines.
117. Institute for Policy Analysis of Conflict, "Update on Indonesian Prio-ISIS Prisoners and Deradicalization Efforts" (2016), 7–8.
118. The main exception was, around 2012 and 2013, with initial recruits to go to Syria to join ISIS. Recruiters promised their debts would be paid and they would be given a generous salary.

## Chapter 2

1. Interview with Abu Muslim, former member of Jemaah Islamiyah, Tanah Runtuh, and Mujahidin Indonesia Timor, outside Solo, Central Java, Indonesia.
2. Interview with Abu Muslim, former member of Jemaah Islamiyah, Tanah Runtuh, and Mujahidin Indonesia Timor, outside Solo, Central Java, Indonesia.
3. Interview with Abu Muslim, former member of Jemaah Islamiyah, Tanah Runtuh, and Mujahidin Indonesia Timor, outside Solo, Central Java, Indonesia.
4. Interview with Abu Muslim, former member of Jemaah Islamiyah, Tanah Runtuh, and Mujahidin Indonesia Timor, outside Solo, Central Java, Indonesia.
5. See Randy Borum, "Understanding the Terrorist Mindset," *FBI Law Enforcement Bulletin* (2003, July); J. M. Berger, *Extremism* (Boston: MIT Press, 2018); Quintan Wiktorowicz, *Radical Islam Rising* (Oxford, UK: Rowman & Littlefield, 2005); Fathali Moghaddam, *From the Terrorists' Point of View* (New York: Praeger, 2006).
6. See Mark Sageman, *Understanding Terror Networks* (Philadelphia: University of Pennsylvania Press, 2004); Clarke McCauley and Sophia Moskalenko, *Friction: How Conflict Radicalizes Them and Us* (London: Oxford University Press, 2016); John Horgan, "From Profiles to Pathways and Roots to Routes: Perspectives from Psychology on Radicalization into Terrorism," *Annals of the American Academy of Political and Social Science* 618 (2008): 80–94; Andrew Silke, "Becoming a Terrorist," in *Terrorists, Victims and Society*, ed. Andrew Silke (London: Wiley, 2003): Chapter 2; Max Taylor and John Horgan, "A Conceptual Framework for Addressing Psychological Process in the Development of the Terrorist," *Terrorism and Political Violence* 18, no. 4 (2006): 585–601; Daniel Koehler, *Understanding Deradicalization* (London: Routledge, 2017).
7. Fieldwork notes, July 2019, Marawi, Philippines.
8. See Horgan, "From Profiles to Pathways, from Roots to Routes"; Mohammed Hafez, "The Ties That Bind: How Terrorists Exploit Family Bonds," *CTC Sentinel* 9, no. 2 (2016): 15–17; Sulastri Osman, "Jemaah Islamiyah: Of Kin and Kind," *Journal of Current Southeast Asian Affairs* 29, no. 2 (2010): 157–175; Donatella Della Porta, "On Individual Motivations in Underground Political Mobilizations." *International Social Movement Research* 4 (1992).
9. Sophia Moskaleno and Clark McCauley, *Radicalization to Terrorism* (London: Oxford University Press, 2020), 50.
10. See Osman, "Jemaah Islamiyah," 164.
11. Sidney Jones, "Inherited Jihadism: Like Father, Like Son," *Australian Financial Review* (2007, July 4).
12. Julie Chernov Hwang and Kirsten Schulze, "Why They Join: Pathways into Indonesian Jihadist Organizations," Terrorism and Political Violence 30, no. 6 (2018): 911–932, https://doi.org/10.1080/09546553.2018.1481309 (Chernov Hwang wrote the segment on parental socialization).
13. Sidney Jones, "Darul Islam's Ongoing Appeal," International Crisis Group (2010, August 18), https://www.crisisgroup.org/asia/south-east-asia/indonesia/darul-islam-s-ongoing-appeal.

14. Interview with Abu Rusydan, former member of Jemaah Islamiyah, August 8, 2017, Kudus.
15. Jones, "Inherited Jihadism."
16. Noor Huda Ismail, "Al Qaeda's Southeast Asia, Jemaah Islamiyah and Regional Terrorism: Kinship and Family Links," *Asia-Pacific Journal* 5, no. 1 (2007), 51.
17. He cannot recall whether it was 1991, 1992, or 1993.
18. Interview with Hisham, member of Jemaah Islamiyah, July 2015, Surabaya.
19. Interview with Hisham, member of Jemaah Islamiyah, July 2012, Surabaya.
20. Chernov Hwang and Schulze, "Why They Join" (Schulze wrote this paragraph).
21. Dandy Koswaraputra, "Imam Samudra's Son Killed in Syria," *Jakarta Post* (2015, October 16).
22. "Rusydan Putra Dr Amir Mahmud Hijrah ke Daulah Islamiyah, Syahid di Jabal Khilafah," *Panjimas*, (2015, May 19).
23. Interview with Muhammad Jibril Abdurrahman, brother of Ridwan, August 2, 2017, Jakarta. See also A. Z. Muttaqin, "Ta'ziyah sekaligus tahniah atas gugurnya Ridwan," *Arrahmah*. 26 (2015, March 2).
24. Interview with Abu Islam, former member of the Maute group, February 2019, Marawi, Philippines.
25. Interview with Abu Hamdan, former member of the Maute group, February 2019, Marawi, Philippines.
26. Chernov Hwang and Schulze, "Why They Join" (Chernov Hwang wrote this section on sibling recruitment).
27. Interview with Ali Imron, member of Jemaah Islamiyah, Jakarta police headquarters prison, August 3, 2017, Jakarta, Indonesia.
28. Sally Neighbour, *In the Shadow of Swords* (Sydney, Australia: Harper Collins, 2004), 61.
29. Neighbour, *In the Shadow of Swords*, 61–62.
30. Interview with Abu Hamdan, former member of the Maute group, February 2019, Marawi, Philippines.
31. Interview with Amar, former member of FPI and Tim Hisbah and the Bahrum Naim cell within Tim Hisbah, July 2019, Solo, Indonesia.
32. Fieldwork notes from February 2019 and July 2019, Marawi, Philippines.
33. Interview with Ryan, former member of the Maute group, February 2019, Marawi, Philippines.
34. Interview with Jabir, former member of the Maute group, February 2019, Marawi, Philippines.
35. Chernov Hwang and Schulze, "Why They Join" (Chernov Hwang wrote this section on extended family).
36. Interview with Abu Azzam, former member of Al-Qaeda in the Malaysian Archipelago, August 1, 2017, Jakarta, Indonesia.
37. Interview with Abu Azzam, former member of Al-Qaeda in the Malaysian Archipelago, August 1, 2017, Jakarta, Indonesia
38. Interview with Ari, former member of ISIS and returnee from Syria, July 2019, Jakarta, Indonesia.

39. Interview with Ari, former member of ISIS and returnee from Syria, July 2019, Jakarta, Indonesia.
40. See Osman, "Jemaah Islamiyah."
41. Deposition of Parawijayanto, Berita Acara Pemeriksaan (BAP) alias Abang, alias Mas, Alias Abu Askary, alias Abu Faiz, July 19, 2019, 4.
42. Chernov Hwang and Schulze, "Why They Join" and Political Violence (Schulze wrote this paragraph).
43. See the Deposition of Dian Yulia Novi alias Dian alias Ukhti alias Ayatul Nissa Binti Asnawi, MarkaBesar Kepolisian Negara Republik Indonesia Detasemen Khusus 88 Anti Terror, Berita Acara Pemeriksaan, December 16, 2016.
44. S. Yunanto and Badrudin Harun, "Terminology, History and Categorization," in *Islamic Education in South and Southeast Asia* (Jakarta: RIDEP Institute, 2005), 30.
45. There are conflicting estimates of the number of JI *pesantren*. Amru counted 40 *pesantren*. In the course of research for his dissertation, Noor Huda Ismail counted 60. The Institute for the Policy Analysis of Conflict counted 71.
46. Tom Allard and Agustinus Beo Da Costa, "Students Sent Home from Indonesian Islamic School, Linked to Child Fighters," Reuters (2017, September 17), https://www.reuters.com/article/cnews-us-indonesia-militants-school-idCAKCN1BS003-OCATP.
47. Solahudin, *The Roots of Terrorism in Indonesia* (Ithaca, NY: Corrnell University Press, 2013), 161.
48. Jones, "Inherited Jihadism."
49. Jones, "Inherited Jihadism."
50. Conversations with Amru, former member of Jemaah Islamiyah, June 2016, Semarang, Indonesia. His children attend JI elementary schools.
51. Conversations with Amru, former member of Jemaah Islamiyah, June 2016, Semarang, Indonesia.
52. Correspondence with Taufik Andrie, Executive Director of the Institute for International Peacebuilding, November 21, 2017.
53. Osman, "Jemaah Islamiyah: Of Kin and Kind," RSIS Working Paper no. 194 (2010), 10.
54. Interview with Amru, former member of Jemaah Islamiyah, June 2016, Semarang, Indonesia.
55. Interview with former Aceh camp member and former student at Ngruki and Darul Syahadah *pesantren*, July 2018, Magelang, Indonesia.
56. Interview with former Aceh camp member and former student at Ngruki and Darul Syahadah *pesantren*, July 2018, Magelang, Indonesia.
57. Interview with MB, member of Jemaah Islamiyah, POLDA Metrojaya, August 3, 2017, Jakarta, Indonesia.
58. Solahudin, *The Roots of Terrorism in Indonesia*, 162.
59. Solahudin, *The Roots of Terrorism in Indonesia*, 162.
60. Solahudin, *The Roots of Terrorism in Indonesia*, 162.
61. Interview with Hisham, member of Jemaah Islamiyah, July 2015, Surabaya.
62. Interview with Hisham, member of Jemaah Islamiyah, July 2015, Surabaya.
63. Interview with Hisham, member of Jemaah Islamiyah, July 2015, Surabaya.

64. Interview with Hisham, member of Jemaah Islamiyah, July 2015, Surabaya.
65. Interview with Hisham, member of Jemaah Islamiyah, July 2015, Surabaya.
66. Interview with Hisham, member of Jemaah Islamiyah, July 2015, Surabaya.
67. Interview with Haris, former student at Al-Islam, July 2019, Jakarta, Indonesia.
68. Interview with Haris, former student at Al-Islam, July 2019, Jakarta, Indonesia.
69. Interview with Haris, former student at Al-Islam, July 2019, Jakarta, Indonesia.
70. Interview with Haris, former student at Al-Islam, July 2019, Jakarta, Indonesia.
71. Interview with Haris, former student at Al-Islam, July 2019, Jakarta, Indonesia.
72. Tom Allard, "Indonesian School a Launchpad for Child Fighters in Syria's Islamic State," Reuters (2017, July 19).
73. Allard, "Indonesian School a Launchpad."
74. Allard, "Indonesian School a Launchpad."
75. Institute for Policy Analysis of Conflict, "The Decline of ISIS in Indonesia and the Emergence of New Cells," report no. 69 (2021, January 21), 27–28.

# Chapter 3

1. Interview with Hakim, former member of Tauhid wa'al Jihad, July 2017, Jakarta, Indonesia.
2. Interview with Hakim, former member of Tauhid wa'al Jihad, July 2017, Jakarta, Indonesia.
3. Interview with Hakim, former member of Tauhid wa'al Jihad, July 2017, Jakarta, Indonesia.
4. Interview with Hakim, former member of Tauhid wa'al Jihad, July 2017, Jakarta, Indonesia.
5. Interview with Hakim, former member of Tauhid wa'al Jihad, July 2017, Jakarta, Indonesia.
6. Interview with Hakim, former member of Tauhid wa'al Jihad, July 2017, Jakarta, Indonesia.
7. Interview with Hakim, former member of Tauhid wa'al Jihad, July 2017, Jakarta, Indonesia.
8. Interview with Hakim, former member of Tauhid wa'al Jihad, July 2017, Jakarta, Indonesia.
9. Interview with Hakim, former member of Tauhid wa'al Jihad, July 2017, Jakarta, Indonesia.
10. Interview with Hakim, former member of Tauhid wa'al Jihad, July 2017, Jakarta, Indonesia.
11. Interview with Zed, former attendee of study groups led by Abdullah Sunata and Aman Abdurrahman, July 2019, Jakarta, Indonesia.
12. Discussion with Amru on the road to Magetan, July 2017, Indonesia.
13. Discussion with Amru on the road to Magetan, July 2017, Indonesia.

14. Interview with Joko, former member of Jemaah Islamiyah, July 2018, Semarang, Indonesia.
15. Interview with Samir, former head of JAT-Semarang and former member of JI, July 2018, Semarang, Indoensia.
16. These stages according to Solahudin were *tabligh* (public religious meeting), *taklim* (smaller Islamic study group), *tamrin* (closed Islamic study group), and *tamhish*; see Sohahuddin, *The Roots of Terrorism in Indonesia* (Ithaca, NY: Corrnell University Press, 2013), 160–161. Similarly, Nasir Abas explains the stages as tabligh, taklim, tamrin, and tamhish; see Nasir Abas, *Membongkar Jamaah Islamiyah: Pengakuan Mantan Ketua JI* (Jakarta: Abdika Press, 2009), p. 99. These stages and terminology are JI specific.
17. Section on Amru's pathway taken from Julie Chernov Hwang and Kirsten Schulze, "Why They Join: Pathways into Indonesian Jihadist Organizations," *Terrorism and Political Violence* 30, no. 6 (2018): 911–932. Both Chernov Hwang and Schulze were present for the interview. Schulze took the lead in writing up the narrative around Amru's pathway.
18. Interview with Hisham, inactive member of JI, July 2018, Surabaya, Indonesia.
19. Interview with Amru, former JI member, August 8, 2017, Semarang, Indonesia.
20. Solahudin, *The Roots of Terrorism in Indonesia*, 159.
21. Interview with Amru, former JI member, August 8, 2017, Semarang, Indonesia.
22. For a detailed analysis of the "new" JI, see Institute for Policy Analysis of Conflict (IPAC), "The Re-Emergence of Jemaah Islamiyah," report no. 36 (2017, April 27).
23. Conversation with former member of JI, JAT, and current member of JAS, July 2018, Magetan, Indonesia.
24. Conversation with former member of JI, JAT, and current member of JAS, July 2018, Magetan, Indonesia.
25. Conversation with former member of JI, JAT, and current member of JAS, July 2018, Magetan, Indonesia.
26. Conversation with former member of JI, JAT, and current member of JAS, July 2018, Magetan, Indonesia.
27. Interview with Ustad Achwan, former deputy to Abu Bakar Ba'asyir in JAT, current JAS leader, July 2019, Malang, Indonesia.
28. Conversation with an Indonesian jihadi, July 2017, Jakarta, Indonesia.
29. Interview with Ustad Syamudin Uba, Al-Aqsha Al-Haqquna, July 2017, Bekasi, Indonesia.
30. Interview with BeWe, ISIS recruiter, July 2017, Bekasi, Indonesia.
31. Interview with Ustad Syamudin Uba, Al-Aqsha Al-Haqquna, Bekasi, July 2017, Bekasi, Indonesia.
32. Interview with BeWe, ISIS recruiter, July 2017, Bekasi, Indonesia.
33. Two paragraphs on ISIS taken from Chernov Hwang and Schulze, "Why They Join" (Schulze took the lead on these two paragraphs).
34. Chernov Hwang and Schulze, "Why They Join," 12–13 (Schulze wrote this paragraph).
35. Sidney Jones, "Radicalisation in the Philippines: The Cotabato Cell of the 'East Asia Wilayah,'" *Terrorism and Political Violence* 30, no. 6 (2018): 933–943.

36. Jones, "Radicalisation in the Philippines," 936–940.
37. Jones, "Radicalisation in the Philippines," 936–940.
38. See Kirsten E. Schulze and Joseph Liow, "Making Jihadis, Waging Jihad: Transnational and Local Dimensions of the ISIS Phenomenon in Indonesia and Malaysia," *Asian Security* 15, no. 2 (2019): 122–139.
39. Idul Fitri is the feast holiday marking the end of Ramadan.
40. Dave McRae, *A Few Poorly Organized Men: Interreligious Violence in Poso, Indonesia* (Sydney, Australia: Brill, 2013), 75.
41. These conflicts broke out several months after the police was separated from the military. Thus, both forces faced a learning curve with regard to their new roles and conflict over turf. This hindered the ability of either force to effectively respond to the initial outbreak of violence.
42. Interview with Khaled, former member of Mujahidin KOMPAK, JI, AQMA, JAT, JAD, and JAS Solo, August 2015, Solo, Indonesia.
43. Interview with "Abu Sayyaf," former member of Mujahidin KOMPAK, August 2015, Solo, Indonesia.
44. Chernov Hwang and Schulze, "Why They Join" (Schulze wrote this paragraph).
45. Julie Chernov Hwang, Rizal Panggabean, and Ihsan Ali Fauzi, "When We Were Separated, We Began to Think for Ourselves Again: The Disengagement of Jihadists in Poso, Indonesia," *Asian Survey* 53, no. 4 (2013): 754–777, 762.
46. Chernov Hwang et al., "When We Were Separated."
47. Interview with BR, former member of Tanah Runtuh, August 2017, Palu, Indonesia.
48. Interview with BR, former member of Tanah Runtuh, August 2017, Palu, Indonesia.
49. Interview with former member of Tanah Runtuh, August 2017, Palu, Indonesia.
50. Interview with former member of Tanah Runtuh, August 2017, Palu, Indonesia.
51. Interview with Cecep, former member of Tanah Runtuh, August 2017, Palu, Indonesia.
52. Interview with BR, former member of Tanah Runtuh, August 2017, Palu, Indonesia.
53. Interview with Ambo, former member of Tanah Runtuh, August 2017, Palu Indonesia.
54. Chernov Hwang and Schulze, "Why They Join" (Schulze wrote this paragraph).
55. Interview with Gungun, former member of MIT, July 2019, Poso, Indonesia.
56. Interview with Abu Muslim, former member of MIT, July 2019, outside Solo, Indonesia.
57. Interview with Gungun, former member of MIT, July 2019, Poso, Indonesia.
58. Interview with Gungun, former member of MIT, July 2019, Poso, Indonesia.
59. Interview with Mat, former member of MIT, July 2019, Poso, Indonesia.
60. Interview with Mat, former member of MIT, July 2019, Poso, Indonesia.
61. Interview with Mat, former member of MIT, July 2019, Poso, Indonesia.
62. Jones, "Radicalisation in the Philippines," 936.
63. Interviews with 20 former members of the Maute group, February and June 2019, Marawi, Butig, and Piagapo, Philippines.
64. Interviews with 20 former members of the Maute group, February and June 2019, Marawi, Butig, and Piagapo, Philippines.

65. See Martha Crenshaw, "Causes of Terrorism," *Comparative Politics* 13, no. 4 (1981): 379–399.
66. Interview with Subair, former member of the Maute group, July 2019, Marawi, Philippines.
67. IPAC, "Update on Indonesian Pro-ISIS Prisoners and Deradicalization Efforts" (2016), 9.
68. Joshua Sinai, "Developing a Model of Prison Radicalization," in *Prisons, Terrorism and Extremism*, ed. Andrew Silke (London: Routledge, 2014), 36.
69. Arie Kruglanski, Michele Gelfand, Jocelyn Belanger, Rohan Gunaratna, and Malkanthi Hettiarachichi, "Deradicalizing the Liberation Tigers of Tamil Eelam," in *Prisons, Terrorism and Extremism*, ed. Andrew Silke (London: Routledge, 2014), 184.
70. IPAC, "Update on Indonesian Pro-ISIS Prisoners and Deradicalization Efforts," 1–7.
71. Sulastri Osman, "Radicalization, Recidivism and Rehabilitation," in *Prisons, Terrorism and Extremism*, ed. Andrew Silke (London: Routledge, 2014), 217.
72. Osman, "Radicalization, Recidivism and Rehabilitation," 217.
73. Osman, "Radicalization, Recidivism and Rehabilitation," 217.
74. Interview with former member of the "bombing wing" of Jemaah Islamiyah, July 2018, Jakarta, Indonesia.
75. Osman, "Radicalization, Recidivism and Rehabilitation," 218.
76. Osman, "Radicalization, Recidivism and Rehabilitation," 219.
77. IPAC, "Prison Problems: Planned and Unplanned Releases of Convicted Extremists in Indonesia" (2013), 18.
78. IPAC, "Update on Indonesian Pro-ISIS Prisoners and Deradicalization Efforts," 9–10.
79. IPAC, "Update on Indonesian Pro-ISIS Prisoners and Deradicalization Efforts," 9–10.
80. Interview with Khaled, former members of JI, Mujahidin KOMPAK, AQMA, JAD, JAT, JAS, July 2016, Solo, Indonesia.
81. Interview with Ahmed, former member of Mujahidin Indonesia Timor and JI, July 2018, Jakarta, Indonesia.
82. Interview with Badrol, former member of Neo-JI, July 2019, Semarang, Indonesia.
83. Interview with Badrol, former member of Neo-JI, July 2019, Semarang, Indonesia.
84. IPAC, "Support for the Islamic State in Indonesian Prisons," report no. 15 (2015, January 25), 8.
85. IPAC, "Support for the Islamic State in Indonesian Prisons," 10.
86. IPAC, "Support for the Islamic State in Indonesian Prisons," 10.
87. IPAC, "Support for the Islamic State in Indonesian Prisons," 10.
88. IPAC, "Support for the Islamic State in Indonesian Prisons," 10.
89. IPAC, "Support for the Islamic State in Indonesian Prisons," 10.
90. IPAC, "Support for the Islamic State in Indonesian Prisons," 10.
91. See Mia Bloom and Chelsea Daymon, "Assessing the Future Threat: ISIS' Virtual Caliphate," *Orbis* 62, no. 3 (2018): 372–388; Mia Bloom, Hicham Tiflati, and John Horgan, "Navigating ISIS' Preferred Platform: Telegram," *Terrorism and Political Violence* 231, no. 6 (2017): 1242–1254; Maura Conway, "From al Zarqawi to al-Awlaki: The Emergence and Development of an Online Radical Milieu," *Combatting Terrorism Exchange* 2, no. 4 (2012); Scott Gates and Sukanya Podder, "Social Media,

Recruitment, Allegiance and the Islamic State," *Perspectives on Terrorism* 9, no. 4 (2015): 107–116; Antonia Ward, "ISIS' Use of Social Media Still Poses a Threat to the Stability of the Middle East," *Georgetown Security Studies Review* (2018, December 11); Maura Conway, Ryan Scrivens, and Logan McNair, "Right-Wing Extremists' Persistent Online Presence: History and Contemporary Trends," ICCT Policy Brief (2019, October); Maura Conway, "Reality Bytes: Cyberterrorism and Terrorist 'Use' of the Internet," *First Monday Y*, no. 11 (2002); Maura Conway, "Terrorist Websites: Their Contents, Functioning and Effectiveness," in *Media and Conflict in the Twenty First Century*, ed. Philip Seib (New York: Palgrave, 2005): 185–216; J. M. Berger, "Nazis vs. ISIS on Twitter," George Washington University Program on Extremism (2016).

92. Bloom et al., "Navigating ISIS' Preferred Platform."
93. Conway, "From al Zarqawi to al-Awlaki," 4.
94. Conway et al., "Right-Wing Extremists' Persistent Online Presence," 6–16.
95. IPAC, "Online Activism and Social Media Usage Among Indonesian Extremists," report no. 24 (2015, October 30), 1.
96. IPAC, "Online Activism and Social Media Usage," 20.
97. IPAC, "Online Activism and Social Media Usage," 1.
98. IPAC, "Online Activism and Social Media Usage," 15.
99. Interviews with 25 former members of the Maute group.
100. IPAC, "The Evolution of ISIS in Indonesia" (2014), 3.
101. IPAC, "The Evolution of ISIS in Indonesia," 3.
102. IPAC, "The Evolution of ISIS in Indonesia," 3.
103. IPAC, "The Evolution of ISIS in Indonesia," 3.
104. IPAC, "The Evolution of ISIS in Indonesia," 9.
105. IPAC, "The Evolution of ISIS in Indonesia," 10.
106. IPAC, "Mothers to Bombers: The Evolution of Indonesian Women Extremists," report no. 35 (2017, January 31), 21.
107. IPAC, "Mothers to Bombers," 20.
108. IPAC, "Online Activism and Social Media Usage," 6.
109. IPAC, "Online Activism and Social Media Usage," 15.
110. Aisyah Llewellyn and Arif Budi Setyawan, "Why Are More Women Getting Involved in Bomb Attacks," Al Jazeera (2021, May 25).
111. IPAC, "Mothers to Bombers," 12.
112. IPAC, "Mothers to Bombers," 12.
113. IPAC, "Mothers to Bombers," 12.
114. IPAC, "Online Activism and Social Media Usage," 10.
115. IPAC, "Online Activism and Social Media Usage," 10.
116. Interview with Arif, networker and facilitator connecting various jihadists from different jihadi groups through online social media, July 2018, Jakarta, Indonesia.
117. Interview with Arif, networker and facilitator connecting various jihadists from different jihadi groups through online social media, July 2018, Jakarta, Indonesia.
118. Interview with Muhammad, former member of JI and JAT, July 2018, Surabaya, Indonesia.

119. Interview with Muhammad, former member of JI and JAT, July 2018, Surabaya, Indonesia.
120. Interview with Jamal, former member of the Maute group, February 2019, Piagapo, Philippines.
121. Interview with Jamal, former member of the Maute group, February 2019, Piagapo, Philippines.
122. IPAC, "Online Activism and Social Media Usage," 1.
123. Interview with Arif, former jihadi networker among several groups who utilized the internet to connect members with one another, July 2018, Jakarta, Indonesia.
124. Interview with Farah, returnee from Syria, July 2019, Depok, Indonesia.
125. Interview with Farah, returnee from Syria, July 2019, Depok, Indonesia.
126. Interview with Farah, returnee from Syria, July 2019, Depok, Indonesia.
127. Interview with Farah, returnee from Syria, July 2019, Depok, Indonesia.
128. Interview with Farah, returnee from Syria, July 2019, Depok, Indonesia.

# Chapter 4

1. Michael Kenney speaks of "learning" in becoming a member in *Islamic State in Britain* (Cambridge, UK: Cambridge University Press, 2018), 101; Karsten Hundeide develops the idea of "committed insider" in "Becoming a Committed Insider," *Culture and Psychology* 9, no. 2 (2003): 107–127, 108.
2. Hundeide, "Becoming a Committed Insider," 108.
3. Hundeide, "Becoming a Committed Insider," 111.
4. Hundeide, "Becoming a Committed Insider," 113.
5. Hundeide, "Becoming a Committed Insider," 113.
6. Hundeide, "Becoming a Committed Insider," 112–113. See also Thomas Hegghammer, *Jihadi Culture* (Cambridge, UK: Cambridge University Press, 2017), 1.
7. Interview with BR, former member of Tanah Runtuh, July 2018, Palu, Indonesia.
8. Interview with Ali Imron, member of JI, July 2017, POLDA Metrojaya Prison, Jakarta, Indonesia.
9. Interview with Haroun, former leader of Poso branch of JI, July 2018, Poso, Indonesia.
10. Interview with BeWe, recruiter for pro-ISIS community, July 2018, Depok, Indonesia.
11. Interview with Syamsuddin Uba, pro-ISIS cleric, July 2018, Bekasi, Indonesia.
12. Interview with Firdaus, former leader of JI-Palu, July 2019, Palu, Indonesia.
13. Interview with Badrol, member of JI/Neo-JI, July 2019, Semarang, Indonesia.
14. See Doug McAdam, "High and Low Risk/Cost Activism," in *Wiley Encyclopedia of Social and Political Movements* (London: Wiley, 2013), https://doi.org/10.1002/9780470674871.wbespm101.
15. Interviews with former members of the Maute group, February 2019, Marawi, Philippines.

16. Fieldwork notes from February and July 2019. Interviews with four female former members.
17. Interview with Abu Usama, former member of the Maute group, February 2019, Marawi, Philippines.
18. Fieldwork notes, February and July 2019, Marawi, Philippines.
19. Interview with Abu Rusydan, spiritual leader, JI, July 2018, Kudus, Indonesia.
20. Interview with Hisham, preacher with JI, July 2016, Surabaya, Indonesia.
21. Interview with Firdaus, preacher with JI, July 2018, Palu, Indonesia.
22. Interview with Haris, candidate for membership in JI, July 2019, Jakarta, Indonesia.
23. Interview with Syamsuddin Uba, pro-ISIS cleric, July 2018, Bekasi, Indonesia.
24. Interview with Abu Muslim, former member of JI and MIT, July 2018, outside Solo, Indonesia.
25. Interview with Hakim, former member of Tauhid wa'al Jihad, July 2016, Jakarta, Indonesia.
26. Interview with Hakim, former member of Tauhid wa'al Jihad, July 2016, Jakarta, Indonesia.
27. Interview with Amru, inactive member of JI, July 2018, Semarang, Indonesia.
28. Interview with Amru, inactive member of JI, July 2018, Semarang, Indonesia.
29. Interview with Amru, inactive member of JI, July 2018, Semarang, Indonesia.
30. Interview with Amru, inactive member of JI, July 2018, Semarang, Indonesia.
31. Interview with Munira, wife of Hassan, daughter of Haji Adnan Arsal, July 2010, Poso, Indonesia.
32. Interview with Umm Farish, second wife of "Yasir," former member of JI and Mujahidin KOMPAK, July 2012, Jakarta, Indonesia.
33. Discussion with Umm Farish's father, Umm Farish's house, July 2012, Jakarta, Indonesia.
34. Discussion with Umm Farish's father, Umm Farish's house, July 2012, Jakarta, Indonesia.
35. Hundeide, "Becoming a Committed Insider," 114.
36. Interview with "Badrol," a senior leader of JI and later what the police termed Neo-JI, July 2018, Semarang, Indonesia.
37. Interview with "Amir," a former member of Al Qaeda in the Malay Archipelago, Interviews in 2012 and 2018, Jakarta, Indonesia.
38. Interview with Maresh, former head of JI's Palu Branch, July 2018, Solo, Indonesia.
39. Interview with Joko, a former member of AQMA, July 2018, Solo, Indonesia.
40. Interview with Khaled, a former member of JI, Mujahidin KOMPAK, AQMA, Jemaah Ashorut Tauhid, Jemaah Anshorut Daulah, and Jemaah Anshorusy Sharia, July 2018, Solo, Indonesia.
41. Interview with Zed, former participant in study sessions run by Aman Abdurrahman and Abdullah Sunata, July 2019, Jakarta, Indonesia.
42. Interview with Mat, former member of MIT, July 2019, Poso, Indonesia.
43. Interview with Gungun, former member of MIT, July 2019, Poso, Indonesia.
44. Julie Chernov Hwang, *Why Terrorists Quit: The Disengagement of Indonesian Jihadists* (Ithaca, NY: Cornell University Press, 2018), 75.

45. Chernov Hwang, *Why Terrorists Quit*, 75.
46. Chernov Hwang, *Why Terrorists Quit*, 75.
47. Chernov Hwang, *Why Terrorists Quit*, 112.
48. Chernov Hwang, *Why Terrorists Quit*, 112.
49. This example was provided by Hakim in a 2018 interview. He discussed it in the context of his broader realization while in prison that Aman Abdurrahman's brand of extremism was inhumane and he wanted nothing to do with it any longer. This was just one in a long line of incidents that contributed to that realization.
50. This was another example provided by Hakim from the same 2018 interview.

# Chapter 5

1. Doug McAdam, "Recruitment into High Risk Activism: The Case of Freedom Summer," *American Journal of Sociology* 92, no. 1 (1986): 64–90, 66.
2. McAdam, "Recruitment into High Risk Activism," 66.
3. Nasir Abas, *Inside Jama'ah Islamiyah: A Former Member's True Story* (South Jakarta: Grafindo, 2011), 95–98.
4. Abas, *Inside Jama'ah Islamiyah*, 95–98.
5. Abas, *Inside Jama'ah Islamiyah*, 95–98.
6. Conversation with Amru, inactive member of JI, July 15, 2021, via WhatsApp.
7. Conversation with Amru, inactive member of JI, July 15, 2021, via WhatsApp.
8. Conversation with Amru, inactive member of JI, July 15, 2021, via WhatsApp.
9. This was a members-only study session led by Abu Fida, when he was associated with Al Qaeda in the Malay Archipelago (AQMA). "Jali" reported attending it during our interview in February 2019, Jakarta, Indonesia.
10. Deposition of Ahmed Junaidi, Berita Acara Pemeriksaan (BAP) Ahmed Junaidi alias Abu Salman alias Jun alias Ju, 11, May 2015, 3–4.
11. Interview notes for members of JI, 2016–2019. Each of those interviewed who graduated from pesantren was assigned either to teach at a pesantren or to dakwah following graduation, irrespective of school and irrespective of generation. This holds true for those who joined in the 1980s, when it was still Darul Islam, the 1990s, or the 2000s.
12. Thomas Hegghammer, "The Recruiters Dilemma: Signalling and Rebel Recruitment Tactics," *Journal of Peace Research* 50, no. 1 (2012): 3–16, 3.
13. Hegghammer, "The Recruiters Dilemma," 3.
14. Hegghammer, "The Recruiters Dilemma," 3–4.
15. Hegghammer, "The Recruiters Dilemma," 6.
16. Interview with Ali Imron, JI operative and participant in the 2002 Bali bombing, July 2017, Polda Metrojaya prison, Jakarta, Indonesia.
17. Interview with "Abu Tsabita," former member of JAD, July 2019, Semarang, Indonesia.
18. Interview with Abu Tsabita, former member of JAD, July 2019, Semarang, Indonesia.
19. Interview with Hakim, former member of Tauhid Wa'al Jihad, July 2016, Jakarta, Indonesia.

20. Interview with Gungun, former recruiter and logistician for MIT, July 2018, Poso, Indonesia.
21. Interview with Aisyah, former Maute recruiter, February 2019, Marawi, Philippines.
22. Interview with Aisyah, former Maute recruiter, February 2019, Marawi, Philippines.
23. Interview with Abu Ayyas, former trainer in the Aceh training camp, July 2017, Jakarta, Indonesia.
24. Interview with Abu Ayyas, former trainer in the Aceh training camp, July 2017, Jakarta, Indonesia.
25. Interview with Ali Imron, JI member, former participant in the Bali bombing in 2002, July 2010, Polda Metrojaya, Jakarta, Indonesia.
26. Interview with MB, JI member, former participant in the Bali bombing in 2002, July 2012, Polda Metrojaya, Jakarta.
27. Interview with Pepen, former JI member, Afghan veteran, July 2012, Jakarta, Indonesia.
28. Interview with Nasir Abas, Umar Patek's boss at MILF Camp Abu Bakar/Camp Hudaibiyah, July 24, 2022.
29. Deposition of Parawijayanto, Berita Acara Pemeriksaan (BAP) alias Abang, alias Mas, Alias Abu Askary, alias Abu Faiz, July 19, 2019, 47.
30. Institute for Policy Analysis of Conflict (IPAC), "The Reemergence of Jemaah Islamiyah," report no. 36 (2017, April 27), 7.
31. IPAC, "The Reemergence of Jemaah Islamiyah," 7.
32. BAP Parawijayanto, 47.
33. BAP Parawijayanto, 47.
34. BAP Parawijayanto, 47.
35. Interview with Anas, former member of JI, July 2012, Jakarta, Indonesia.
36. Interview with Anas, former member of JI, July 2012, Jakarta, Indonesia.
37. Interview with Anas, former member of JI, July 2012, Jakarta, Indonesia.
38. Interview with Hisham, former member of JI, July 2012, Surabaya, Indonesia.
39. Kirsten Schulze, "From Ambon to Poso: Comparative and Evolutionary Aspects of Local Jihad in Indonesia," *Contemporary Southeast Asia* 41, no. 1 (2019): 35–62, 42.
40. Kirsten Schulze, "From Ambon to Poso," 45.
41. Kirsten Schulze, "From Ambon to Poso," 46.
42. Kirsten Schulze, "From Ambon to Poso," 46.
43. Interview with Haroun, JI member, Tanah Runtuh member, July 2018, Poso, Indonesia.
44. Interview with Anas, former member of JI, July 2012, Jakarta, Indonesia.
45. Interview with Hisham, former member of JI, July 2018, Surabaya, Indonesia.
46. Interview with Ali Fauzi, former trainer with JI and Mujahidin KOMPAK, July 2011, Surabaya, Indonesia.
47. Interview with Ali Fauzi, half-brother of Mukhlas, Amrozi and Ali Imron, former trainer for JI and KOMPAK, July 2011, Surabaya, Indonesia.
48. International Crisis Group, "Indonesia Backgrounder: Jihad in Central Sulawesi," report no. 74 (2004, February 3), 11; IPAC, "ISIS in Ambon: The Fallout from

Communal Conflict," report no. 28 (2016, May 13), 1; International Crisis Group, "Weakening Indonesia's Mujahidin Networks," report no. 103 (2005, October 13), 7.
49. The time of the training varied. The early trainings on the Afghan–Pakistan border at Camp Saada were 3 years in duration. The trainings at Al Qaeda Camp al Faruq lasted 2 or 3 months. Hudaibiyah had two separate training tracks: the Military Training and Education Academy that lasted 1½–2 years and a Basic Military Course that ran for shorter periods: 2 weeks, 1 month, 2 months, 4 months, and 6 months. Training at Pawas lasted upwards of 6 months. In Syria, the duration of ISIS training camps varied from 3 weeks at Muadzkar to 2½ months at Harari, according to the interrogation deposition of Ahmad Junaidi, who spent 5 months in Syria. JI members who trained with Jabhat al Nusra went to Syria for periods of 6–12 months with explicit instructions to focus on gaining military capacity and battlefield experience. Local trainings tended to be fairly short. Participants in the Ambon jihad who attended trainings at Waimorat quoted a figure of 3 or 4 months, whereas trainings on the island of Seram lasted 2 months. Poso jihadis from Tanah Runtuh cited 1 week.
50. Interview with Yasir, member of JI, July 2018, Jakarta, Indonesia.
51. Interview with Rashid, former member of JI and AQMA, August 2017, Pekanbaru, Indonesia.
52. Nasir Abas, *Inside Jemaah Islamiyah* (Jakarta: Grafindo, 2011), 147.
53. Abas, *Inside Jemaah Islamiyah*, 147.
54. V. Arianti, "Jemaah Islamiyah's Hierarchical Structure," *Counter Terrorist Trends and Analyses* 13, no. 3 (2021, June), 15–21, 19.
55. BAP Parawijayanto, 22, 24.
56. BAP Parawijayanto, 41.
57. Interview with Umar, former member of JI and JAT, July 2016, Magetan, Indonesia.
58. Interview with Umar, former member of JI and JAT, July 2016, Magetan, Indonesia.
59. Interview with Abu Usama, former member of the Maute group, February 2019, Marawi, Philippines.
60. Interview with Abu Usama, former member of the Maute group, February 2019, Marawi, Philippines.
61. This was not true for Abu Usama, who went home and, as many an alcoholic does, soon returned to drinking.
62. IPAC, "ISIS in Ambon," 9.
63. IPAC, "ISIS in Ambon," 2.
64. Interview with Jali, former member of AQMA, July 2018, Depok, Indonesia.
65. Interview with Jali, former member of AQMA, July 2018, Depok, Indonesia.
66. IPAC, "Post-Marawi Lessons from Detained Extremists in the Philippines," report no. 18 (2017, November 27), 3.
67. IPAC, "The Failed Solo Suicide Bombing and Bahrun Naim's Network," report no. 30 (2016, July 29), 6.
68. Kirsten Schulze, "The Surabaya Bombings and the Evolution of the Jihadi Threat in Indonesia," *CTC Sentinel* 11, no. 6 (2018), 1.

69. Tom Smith and Kirsten Schulze, "Introduction: Examining the Global Linkages of Asian and North American Jihadis," in *Exporting Global Jihad*, ed. Tom Smith and Kirsten Schulze (New York: IB Taurus, 2020), 1.
70. Schulze, "The Surabaya Bombings," 1.
71. Schulze, "The Surabaya Bombings," 1.
72. Jones, "The Surabaya Bombings and the Future of ISIS in Indonesia," 1.
73. Schulze, "The Surabaya Bombings," 4.
74. International Crisis Group, "Terrorism in Indonesia: Noordin's Networks," report no. 114 (2006, May 5), 2.
75. International Crisis Group, "Terrorism in Indonesia," 4.
76. International Crisis Group, "Terrorism in Indonesia," 4.
77. International Crisis Group, "Terrorism in Indonesia," 4.
78. Sidney Jones, "Radicalisation in the Philippines: The Cotabato Cell and the 'East Asia Wilayah,'" *Terrorism and Political Violence* 30, no. 6 (2018): 933–943, 935.
79. IPAC, "Post-Marawi Lessons," 3.
80. Jones, "Radicalisation in the Philippines, 935.
81. Jones, "Radicalisation in the Philippines," 935.
82. Jones, "Radicalisation in the Philippines," 935.
83. Deposition of Ibadurrahman, Berita Acara Pemeriksaan. Alias Ali Rabani, Alias Azis alias Ibad. August 18, 2015
84. BAP Ibadurrahman, 11–12.
85. BAP Ibadurrahman, 11–12.
86. IPAC, "The Failed Solo Suicide Bombing," 8.
87. They chose the church to avenge the destruction of a mosque in Tolikara, Papua, and the Buddhist temple to avenge the deaths of Rohingya Muslims in Myanmar. IPAC, "The Failed Solo Suicide Bombing," 8.
88. IPAC, "The Failed Solo Suicide Bombing," 6.
89. IPAC, "The Failed Solo Suicide Bombing," 8.

# Conclusion

1. Interview with Arif Tuban, former JI member, July 2018, Jakarta, Indonesia.
2. Interview with Arif Tuban, former JI member, July 2018, Jakarta, Indonesia.
3. Interview with Arif Tuban, former JI member, July 2018, Jakarta, Indonesia.
4. Interview with Arif Tuban, former JI member, July 2018, Jakarta, Indonesia.
5. Interview with Arif Tuban, former JI member, July 2018, Jakarta, Indonesia.
6. Interview with Arif Tuban, former JI member, July 2018, Jakarta, Indonesia.
7. Interview with Arif Tuban, former JI member, July 2018, Jakarta, Indonesia.
8. I interviewed a hit man, a methamphetamine addict, as well as multiple farmers. The farmers were recruited by Imam Abilino Dimakaling in Piagapo. Thus, these are not abstractions. The Maute group would enlist anyone willing to fight and coerce individuals who were not.

# Glossary

**Aklak:** ethics and morals

**Amaliyat:** actions; used to refer to terrorist attacks

**Amar Ma'aruf Nahi Mungkar:** enjoining the good and forbidding the bad

**Aqidah:** creed

**Askari:** military

**Bai'at:** loyalty oath

**Da'i:** preachers

**Dakwah:** Islamic propagation

**Daulah Islamiyah:** Islamic state

**Dauroh:** internal group study sessions

**Fa'i:** robbery in the name of Islam

**Fardu Ayn:** individual obligation; term used to refer to jihad as an individual obligation, incumbent on every able-bodied Muslim man

**Fardu Kifaya:** collective obligation; term used to refer to jihad as a collective obligation, incumbent upon Muslim leaders

**Fiqh:** the operationalization of the broad principles and values of the sharia into distinct laws by Islamic jurists

**Ghazwul Fikri:** war of thought against Western civilization

**Halaqoh:** specialized small group study sessions

**Haram:** forbidden according to Islam

**Hijab:** headscarf

**Hijrah:** migration

**I'dad:** preparations for jihad

**Ikhwan:** brothers

**Iman:** Islamic belief

**Irhaabii:** terrorists

**Jamaah Islam:** Islamic community

**Jihad fisabililah:** Jihad in the name of Allah

**Jihad Qital:** battle

**Jilbab:** headscarf (Indonesia)

**Kafir:** infidel

**Kimon:** black garmet warn by the Maute group members

**La ilaha illallah:** there is no God but Allah

**Manhaj:** a methodology for receiving and applying knowledge

**Medan jihad yang sah:** a legitimate field of battle

**Mujahid:** holy warrior

**Niqab:** face veil

**Pengajian:** study sessions

**Pesantren:** Islamic boarding school

**Qital fisabililah:** battle in the name of Allah

**Salaf:** to go before

**Salafi:** refers to those Muslims who adhere to the model of conduct set out by the Prophet and his companions and who take the injunctions of the Quran and Hadith literally

**Sami'na wa'ato'na:** I hear and I obey

**Sharia:** Islamic law

**Tabligh:** mass prayers

**Tadrib:** paramilitary training

**Tajwid:** the correct pronunciation of Quranic Arabic; this is a class in many Islamic boarding schools

**Takfir:** excommunication

**Takfiri:** individuals and groups that declare individual Muslim, Islamic, and Islamist groups and governments that do not conform to their rigid and doctrinaire norms of behavior as infidels

**Taklim:** study circles

**Tauhid:** the divine oneness of god

# Index

*For the benefit of digital users, indexed terms that span two pages (e.g., 52–53) may, on occasion, appear on only one of those pages.*
Figures are indicated by *f* following the page number

Abas, Nasir, 2, 128
Abd al-Salam Faraj, Muhammad, 8–9
Abdurrahman, Aman
   fragmentation of groups due to teachings of, 19–21
   hate in teachings of, 160–61
   Ibnu Mas'ud school, 78
   Muhammad Fachry and, 103–4
   reaction to defiance of orders, 121–22
   role in motivation, 42–43, 46–47
   study circles, 35
Abu Jandal (Salim Mubarok), 19–20, 22, 38
Abu Sayyaf Group (ASG), 3, 24–25, 25*f*
activism, Jihadi. *See* Jihadi activism
Adnani, Abu Muhammad al, 20–21
affinity ties, 159–60
Afghanistan, training in, 15–16, 140–41
Ahmad, Farihin, 144–45
Aini, Zakiah, 105
AKP (Ansar al Khilafah Philippines), 24–25, 25*f*
Al Ghozi, Faturrahman, 65
al Irsyad, 72
Al Qaeda
   JI members involved in, 16
   research on Southeast Asian involvement, 14–15
   training at Camp al Faruq, 140–41
Al Qaeda in the Malay Archipelago (AQMA), 17–19, 69–70, 119
Al-Amanah pesantren (Indonesia), 62
alcoholism, search for redemption for, 53–57
Al-Islam pesantren (Indonesia), 75–77
Al-Muhajiroun, 103–4
al-Muttaqin school in Jepara, Central Java, 62

Altier, Mary Beth, 12–13
altruistic motivations, 45–50
Ambon conflict (Indonesia)
   conflict pathway, 91–95
   jihad experiences, 136–40
Amrozi, 67, 68, 139–40, 144–45
Ansar al Khilafah Philippines (AKP), 24–25, 25*f*
anti-vice motivations, 45–49
AQMA (Al Qaeda in the Malay Archipelago), 17–19, 69–70, 119
armaments, member activities related to, 127–28, 133–36
Arrahmah.com, 103–4, 105–6
Arsal, Haji Adnan, 62
Aryan free spaces, 12
ASG (Abu Sayyaf Group), 3, 24–25, 25*f*
Azis, Umar Abdul, 66
Azzam, Abdullah, 8–9

Ba'asyir, Abu Bakar, 15–16, 19, 21, 38, 100–1
*bai'at* (loyalty oath), 35, 38
Baitul Amin Muhammadiyah pesantren, 87
Bali bombing in 2002
   following of orders by Ali Imron, 120–21
   kinship ties among attackers, 144–45
   Mukhlas's justification of, 9
   participation of Umar Patek in, 3
   social ties among attackers, 146
Ballen, Ken, 10
Bangasamoro Islamic Freedom Fighters (BIFF), 24–25, 25*f*
behavioral norms, commitment to obeying, 112–15

Berger, J. M., 11
Bloody Idul Fitri Tragedy (Indonesia), 91–95
boarding schools, Islamic. *See* pesantren
brotherhood. *See* social bonds

#cafeIslam forum, 106
Camp Hudaibiyah (Philippines), 140, 141–42
Carter, Lynn, 11
chats, online. *See* social media
Chernov Hwang, Julie, 10, 14
Christmas Eve bombing in 2000, 3
commitment
　correct practice of religion, 115–16
　deep emotions involved in, 157–61
　following orders, 118–22
　as fundamentally social experience, 153–57, 154f, 156f
　obeying group norms, 112–15
　overview, 6, 111–12
　prioritizing in-group social relationships, 116–18
　trust reinforced by, 159
　types of, 122–24, 123f
　variation by pathway to entry, 152–53
communities, living in, 117–18
conflict pathway
　commitment and, 122–24, 123f, 152–53
　in Indonesia, 84f, 91–95
　overview, 5, 14
　in Philippines, 84f, 95–97
Cotabato cell, 90, 143, 145–46

da'i (preachers), 130
dakwah (Islamic propagation), 126, 129–30
Darul Islam (DI)
　history of, 15–16
　kinship pathway, 64–67, 71
　motivation to join, 34–36
　school pathway, 73, 77
　terrorist attacks by, 17–18
Davao night market bombing in 2016, 146
day schools (madrasas), 72–73
Deneoux, Guilian, 11
Densus 88, revenge for raids by, 52–53
DI. *See* Darul Islam

Dilangalen, Fakhrudin, 145–46
Dimakaling, Imam Abilino, 39, 95–96, 107
divorce, search for redemption after, 55–56
dress, obeying norms on, 112, 113–14
drug abuse, search for redemption after, 55–56
Dulmatin, 1, 3–4

education by members, 129–30
emotional component of membership, 157–61
excommunication of members, 121–22
extended family, as pathway, 69–71
external pathways
　local conflicts, 91–97
　overview, 5, 80–84, 84f
　prisons, 97–102
　social media and Internet, 102–9
　study sessions, 84–90
　variation in, 151–53

Facebook, 102
Fachry, Muhammad, 103–4
FAKSI (Forum of Islamic Law Activists), 104
family
　as internal pathway, 62, 64–72
　prioritizing in-group relationships over, 116–18
　role in motivation, 34–40, 36f
Fauzi, Ali, 67, 68, 139–40
Febrianto, Anton, 144
fieldwork, 27–30
financial assistance, as motivation, 39–40, 57–59
Firqoh Abu Hamzah, 21–22
Forum al Busryo, 106
Forum Jihad al-Tawbah, 106
Forum of Islamic Law Activists (FAKSI), 104
forums. *See* social media
FPI (Islamic Defenders Front), 45–48, 49
fragmentation of Indonesian extremist groups, 18–24
free spaces, Aryan, 12
friendships
　among terrorist attackers, 146
　formed at boarding schools, 77

formed in jihad experiences, 138–40
formed in paramilitary training, 141
formed in study sessions, 85–87
as pathway, 13–14
prioritizing in-group social relationships, 116–18
role in motivation, 35, 36$f$, 37, 39–40, 45
Futrell, Robert, 12

gender relations, obeying norms on, 112
*ghazwul fikri* (war of thought), 42
Ghuraba, 24–25
group norms, commitment to obeying, 112–15
Gufron, Ali. *See* Mukhlas
guns, member activities related to, 127–28, 133–36

Hadi, Rusydan Abdul, 66
Hafez, Mohammed, 10
halaqoh (Islamic studies circle), 85–86, 87–88
Hambali, 16
Hapilon, Isnilon, 24–25
Haq, Huda Bin Abdul. *See* Mukhlas
Harbiy Pohantun Military Academy (As Saada), 15–16
hate, as motivation in radicalization, 160–61
Hayyie, Ridwan Abdul, 66
historical approach to Islamist terrorist organizations, 14
Horgan, John, 12–13
Husna, Abu, 22, 78, 100–1

Ibnu Mas'ud school (Indonesia), 78
ideology affinity, as motivation, 41–45
Imron, Ali
  bonding with brothers, 139–40
  following of orders, 120–21
  gun procurement by, 135
  obedience to group norms, 112
  recruitment by Mukhlas, 67–68, 144–45
  relationship with students, 75–76
  trust in Umar Patek, 3–4
Indonesia
  altruistic motivations in, 45–49
  commitment in, 111–12

conflict pathway in, 91–95
correct practice of religion in, 115–16
financial benefit motivation in, 59
fragmented Islamist extremist ecosystem in, 18–24
history of Islamist terrorism in, 15–16
jihad experiences in, 136–40
kinship pathway in, 63–72
obedience to group norms in, 112–14
overview, 17
prioritizing of in-group relationships in, 116–18
prison pathway in, 97–102
pull factors in, 34–38, 36$f$
push factors in, 41$f$
redemption motivation in, 55
revenge motivation in, 50–53
school pathway in, 72–78
seeking knowledge/ideology affinity motivation in, 41–44
social bonds in joining and commitment, 153–55, 154$f$
study session pathway in, 84–90
terrorist attacks in, 17–18
induction of candidates, 131
Ingram, Kiraloi, 14
in-group marriage, 71
in-group social relationships, prioritizing, 116–18
injustices, motivation to redress past, 49–50
insurgency pathway. *See* conflict pathway
intentional socialization, 64–67
internal pathways
  kinship, 64–72
  overview, 5, 62–63
  schools, 72–78
  variation in, 151–53
Internet pathway, 89, 102–9
interpersonal relationships. *See* social bonds
interview process in research, 27–29
ISIS (Islamic State of Iraq and Syria)
  correct practice of religion in, 116
  Filipino groups affiliated with, 24–25
  Indonesian groups affiliated with, 19–24, 23$f$
  kinship pathway, 66, 70–71

ISIS (Islamic State of Iraq and Syria) (*cont.*)
  motivation to join, 47–48, 56
  prison pathway, 98–99, 100–2
  research on Southeast Asian involvement, 14–15
  school pathway, 78
  study session pathway, 89–90
Islam
  altruistic motivation to protect Muslims, 45–50
  commitment to correct practice of religion, 115–16
  prison education in, 99–100
  redemption motivation, 53–57
  seeking knowledge motivation, 41–45
Islamic boarding schools. *See* pesantren
Islamic Defenders Front (FPI), 45–48, 49
Islamic propagation (dakwah), 126, 129–30
Islamic State of Iraq and Syria. *See* ISIS
Islamic terminology, 8–9
Islamist extremist groups. *See also by name*
  in Indonesia, 18–24
  in Philippines, 24–27
Ismail, Noor Huda, 14

Jabar, Abdul, 144–45
Jabidah massacre of 1968 (Philippines), 15
JAK (Jemaah Asharul Khilafa), 21–22, 78
JAS (Jemaah Ansharusy Syariah), 19–20, 87–88
JAT. *See* Jemaah Anshorut Tauhid
Jemaah Ansharud Daulah (JAD)
  Dita Oepriarto cell, 36–37
  recruitment in, 131
  social bonds in, 4–5
  support for ISIS, 20–21, 22
  terrorist attacks by, 18
Jemaah Ansharusy Syariah (JAS), 19–20, 87–88
Jemaah Anshorut Tauhid (JAT)
  motivation to join, 38
  overview, 19
  role of social media in joining, 107
  study sessions, 87–88, 130
  support for JAD, 21
Jemaah Asharul Khilafa (JAK), 21–22, 78

Jemaah Islamiyah (JI)
  affiliates, 19, 20*f*
  attacks by Malaysia-based pro-bombing faction within, 17–18
  conflict pathway, 91–95
  correct practice of religion in, 115–16
  gun procurement in, 135–36
  history of, 15–16
  importance of following orders in, 118–19
  jihad experiences, 136–37
  kinship pathway, 62–63, 64–67, 71
  motivation to join, 38, 42, 52
  obeying group norms in, 112
  opposition to ISIS, 19–20
  paramilitary training in, 140–42
  participation of Umar Patek in, 1–4
  prioritizing in-group relationships, 116–18
  prison pathway, 97–100
  recruitment in, 131
  role of Mukhlas in, 1
  school pathway, 73–78
  study session pathway, 86–89
  study sessions and education by members, 130
  time horizons for joining, 152
jihad
  member participation in, 127, 136–40
  seeking knowledge about (as motivation), 41–44, 45
Jihadi activism
  armaments, 133–36
  deep emotions involved in, 157–61
  forms of, 127*f*
  jihad, 136–40
  overview, 126–29
  paramilitary training, 140
  recruitment, 131–33
  study sessions, dakwah, and education, 129–30
  terrorism, 143–47
jihadis (Salafi), 8–9
joining process. *See also* external pathways; internal pathways
  emotions involved in, 157–61
  in Indonesia, 22–24
  literature on, 10–15

Maute group, 26–27
  overview, 6–8
  social bonds in, 153–57, 154f, 156f
  in Southeast Asia, 15–16
  variation in, 151–53
Jones, Sidney, 14
Junaidi, Ahmed, 38
JW Marriott bombing in 2003, 13, 145, 146

kinship ties
  commitment and, 122–24, 123f
  extended family, 69–71
  in joining and commitment, 156f, 156–57
  marriage, 65, 71–72
  overview, 5
  parents, 62, 64–67
  research on, 10, 13–14
  role in motivation, 34–40
  siblings, 65, 67–68
  in terrorist attacks, 144–45
  trust in, 158
  variations in commitment, 152–53
knowledge-seeking, as motivation, 41–45
KOMPAK (Komite Aksi Penanggulangan Akibat Krisis), 92–93, 137–38
Kressel, Neil J., 10
Kruglanski, Arie, 10

literature on joining and radicalization, 10–15
local conflicts pathway. *See* conflict pathway
love, as motivation in radicalization, 10, 160
loyalty oath (*bai'at*), 35, 38
Luqmanul Hakim boarding school (Malaysia), 35, 68, 73, 145

madrasas (day schools), 72–73
Makmun, Halawi, 34–35
Malaysia, history of Islamist terrorism in, 15–16
Maranao community, desire to rectify injustices against, 49–50
Marawi City takeover (Philippines), 25–26, 58, 95–97

marriage
  as binding agent, 101, 113
  as expression of commitment, 118
  as pathway, 65, 71–72
Maskuron, Bagus, 22
Masyaariq, Katibah, 22
material assistance motivation, 39–40, 57–59
Matesan, Emy, 14
Maute, Abdullah, 26, 53–55
Maute, Omar, 26, 53–55
Maute group
  commitment to group norms, 114–15
  commitment in, 111–12
  conflict pathway, 95–96
  financial benefits as motivation to join, 57–59
  kinship pathway, 38–40, 65, 68–69
  overview, 24–27, 25f
  paramilitary training in, 142
  pathways to joining, 63
  recruitment in, 132–33
  redemption motivation, 53–56
  seeking knowledge motivation, 44–45
  social bonds in joining and commitment, 156f, 156–57
  social media pathway, 107
  time horizons for joining, 152
McCauley, Clark, 12
mechanisms of radicalization research, 12–15
members of extremist groups. *See also* commitment; Jihadi activism; social bonds
  correct practice of religion, 115–16
  emotions felt by, 157–61
  excommunication of, 121–22
  following of orders, 118–22
  obedience to group norms, 112–15
  prioritizing in-group social relationships, 116–18
  roles of, 6–8
  time horizons for joining, 152
mentors, role in motivation, 37–38
methodology, 27–30
military training. *See* paramilitary training
MIT. *See* Mujahidin Indonesia Timor
Moghaddam, Fathali M., 11–12

Mohammed, Khaled Sheikh, 16
Moro Islamic Liberation Front (MILF)
   motivation to join, 49–50
   multigenerational jihadi families, 66–67
   overview, 24–25, 25f
Moro National Liberation Front (MNLF), 24–25, 25f, 49–50
Moskalenko, Sophia, 12
motivation to join
   altruism and purpose, 45–50
   financial and material assistance, 57–59
   kinship ties, 34–40, 36f
   overview, 33–34
   purpose-driven push factors, 40–50
   redemption, 53–57
   research on causes of and, 10–11
   revenge, 50–53
   seeking knowledge and ideology affinity, 41–45
Mubarok, Salim (alias Abu Jandal), 19–20, 22, 38
Muhammadiyah, 38–149
Mujahidin Indonesia Timor (MIT)
   conflict pathway, 94–95
   friendship as pull factor to join, 37
   importance of following orders in, 120
   overview, 21–22, 52
   recruitment in, 132
   terrorist attacks by, 18
Mujahidin Kayamanya, 94–95
Mujahidin KOMPAK
   conflict pathway, 92–93
   importance of following orders in, 120
   jihad experiences, 136–40
   motivation to join, 48, 52
   overview, 18–19, 22–23
mujahidin struggle, role in motivation, 41–43
Mukhlas (Ali Gufron, Huda Bin Abdul Haq), 163n.2
   Bali bombing in 2002, 144–45
   bonding with brothers, 139–40
   on martyrdom of terrorists, 9
   recruiting of brothers, 67–68
   role in motivation, 34–35
multidimensional personal crisis, motivation from, 55–56, 108–9

multigenerational jihadi families, 64–67, 73–74
Muslims, motivation to better lives of, 45–50

Naim, Bahrun, 22, 104–5, 146–47
negative emotions felt by members, 158, 160–61
neighborhoods, importance of, 117–18, 145–46
New Order era, 17
Ngruki pesantren (Indonesia), 35, 74–75, 145
Novi, Dian Yulia, 71–72, 104–5
Nur, Abu, 33–35
Nuraniyah, Nava, 14

obedience in extremist groups
   adopting group norms, 112–15
   correct practice of religion, 115–16
   following orders, 118–22
Oepriarto, Dita, 36–37, 144, 146–47
orders, commitment to following, 118–22
Osman, Sulastri, 10, 14

Pakistan, training in, 15–16, 140
paramilitary training
   conflict pathway, 91–95
   member participation in, 127, 140
   social bonds formed in, 156–57
   time of, 189n.49
parents, influence of, 62, 64–67
Patek, Umar, 1–4
pathways of radicalization. *See also* external pathways; internal pathways
   research on, 11–12
   social bonds in, 13–14, 120–21
peer pressure to join, 39–40, 48
pesantren (Islamic boarding schools)
   as pathway, 62, 72–78
   terrorist attacks by friends from, 145
Philippines
   altruistic motivation in, 49–50
   commitment in, 111–12
   conflict pathway in, 95–97
   financial benefit motivation in, 57–59
   history of Islamist terrorism in, 15–16
   Islamist extremist groups in, 24–27

kinship pathway in, 66–67, 68–69, 72
obedience to group norms in, 114–15
overview, 24
paramilitary training in, 140, 141
pull factors in, 36f, 38–39
push factors in, 41f
redemption motivation in, 53–56
seeking knowledge/ideology affinity motivation in, 44–45
social bonds in joining and commitment, 156–57, 156f
study sessions in, 90
politicos (Salafi), 8
positive emotions felt by members, 157–61
Poso conflict (Indonesia)
conflict pathway, 91–95
jihad experiences, 136, 138
Walisongo massacre, revenge after, 50–53
practice of religion, commitment to, 115–16
preachers, members as, 130
prisons
commitment in pathway, 122–24, 123f
expulsion for conjugal visit in, 121–22
financial benefits as motivation to join in, 59
as pathway, 5, 23–24, 84f, 97–102
probing of candidates, 131
psychological approach to radicalization, 10
pull factors, 34–40, 36f
purists (Salafi), 8
push factors
altruism and purpose, 45–50
financial and material assistance, 39–40, 57–59
overview, 40–41, 41f
redemption, 53–57
revenge, 50–53
seeking knowledge and ideology affinity, 41–45
puzzle metaphor, 11–12

radicalization, literature on, 10–15
Ramakrishna, Kumar, 14
recruitment by members, 131–33
redemption motivation, 53–57

relational pull factors, 34–40, 36f
relatives, role in motivation, 38–39
religion. *See* Islam
research methodology, 27–30
revenge motivation, 50–53, 91–92, 160–61
Ring Banten, 18–19, 21–22, 36
robberies, by members, 127–28
Rochman, Nur, 143
role assignment, 155
roles of members in terrorist groups, 6–8
Rosenau, William, 11
Rusbult model, 12–13
Rusydan, Abu, 65

Sageman, Marc, 12, 13
Salafi, defined, 8
Salafi-Jihadis, defined, 8–9
sampling methods, 27–28
Samudra, Imam, 3–4
school pathway
commitment in, 122–24, 123f
general discussion, 72–78
overview, 5, 13–14, 62
trust in, 158
Schulze, Kirsten, 10, 14
siblings, as pathway, 65, 67–68
Silke, Andrew, 11
Simi, Pete, 12
social bonds
among terrorist attackers, 144–46
in conflict pathway, 94–95
formed at boarding schools, 74–76, 77
formed in jihad experiences, 138–40
formed in paramilitary training, 141
formed in study sessions, 85–87, 90
importance in joining and commitment, 153–57, 154f, 156f
overview, 3–5
in pathways, 149–51
prioritizing of in-group relationships, 116–18
prison pathway, 99, 101–2
role in radicalization, 13–14
social media
commitment in pathway, 122–24, 123f
invitations to study sessions, 89
nonviolent roles related to, 7
as partial pathway, 5, 84f, 102–9

social norms, commitment to obeying, 112–15
socialization, intentional, 64–67
Solahudin, 14
Southeast Asia, history of Islamist terrorism in, 15–16
Soviet–Afghan war, 15–16
special study sessions, 85–86, 87–88
speech, among members, 112–13
stages of radicalization research, 11–12
staircase of terrorism metaphor, 11–12
Stern, Jessica, 11
study sessions
  after local conflicts, 93–94
  attending as sympathizers, 85
  commitment in pathway, 122–24, 123f
  JI, 86–89
  journey to becoming members, 80–84
  member attendance, 126, 129–30
  overview, 84–85
  as pathway, 5, 13–14, 84–90, 84f
  in Philippines, 90
  in prisons, 99–100, 101
  of pro-ISIS groups, 89–90
  role in motivation, 37, 44
  social bonds formed in, 85–87
  social media involvement after, 105–6
  terror cells from, 145–46
  thick social bonds in, 4–5
  trust in, 158–59
  types of, 85–86
suicide bombing, 9
Sungkar, Abdullah, 15–16, 34, 35, 65–66
Syah, Bahrum, 19–20
Syria
  making hijrah to, 20–21
  paramilitary training in, 141
  role of social media in migration to, 108–9

takfiri, defined, 9
Tanah Runtuh, 18–19, 50–53, 93, 112
Tarbiyah movement, 42
Tauhid wa'al Jihad, 132
Taylor, Max, 12
teachers
  members as, 130
  role in motivation, 36f, 37–38
  school pathway, 72–78

Telegram, 102
Temby, Quinton, 14–15, 26
terminology, Islamic, 8–9
terrorist attacks. *See also specific attacks*
  in Indonesia, 17–18
  member participation in, 127, 143–47
  roles of members in, 6–8
  trust among participants, 159
thick social bonds
  formed at boarding schools, 74–76, 77
  importance in joining and commitment, 153–57, 154f, 156f
  overview, 3–5
thin social bonds, 95–97
Tholut, Abu, 2
Thoroughgood, Christian, 12–13
Tim Hisbah
  motivation to join, 46–47, 49
  overview, 19, 21–22
  terrorist attacks, 143
time horizons for joining, 152
Top, Noordin M., 17–18, 144–45
trust
  emotional component of membership, 158–59
  formed in jihad experiences, 138–40
  formed in paramilitary training, 141
  overview, 3–5
  role in motivation, 40
  role in terrorist activities, 128, 143
  teacher–student discipleship relationship, 75–76

Uba, Syamsudin, 89
uncles, influence of, 69–71
unfreezing/refreezing mechanisms, 12

vengeance motivation, 50–53, 91–92, 160–61

Walid, Abu, 22
Walisongo massacre (Indonesia), 49–50, 91–95, 138
war of thought (*ghazwul fikri*), 42
Ward, Ken, 14
weapons, member activities related to, 127–28, 133–36
WhatsApp, 108

Wiktorowicz, Quintan, 11
women
   financial benefits as motivation for, 57–59
   marriage pathway, 71–72
   motivation for joining, 10, 14
   recruitment by, 132–33
   redemption motivation in, 55, 56
   role in terrorist groups, 7
   social media involvement, 104–6
   social norms, commitment to obeying, 113, 114

YouTube, 102

Zuhri, Saifuddin, 144–45